# Energy Research and Development

A Report to the Energy Policy Project of the Ford Foundation

# Energy Research and Development

*ohn*

J. Herbert Holloman
Michel Grenon

**Ballinger Publishing Company** ● **Cambridge, Mass.**
*A Subsidiary of J. B. Lippincott Company*

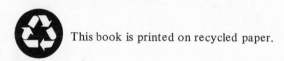 This book is printed on recycled paper.

Published in the United States of America by Ballinger Publishing Company,
Cambridge, Mass.

First Printing, 1975

Library of Congress Catalog Card Number: 74-23368

International Standard Book Number: 0-88410-316-1 (H.B.)
                                    0-88410-317-X (Pbk.)

Printed in the United States of America


**Library of Congress Cataloging in Publication Data**

Holoman, John Herbert.
    Energy research and development.

    1. Energy policy—United States.   2.  Research, Industrial—United States.
I. Grenon, Michel, joint author.   II.  Ford Foundation. Energy Policy Project.
III.  Title.
HD9502.U52H64                    333.7                    74-23368
ISBN 0-88410-316-1
ISBN 0-88410-317-X pbk.

# Contents

*v*

# List of Figures

# List of Tables

# Foreword

In December 1971 the Trustees of the Ford Foundation authorized the organization of the Energy Policy Project. In subsequent decisions the Trustees have approved supporting appropriations to a total of $4 million, which is being spent over a three-year period for a series of studies and reports by responsible authorities in a wide range of fields. The Project Director is S. David Freeman, and the Project has had the continuing advice of a distinguished Advisory Board chaired by Gilbert White.

This analysis and survey of energy R&D policies and program, entitled "Energy Research and Development," is one of the results of the Project. As Mr. Freeman explains in his Preface, neither the Foundation nor the Project presumes to judge the specific conclusions and recommendations of the authors who prepared this volume. We do commend this report to the public as a serious and responsible analysis which has been subjected to review by a number of qualified readers.

These studies, like many others in the Project, deal with a sensitive and difficult question of public policy. Not all of it is easy reading, and not all those we have consulted have agreed with all of it. Nor does it exhaust a subject which is complex, controversial, and partly obscured by gaps in the available data. The matters it addresses are of great and legitimate interest not only to those who are faced with difficult decisions about energy R&D policy but also to those in current and future generations who will have to live with the economic, political, social and environmental implications of those decisions. The perspectives of these interested parties are not likely to be identical.

In this last respect the present studies reflect tensions which are intrinsic to the whole of the Energy Policy Project—tensions between one set of objectives and another. As the worldwide energy crisis has become evident to us all, we have had many graphic illustrations of such tensions, and there are more ahead. This is what usually happens when a society faces hard choices, all of them carrying costs that are both human and material.

But it is important to understand that there is a fundamental difference between present tension and permanent conflict. The thesis accepted by our Board of Trustees when it authorized the Energy Policy Project was that the very existence of tension, along with the inescapable necessity for hard choices, argued in favor of studies which would be, as far as possible, fair, responsible, carefully reviewed, and dedicated only to the public interest. We do not suppose that we can evoke universal and instantaneous agreement, and still less do we presume that this Project can find all the answers. We do believe that it can make a useful contribution to a reasonable and democratic resolution of these great public questions, one which will serve the general interest of all.

The current studies are a clear example of what we aim at. It draws on principles of economics and organization, and on the considerable experience of the authors, to make recommendations about the general nature of public policy toward energy research and development; and it surveys the state of current technological options and of energy R&D programs in other nations to provide an enlightening information base. A wide range of outside experts and organizations reviewed the book; and, although not all of them agreed with all of the analysis and conclusions, we do believe that the authors have treated their hard subject with the respect it deserves. I commend their analysis to the attention of the American public.

**McGeorge Bundy**
President, Ford Foundation

# Preface

The Energy Policy Project was initiated by the Ford Foundation in 1971 to explore alternative national energy policies. The papers in this book, *Energy Research and Development,* are part of a series of studies commissioned by the Project. They are presented here as a carefully prepared contribution by the authors to today's public debate about research and development in energy. It is our hope that each of these special reports will stimulate further thinking and questioning in the specific areas it addresses. At the very most, however, each special report deals with only a part of the energy puzzle; the Energy Policy Project's final report, *A Time to Choose,* which was published in October 1974, attempts to integrate these parts into a comprehensible whole, setting forth the energy policy options available to the nation as we see them.

The papers in this book, like the others in the series, have been reviewed by scholars and experts in the field not otherwise associated with the Project in order to be sure that differing points of view were considered. With each book in the series, we offer reviewers the opportunity of having their comments published in an appendix to the volume. I believe the comments in this volume will be most useful to the reader in appraising the policy issues that are discussed. (See pages 109 ff.)

*Energy Research and Development* comprises the authors' reports to the Ford Foundation's Energy Policy Project and neither the Foundation, its Energy Policy Project or the Project's Advisory Board have assumed the role of passing judgement on its contents or conclusions. We have expressed our views in *A Time to Choose.*

**S. David Freeman**
Director
Energy Policy Project

# Introduction

The two papers which make up this book were originally commissioned by the Energy Policy Project because they delve into the two aspects of energy research and development where data and analyses are most scanty. Their subjects and purposes are quite different. In one, Michel Grenon, international consultant (now associated with the International Institute of Applied Systems Analysis) surveys energy research and development efforts outside of the United States, specifically in Canada, France, Germany, Japan, Sweden and the United Kingdom. In the other, J. Herbert Hollomon and his colleagues examine energy research and development policy issues in the U.S. within the conceptual framework of the energy marketplace.

The staff of the Energy Policy Project found these studies, like those commissioned in other fields, useful in clarifying issues and identifying the strengths and weaknesses of our energy system. Supplementing the staff's own research and analysis, the background reports made up a solid base of information for developing the Project's conclusions, published in the Project's final report, *A Time To Choose: America's Energy Future.*

One of the central findings of the Project's three-year inquiry into the energy problem is the need for coherent government policies to conserve energy and slow down growth in energy consumption. Present R&D efforts, the Project noted, are at odds with these goals. Both public and private R&D programs are concentrated in a very few supply-oriented technologies, with allocation of funds tilted heavily toward supporting a high rate of energy growth. The Project found that the nation is ignoring energy conservation technologies, neglecting environmental R&D, and failing even to achieve very much diversity of energy supplies. (See Chapters Twelve and Thirteen of *A Time to Choose.*)

To rectify these weaknesses, the Project recommended a reallocation of federal energy R&D in accord with deliberately chosen goals: energy conservation, diversity of energy supplies (including a major new thrust for solar energy and other relatively untapped energy sources such as geothermal power), environmental protection, and health and safety.

The Project recommended that government energy R&D programs explore promising ideas, perform basic research, and advance the concomitant technology to the demonstration phase. It also urged independent outside assessment of government-supported R&D projects, as well as full public debate on their merits.

The Hollomon group take a different approach. They identify weaknesses in energy R&D, and discuss ways of meeting urgent needs, but their basic perspective on policy diverges from that of the Project. Rather than recommending a government R&D policy with clearly defined goals, they conclude primary reliance for R&D decisions should be placed on the market system. Only where market forces fail to meet certain of society's needs, should it be a major concern of government to correct that failing.

A decision-making process linking R&D decisions closely to the market would be responsive to the needs of the nation's predominantly private energy system, the authors conclude. They believe decisions about energy R&D cannot be separated from other allocative choices, not only for energy but also for other sectors of the economy. The market provides a mechanism for comparing investment in R&D with other means of meeting national needs.

Hollomon and his colleagues rely on this classical economic approach as a basis for determining when government ought to intervene. In the authors' judgment a number of vital energy areas are in fact neglected by market forces; their analysis therefore points toward an active Federal role in energy R&D. They recommend a strong new federal energy department to monitor the energy system and to initiate needed programs. The federal actions they propose would be directed toward many of the same goals the Energy Policy Project set. The Hollomon group recommends emphasis on basic science and technology, including manpower training; environmental quality, health and safety; energy utilization and conservation; and preliminary investigation of promising new technologies; they also stress the need to right the present imbalance of energy R&D, which is now dominated by nuclear energy.

The two divergent approaches—the Project's and that of the Hollomon group—thus lead to a considerable area of agreement on the R&D efforts that government should pursue. It is interesting that the two approaches converge in concluding that the present level of government support for the breeder reactor program is unjustified. The Project found that there had been insufficient public consideration of the breeder's total costs, including environmental, health and safety risks. Hollomon and his colleagues conclude that the future development of the breeder reactor is now largely an economic decision; that is, that the technology is far enough advanced for reactor manufacturers and electric utilities to proceed if they are willing to bear the major share of development costs and risks.

This example also illustrates, however, the genuine, fundamental differences in the two perspectives. Energy R&D is a complex part of a complicated system, and the tumultuous events of 1973–1974 have made energy planning more difficult than ever. Differences of opinion and judgment are to be not only expected but welcomed, as contributions to necessary public debate. The reader's attention is called to the comments (pages 109 ff.) of Philip Scorn, former president of the American Electric Power Company; Joel Primack, of the University of California, Santa Cruz, and S. Fred Singer, of the University of Virginia, Charlottesville.

In his survey of foreign R&D, M. Grenon reports on R&D options pursued in Canada, Western Europe, and Japan, and on the respective responsibilities undertaken by governments and industry in the various countries. He outlines the energy situation in each country (Canada, France, Germany, Japan, Sweden, and the United Kingdom) and presents details of their programs, organizations, and funding.

Conditions in these countries—the extent of their domestic supplies, their dependence on imported fuels—vary considerably from those in the U.S., but Grenon found a similar imbalance in their energy R&D programs: most countries rely on nuclear energy as the fuel for the future.

Grenon finds that besides a general over emphasis on the atom there has also been considerable duplication in nuclear energy R&D. He assesses the comparative advantages of coordinating energy R&D on a European Community, international, multi-national, or joint public-private basis.

The economic well-being of the U.S. depends to a considerable extent on the healthy economies of its major trading partners, and for this reason alone energy developments in these countries are important to this nation.

Recent events have alerted all the industrialized countries to their vulnerability to sudden disruptions of energy supplies, and to the economic repercussions of the new balance of power in energy.

Energy R&D is even more crucial to the world's developing countries, as the Project pointed out in *A Time to Choose*. In the Third World, the inter-related impact of soaring fuel, fertilizer, and food prices makes the struggle for survival far more difficult.

The Energy Policy Project is grateful to Grenon and to Hollomon and his colleagues for their work, which will add to the body of knowledge needed to attack energy problems intelligently. The Project offers these reports, like the others in this series, with the hope they will prove useful to citizens who must ultimately decide our energy future.

**Irene Gordon**
Energy Policy Project

Part I

# A Proposal for a U. S. Energy
# Research and Development Policy

*Center for Policy Alternatives*
*Massachusetts Institute of Technology*
*J. Herbert Hollomon, Director*

# Preface to Part I

This report was originally developed during the period from March to October 1973. Between March and July, information concerning the energy system of the United States, the then national activities in Research and Development (R&D), and the legislative changes related to energy then in prospect, was assembled and analyzed. For several weeks during the summer of 1973 those listed below met and discussed the principles governing the government support of R&D in the United States, particularly in relation to energy. A first draft of our report was presented to the Energy Policy Project in October 1973. The report was not intended as a scholarly analysis of the pertinent literature nor an analysis of all the knowledge that related to these complex questions. Time did not permit that approach nor did we believe that the results would have been as useful. Rather, we relied upon our own experience, knowledge, and the advice of consultants with specific knowledge of certain questions, to prepare a basis for consideration of government policy with respect to energy R&D.

The rapidly changing situation with respect to the supply and prices of energy (and other commodities) since October 1973 may make some of the data in this report appear dated although we have tried to bring the factual information in this report as up to date as possible. However, we do not think that the new circumstances require changes in the basic approach or thrust of our recommendations.

The following individuals participated in formulating this report.

**Participants at the summer 1973 conference:**

Jean–Claude Derian
Center for Policy Alternatives
MIT

George Eads
Department of Economics
George Washington University

3

John E. Gray
Consultant, The Energy Policy Project
Washington, D.C.

Walter R. Hibbard, Jr.
Office of Energy R&D
Federal Energy Office
Washington, D.C.

J. Herbert Hollomon
Director, Center for Policy Alternatives
MIT

Charles O. Jones
Department of Political Science
University of Pittsburgh

Judith T. Kildow
Center for Policy Alternatives
MIT

Joseph B. Lassiter
Department of Ocean Engineering
MIT

David J. Rose
Department of Nuclear Engineering
MIT

Roland W. Schmitt
R&D Manager
Physical Science & Engineering
General Electric Company
Schenectady, New York

S. Fred Singer
Department of Environmental Sciences
University of Virginia

Marvin A. Sirbu, Jr.
Center for Policy Alternatives
MIT

David C. White
Director, Energy Laboratory
MIT

**Consultants**

Thomas Baron
President, Shell Development Company
Houston, Texas

Irwin C. Bupp
Kennedy School of Government
Harvard University

Eugene Fubini
Consultant
Arlington, Virginia

Bernard Gelb
The Conference Board
New York, New York

Milton Shaw
Formerly of the AEC

**Staff** (of Center for Policy
Alternatives, MIT)

Alan Fusfeld
T. Jeffrey Jones
Jennifer Lewis
David Marsh
Stephen Resnick
Amit J. Sen

**J. H. Hollomon**

# Chapter One

# Introduction

The nonrenewable nature of America's energy-producing natural resources has become the object of growing attention, and among some, even alarm. For a nation traditionally comfortable in the easy assumption of limitless material resources, evidence of an actual or impending scarcity has caused concern and demands for action.

Many of these demands have focused upon a "technological fix" to our energy supply problems. The atomic bomb program of the 1940s and the space program of the 1960s are commonly cited as models for a high-priority federally funded research and development (R&D) program to provide new energy-conversion technology and new energy-producing resources.

In this report we have taken a different approach. We have focused upon the behavior of the system that delivers energy for consumption and determines its pattern and rate of use. Unlike the aerospace and defense industries, where the ultimate customer is to a large extent the government, the energy system consists mainly of privately owned companies that provide goods and services to individual consumers. The salient characteristic of this system is that it is a market system, even though some of its parts are dominated by a few large firms and cartels, and even though parts of the system are regulated by the government.

Two basic activities characterize the energy system: production and consumption (see Figure 1–1). Production consists of the activities of extraction of energy-producing natural resources, conversion to other forms of energy and delivery to consumers. Considering the production system by sectors, the coal-mining industry consists of several large firms (the fifteen largest control half the total production), many of which are owned either by oil or steel companies. The oil industry is likewise dominated by some twenty integrated multinational companies, each with annual sales of more than $1 billion. These companies coexist with a number of smaller, less vertically integrated "independents."

**Figure 1–1.**   United States Energy Flow Pattern, Actual—1970

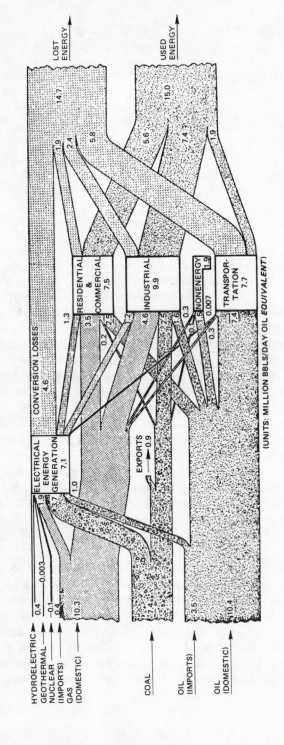

(UNITS: MILLION BBLS/DAY OIL *EQUIVALENT*)

Source:   Dixy Lee Ray, *The Nation's Energy Future*, Report to the President (December 1, 1973).

Many of the large companies have acquired substantial coal and uranium holdings. Most of the natural gas is also extracted by the oil companies and transmitted and distributed by independent gas pipeline companies. There are, about eighty interstate pipeline companies with annual revenues of more than $1 million.

The electric utility industry performs the functions of generation, transmission and distribution of electricity. Most of the investor-owned utilities are vertically integrated and perform all three functions. There are also federal (TVA, Bonneville, etc.), public, nonfederal and cooperative public utilities which are not, on the whole, as fully integrated as the private companies. Although not directly involved in energy production and distribution, several industries are closely related to energy supply. The most important of these are the equipment suppliers to the electric utilities and the engineering-construction industry.

Concerning consumption of energy by sectors in 1968, the industrial sector was the largest, with 41.2 percent of the total. Transportation used 25.1 percent and the residential and commercial sectors consumed 19.2 percent and 14.4 percent of the total, respectively.[1]

Unlike the production sectors, which consist of large, often vertically integrated firms, the consumption sectors consist of some large industrial users and millions of small units (individuals and small businesses). Given the cheap cost and easy availability of energy in the past there has been little concern for utilizing energy efficiently for all but the most intensive energy-using industries.

The federal government operates within the energy/industry-market system as owner and manager of public lands, and buyer and seller of energy, and as overseer of the system. As overseer, the federal as well as state governments set rate structures for utilities. Historically, governmental interest has primarily been concerned with resource development, taxation, and environmental protection, rather than utilization.

At the federal level, government involvement in the energy system has been characterized by near independence among important elements of the decision-making machinery, particularly in the executive branch. Coordinated policy-making with regard to energy production and consumption has been rare, principally because each energy agency has had a narrow mission. Moreover, a variety of other public policies and activities have an indirect impact upon energy supply and consumption. In fact, many of the current energy supply problems are in large part an unintended by-product of governmental action in nonenergy areas.

As a specific example, it is generally conceded that the actions of the Environmental Protection Agency (EPA) have had a significant impact on the total demand and supply of energy. They have also changed the relative attractiveness of various fuels. For example, the level of desulfurization demanded by the EPA determines almost completely whether low-Btu coal gasification is a better alternative than stack gas scrubbing for desulfurization of coal. Apparently in setting environmental standards the EPA has given little or no thought to the consequences of its actions on the energy system.

Another example is the regulation of automobile emissions, where emission-control requirements have increased gas consumption by an average of 10–15 percent per car. Furthermore, government regulation of interstate freight rates has led to a highly inefficient system for the transport of goods. For example, current regulations favor trucks over railroads for interstate shipping, even though trains are generally more efficient. The Civil Aviation Board, in regulating air fares, controls load factors and thereby fuel consumption per passenger mile. The Federal Housing Administration, by not including life cycle costs in its mortgage insurance procedures, indirectly encourages inefficiency of energy consumption.

These examples provide only an indication of the important indirect leverage that governmental action has on energy supply and demand. Some of the areas of government involvement in the energy system are listed in Appendix A of this report. Appendix D describes the federal contribution to total energy research and development fundings. In fiscal year 1973 this contribution was about $640 million, of which two-thirds was devoted to nuclear fission mainly for the project to develop the Liquid Metal Fast Breeder Reactor. Also in Appendix D, it can be seen that the private sector of the energy supply system supported twice as much R&D on energy in 1972 than did the government during the 1973 fiscal year. The bulk of the contribution in the private sector came from the oil companies and the electric utility equipment suppliers.

## APPROACH

The energy sector in the United States is mainly comparable to other industries that provide goods and services for consumption. Although government action has in the past been more important in this area than in many other industrial sectors, the energy system still remains a competitive market system where the behavior of the institutions that operate within its framework is chiefly, though not wholly, determined by costs and prices. Such actions may, under certain circumstances, result in nonoptimal allocation of resources from the point of view of society: the possession of monopoly power by one or more firms, or external costs of production—such as pollution—which are not included in the price, are possible reasons for this misallocation. It should be government's major concern and responsibility to correct this kind of failing in the operation of the market mechanism or to impose restraints on its operation in the public interest.

Obviously, this method of dealing with market failing is in principle applicable only when market imperfections are few in number and their impact reasonably well understood. When imperfections are too many and their effects complex and interdependent, comprehensive planning, including the setting of public priorities, may turn out to be necessary. Although the energy system has some imperfections of the second category, we still believe that the classical economic approach provides a reasonable—if not the only existing—analytical framework for describing the present and future behavior of the energy system and for determining criteria and rules for government intervention.

Our purpose in this report has been to identify the specific failures of the energy supply and demand system related to the allocation of resources for research and development; and to suggest: (1) criteria on which a decision of the federal government to intervene to correct such failures may be based; (2) the method of subsequent intervention; (3) appropriate institutional structures to carry out the intervention; and (4) specific suggestions regarding research and development with respect to energy supply and demand.

Throughout, we have stressed the process by which decisions are made concerning energy research and development. The problem is how to ensure that the energy sector of the economy (including the government) will be responsive to future needs and demands—needs and demands that are not only requirements for more fuel but may also include considerations for cleaner air, preservation of the environment, safety and reliability of supply.

We take this approach because R&D provides one of the bases for new and improved devices or systems for supplying or utilizing energy. For example, resources can be committed either for providing new technical capability through R&D or for enlarging coal production or for expanding mass transit. Comparisons of their potential consequences must somehow be made within the private/public economy that constitutes the energy supply and use system. R&D provides new technical options that may lead to the demonstration of the technical feasibility of new devices and systems—which *may* be adopted and used.

Thus, decisions about R&D *cannot* be separated from other allocative decisions related to energy and other sectors of the economy. Investment in R&D must be compared with other means of meeting national needs. Furthermore, large commitments to technical work related to energy may affect our ability to carry out technical work for other purposes. If we have learned anything about the innovation process[2] during the last 20 years, it is that successful innovation is a result of close coupling between need and capability, and the peculiarities of the institutions adopting the innovation deeply affect and control the process. The process of decision-making by which search for new products and processes is determined influences the nature and extent of R&D and by whom it is done, thus becoming crucial issues of R&D policy.

Our recommendations for a decision-making process on R&D that would be more responsive to needs stem from a particular conception of the appropriate relationship of government to the energy supply system. The government can be thought of as an economic actor in its own right, and as an overseer and regulator of the mostly privately organized system that supplies and uses energy. In its latter capacity, the government needs to monitor the actions of private institutions and, where necessary, intervene to correct specific failures. This function of overseeing in order to encourage rational policies on energy, particularly in the face of recent conflicts between environmental improvement and energy supply and use, has largely been ignored.

It may well be that the absence of a particular type of research and development represents a failure of the energy system for which government corrective action is appropriate. But it may also be that the failure of firms to fund particular R&D programs is entirely rational, even from society's overall perspective. Moreover, the direct funding of R&D by the government is by no means the only method of intervention to correct the inadequacies of industry.

The remainder of Part I has the following four major objectives:

1. To identify the specific failures of supply and use which may cause a misallocation of funds for energy R&D;
2. To contrast various mechanisms and strategies for government intervention to correct these failures;
3. To recommend an organizational framework appropriate to government action on these matters;
4. To identify the deficiencies currently apparent of the energy supply and utilization system, and to identify specific types of intervention that may be justified.

# Chapter Two

# The Government's Role in the Energy System

The government plays an important part in the energy supply system, both as an owner of resources and a consumer of energy. It also is the source of law and regulations that affect and often control the allocation of resources in the largely privately organized energy supply and use system. It is, therefore, by implication an overseer of the economic system, responsible for monitoring and moderating the energy subsystem in the interests of society as a whole. Since the functioning of the market does not take into account all the costs and benefits of particular economic activities, it is the obligation of the government to ensure that these considerations are taken into account by private decision-makers.

The government is also responsible for reconciling the decisions made in the energy system with the decisions made in other spheres of the national interest. Decisions made in the energy system have consequences that are relevant to many other areas of national policy, and vice versa. For example, environmental regulations deeply affect the supply and use of energy, and yet have been promulgated with little consideration of these consequences. Disruption of supplies of Middle East oil has led to severe economic costs for the United States. Changes in energy prices affect the rich and the poor differently, raising legitimate questions of welfare and equity.

Occasionally, the government may intervene in the energy supply and use system to achieve various social goals such as those of equity or national security. When it does, it is desirable that the reasons and objectives for such action be made explicit. Only then is it possible to compare, for example, the consequences of redistributing income by manipulating energy prices or by using taxation or welfare payments to achieve the same ends.[1]

In fact, the government may be involved in the energy supply and use system in two roles:

1. As an "economic actor" responsible for its decisions as owner and consumer of energy;
2. As a monitor and moderator of the energy system for achieving the interests of society as a whole.

       This distinction is crucial. The criteria for evaluating government policies and programs relating to energy R&D are quite different for the two roles. When the government is in the role of an economic actor, the criterion is the familiar one of comparing marginal benefits with marginal costs, similar to a private firm or consumer. Traditionally the United States has refrained from involvement in the production and supply of energy, with some significant exceptions such as the Tennessee Valley Authority. It has instead leased energy-bearing land to others for the purpose of producing fuel. If the government were to become a producer of energy from its own land, it would then become part of the economic system it oversees and regulates. This may have undesirable consequences. When leasing land, however, according to our criteria, the government should act to maximize the net return on its holdings as well as considering the economic and environmental consequences of their exploitation.

       When the government is acting as monitor and moderator of the system, the criteria for judging government actions involve considerations of relevant *social* costs and benefits.[2] Government actions should be judged by comparing whether they bring private decisions about costs and benefits more nearly in line with total social costs and benefits.

       Sometimes the two roles are interrelated and mutually influential: the government may support R&D for its own purposes, which then has a beneficial effect for society at large (e.g., product testing by the General Services Administration). As described later, government procurement of products based on life-cycle performance specifications may provide the stimulus for the development and sale of new products for general consumption. Even so, the rationale for government action should be made clear at the initiation of the proposed program so that the criteria for evaluation are explicit.

## THE GOVERNMENT AS ECONOMIC ACTOR

In its role as an economic actor, it would be rational for the government as a socially responsible owner of energy reserves to try to maximize the returns on its holdings. In evaluating costs and benefits, the government "owner" should assume *the same tax and regulatory circumstances* as would a private owner. In these circumstances, federal funding for energy R&D is warranted when it increases the value of its property. For example, it is in the interest of the government to support research and development of technologies that would indicate more effectively the location of offshore oil reserves or minimize the environmental consequences of their development. With that information the government can more advantageously set the minimum prices of the lands it wishes to lease to oil companies. If it has no idea how much its holdings are worth, it may underprice them, or conversely may adopt policies to underuse them in a time of national need.

There are a few government agencies involved in the process of production of energy, such as the Bureau of Reclamation, Bonneville Power Authority, Tennessee Valley Authority and the U. S. Army Corps of Engineers. Their criteria for investing in R&D should be similar to that of private firms: that is, are the expenditures on R&D likely to produce opportunities for investments for which the benefits exceed the costs?

The federal government is a large user of energy for space conditioning (heating and cooling), transportation, and for the operation of various equipment and products. To minimize costs, it is in the interest of the government to compare the life-cycle costs of different procedures. If the potential savings are large enough to justify innovative activities leading to these savings, the government should clearly support such activities. Even in this case, the new products could be supplied by industry and the mechanism of encouraging the necessary R&D or the use of new techniques must be chosen in a way that minimizes the costs to the government by assuring that industry produces the new products.

## THE GOVERNMENT AS OVERSEER
## OF THE ENERGY SYSTEM

The criteria for government involvement as an overseer of the private energy supply system are more complex.[3] Two broad areas can be identified in which government intervention may be required.

The first relates to areas of national policy concerned with non-economic values; specifically national security, foreign policy, general protection and public welfare and equity. In these matters, the government should seek to coordinate the outcomes of the decisions taken within the energy system with national priorities set by explicit national policies. For example, the government may decide, for reasons of national security, not to be dependent upon foreign supplies of oil. This decision *may* involve federal support (in some form) for encouraging the development and use of new techniques for production of oil from domestic sources. This function of coordination of national policies with policies involving energy has been neglected until now. Recent policies and programs have been ad hoc, unbalanced and difficult to connect with either the needs of society or with the necessity for overcoming deficiencies in the system that supplies and uses energy.

The second broad concern of the government is with structural deficiencies of the system of supply and use. In certain cases, the market may fail to allocate resources in a socially optimal way.[4] Before identifying these failures, which may inhibit the development or the use of new techniques, the process of innovation must be understood. Studies of the process of technological change or innovation have identified six key elements that must be present for industrial innovation to occur:[5] (1) There must be a potential market for the new products or processes; (2) there must be a base of scientific and technical knowledge and information upon which to draw in devising products or processes to take advantage of the potential market; (3) creative invention and design is required to combine what is possible with what is needed; (4) entrepreneurs are needed to implement the innovations; (5) the institution sponsoring the innovation must be able to appropriate to itself a sufficient fraction of the new benefits to justify its investment of time and money; and (6) the organization or firm must be able, at reasonable cost, to assemble the capital and other resources necessary to carry out the development.

The total process of technological change (innovation) includes invention and diffusion. The process does not end when technical feasibility of the new idea has been demonstrated. The process of innovation is complete only when the new product or process is in use, has demonstrated its economic viability, and has started generating a return on the initial investment. In the normal operation of a market economy, we depend upon private industrial firms to innovate, motivated by a desire to maintain or increase their sales, or to reduce costs (e.g., process innovations) to increase profits to their shareholders. However, private firms do not always bring together the necessary conditions for successful innovation.

At least three categories of failures or deficiencies of the market system affecting the innovation process that may require government intervention can be identified.

### Externalities

Externalities refer to situations where the relevant decision-making unit is unable to fully perceive or to compute all the costs or benefits associated with its activities.[6] There are strong economic arguments for the government to support R&D in this instance.

> Government has an appropriate role in R&D even when its results will not be incorporated in Government purchases, because private firms would underinvest in R&D for goods normally purchased by the private sector. Although an investment in R&D may produce benefits exceeding its costs from the viewpoint of society as a whole, a firm considering the investment may not be able to translate enough of these benefits into profits on its own products to justify the investment. This is because the knowledge which is the main product of R&D can usually be readily acquired by others who will compete away at least part of the benefits from the original developer. This is particularly true of basic research, where the output frequently occurs in the first instance not as a marketable product,

but rather as an advance in basic knowledge that can subsequently be used in applied research and development by a wide and often unforseeable range of firms.

One caveat must be mentioned. In many cases, the unit within which all relevant costs and benefits can be captured is far below the federal government in size. The research undertaken by a single firm may benefit all the members of the industry of which this firm is a member, but may not benefit any firm outside this industry. Assuming that the results of the work are not patentable, the way to assure that the proper amount will be undertaken would be to design some form of industry association to tax the members in proportion to the benefits each receives and compensate the firm for undertaking the research (and bearing all of the cost.[8] (The new Electric Power Research Institute, for example, was created for this purpose.) The federal government need intervene only to ensure that any association be designed to minimize the possibility that it could be used for anticompetitive purposes. Since the tax will be passed on to the consuming public, some public participation may be necessary to ensure that the work carried out is in the public interest. Direct federal funding in this case would be neither necessary nor appropriate—except for encouraging the initiation of the association itself. If funds were supplied, the general taxpayers would be bearing a portion of the costs, although not receiving the benefits, and a new distortion would be created.

Pollution, or disruption of the environment are examples of external costs which, if not perceived or consciously avoided by the polluter, may lead to underinvestment in corrective technologies. It is a responsibility of the government to ensure the distribution of these costs in an equitable fashion as determined by the political process. The government, in its role of overseer of the production system, can act through taxes, regulations, or other mechanisms to force internalization of external costs, and this will lead to ameliorative R&D if necessary.

Several other examples of externalities can be given. Since the energy system is complex and interacting, a failure of one part of the system may have consequences on broad sectors of the economy. The blackout on the East Coast in 1965 illustrated the complex interaction of the electricity supply system and its susceptibility to disruption by small events. Increased coal production might lead to increased strip mining and basic changes in the ecosystem. The widespread installation of new systems of supply of energy may have large effects not only on the environment but on the social and economic development of certain regions of the country, with various social costs and benefits. For example, the exploitation of new techniques of obtaining oil from shale will substantially affect large regions of the western part of the United States and hence require study and assessment. The operation of nuclear reactors introduces the risk of accidents and the resulting economic and human losses.

Without government intervention, the investments necessary to reduce such external social costs will not be undertaken by producers or users. To establish the proper mechanism for the determination of social costs and benefits, it may be necessary for the government to sponsor research to enable it to better *evaluate* the social costs and benefits of an externality, and *choose* the kind and degree of intervention that most nearly corrects the market deficiency.

### Indivisibilities
There may be cases in which all benefits and costs are fully perceived and appropriable by the relevant decision-making units, but where the costs of carrying out specific research tasks would be significantly lowered if supported by the government on a nationwide basis.[9] For example, it would be possible (though prohibitively expensive) for individual purchasers of home appliances to test brands to determine which is most efficient in terms of energy utilization. Organizations such as the Consumers' Union take advantage of the economies of scale inherent in such testing procedures by conducting these tests themselves and selling the results.

In some cases, it might be even more efficient for the federal government to test or support the testing of products and then make the results available either free or for a small fee. This is particularly true if the government, in its role as a consumer, already conducts tests for its own purchases. Note, however, the reason for the support of this collective work is that the economies of scale due to indivisibilities are so large as to make the federal government the most economically efficient body to support such work. Clearly this argument also applies to work that would benefit a group of firms cooperatively supporting or performing R&D.

### Public Good
The third broad class of circumstances where government intervention in the energy R&D process would be justified is when the product of such research possesses the characteristics of what economists term "public goods."[10] An example will help to clarify what this term means. Once a decision has been made to provide a given level of national defense, it is impossible to exclude any citizen residing in this country from its full benefit, regardless of how much (or how little) he might desire them. Since the citizen is aware of the impossibility of exclusion, he will understate his preferences if they provide the basis for assessing his share of the costs as they do for ordinary goods. In the case of a public good, therefore, the decision of how much to supply to each unit or individual cannot be made by a market, but must be made by the political system. (Contrast this to the case of externalities where the market provides the appropriate results if the government attaches the costs and benefits to the appropriate decision-making units.)

Energy is an input into all production processes. Substantial disruption of its supply will, therefore, have profound economic and social consequences. Hence, government has a role of assuring reliable supplies and of assessing both the costs of that assurance and costs of the disruption. Such assurance of supply is a "public good" since no one can be excluded from the benefits of an assured supply of energy. This insurance can take many forms— stockpiling, purchase of "futures," or development of alternative technologies.

Consideration of public good is clearly involved in the currently proposed federal R&D directed toward the development of new energy supplies or reduction of energy use. Much of this activity is motivated by a desire to reduce this country's dependence on overseas fuel supplies because of fear that these supplies might be jeopardized in time of war or interrupted in peacetime for political reasons. (Note that we do not here include the balance-of-payments consequences of dependence on overseas supplies. They will be discussed separately below.) Motivation for much of the research and development on coal gasification, coal liquefaction, methods of extracting oil from shale, etc., is to provide insurance against future disruption of supply by reducing dependence upon imports. Nevertheless, governmental restrictions on fuel imports or some form of import tax might be required if world oil prices fall; otherwise, new technologies, even if developed, would not likely be used, since it would be cheaper to import fuels from overseas. If R&D activities are "insurance policies" against disruption of supplies, their effectiveness must be measured against purchasing this "insurance" by another means, for example, stockpiling. They should not be evaluated in comparison with other proposed federal R&D activities aimed at correcting externalities or taking advantage of indivisibilities.

Development of new technologies for producing oil from domestic sources is also a way of insuring against higher prices of imported oil. At present, prices are dependent on the strength of the producers' cartel, the Organization of Petroleum Exporting Countries (OPEC). It also appears to be in the interest of large oil companies when collectively negotiating with OPEC to maintain or even raise the price of oil.

When examined in this light, the public-good aspects of these policies become clear. The benefits of an assured supply of fuel (achieved, perhaps, through the development of new technologies) cannot be confined to a portion of the population. All citizens would receive the benefits of this "insurance policy," even if they did not wish to do so. Private firms clearly would be unwilling to support these activities to the extent that society may desire. A private firm will only invest in new production if the future price is sufficiently high (and reasonably certain) to justify its investment. The government, on the other hand, may see the development of new technologies as a way of putting a lid on OPEC prices, or of reducing dislocations such as those suffered in early 1974 by providing options for future domestic fuel supplies.

As with any insurance policy, the decision to develop domestic self-sufficiency through new technologies should be made after comparing its benefits with its costs. It is difficult to measure the benefits to the nation of assurance against a sudden reduction of foreign sources of fuel. However, the cost of minimizing the risk can be estimated, within limits. It is the additional price that must be paid in terms of R&D and construction costs to provide credible alternatives to imports. This cost can be compared with estimates of the costs of providing assured supplies by means other than by R&D.

There is also a concomitant risk. It is possible, though perhaps unlikely, that R&D on new technologies would demonstrate to OPEC that their oil would be a bargain at a higher price than now prevails.

Finally, classical economic theory argues that in the absence of competition there is little economic incentive to innovate.[11] When an industry is dominated by one or two firms, there may be underinvestment in R&D. In general, the government should treat the *cause* through corrective action (i.e., antitrust action to encourage competition), rather than treat the symptoms by supporting R&D.

## FACTORS NOT JUSTIFYING FEDERAL ENERGY R&D SUPPORT

It is important to note several popular, but in our view, unwarranted justifications of federal support of R&D.

### Long Development Lead Times

It has been occasionally argued that the world will run out of gas or oil, and that the government must begin support of some large ameliorative R&D project now because it will be too late when the fuels on which we now depend are exhausted.

While the earth's resources may indeed be finite, an increase in the price generally encourages an increase in the amount of oil or uranium that can be produced. Thus when examining the arguments for and against developing the breeder reactor to reduce dependence on uranium, the question arises whether an investment should be made now in order to save money in the future, when uranium prices rise. Failure to invest early in R&D for a substitute product or process would not generally result in catastrophic shortages, but only in a temporary period during which prices would be higher than they might otherwise have been. A decision to embark on a twenty-year breeder development program therefore hinges on a comparison of the present value of the investment with the expected value (appropriately discounted) of future savings. These savings are largely due to lower fuel costs, as the breeders would use less uranium than light water reactors, and consequently the price of uranium would rise less quickly.

There are uncertainties in estimating costs and benefits. For example, decisions about breeder reactors hinge on estimates of future prices of uranium and on the construction costs of plants yet to be built. Even so, if the proposed program does not correct externalities or provide a public good, it seems reasonable that the beneficiaries of the development, namely the manufacturers, the utilities and the users of electricity should bear most of the costs.

If the government, in evaluating projects with long lead times, uses a lower interest rate (discount rate)[12] than private industry to judge the future value of its investment for a similar project, it may be able to justify undertaking R&D where the private sector would not. In this connection economists have argued over the question of different public versus private discount rates.

It is first necessary to distinguish between discounting for time and discounting for risk. With regard to the latter, it is clear that the government does face a set of risks different from those a private firm faces. For instance, a firm is less certain about its ability to appropriate all of the benefits of innovation; it must be concerned with the risk of future competition. Moreover, the wise investor calculates the riskiness of his entire portfolio considered all together, not separately. By "covering one's bets" the riskiness of a portfolio of projects may be less than the risk of any single investment. Because the government has a very much larger portfolio of investments, it can benefit from "risk pooling" to a greater extent than private firms. But in no case is it justifiable to invest in an unprofitable portfolio.

To the extent that such factors produce for the government a pattern of expected costs and benefits different from that faced by a private firm, the government might appropriately undertake certain projects that private firms might decide to forego. But the correct way of handling these situations is not for the government to apply a lower discount rate than private industry. This can easily lead to inappropriate decisions as to what projects to support. The correct solution is to indicate the differences in the *expected* benefit and cost streams directly, and discount them at the same rate used by the private sector.

With respect to time, the discount rate is a measure of an individual's willingness to trade present consumption for future gains. The prevailing discount rate in the private market is the result of the complex interplay between factors such as different individuals' willingness to trade present for future value, the distribution of wealth, and the total money supply.

The government, through fiscal and monetary policy, can affect the prevailing private discount rate, and, in general, attempt to regulate it in a way that forces the private discount rate to equal the optimum discount rate as viewed by the society as a whole. That is, it tries to make the private rate coincide with the public discount rate. If it succeeds, there is no difference between public versus private discount rates, and our original question becomes irrelevant.

In practice, due to the many interventions of the federal government and imperfections in capital markets, several discount rates are in use in the U.S. economy. When the government evaluates what are essentially industrial decisions, we see no reason for it to use a discount rate different from what private firms would use in making a similar evaluation. Thus, in evaluating Liquid Metal Fast Breeder Reactors (LMFBR's), the government should use the same rate as would General Electric or Westinghouse.

With respect to time discounting it is our view that the burden is on the proponent of government projects to demonstrate that a discount rate different from the private sector is appropriate. In general, we believe, there is no reason *to assume* that the public sector is justified in adopting a different (lower) time value on money than the private sector. There may, of course, be special cases in which the use of a different rate is justified. But this must *always* be argued on a case-by-case basis.

Furthermore, there is no reason to believe that private industry is not capable of performing the necessary computations and making rational decisions—from society's point of view as well as its own—on whether to invest in such projects, once externalities and other factors are taken care of.

### Balance-of-Payments Considerations

In the discussion of the aspects of energy R&D above, care was taken to distinguish balance of payments consequences resulting from an increased dependence on foreign energy supplies from other considerations. Increased payments for imported fossil fuels may affect the balance of payments and even require adjustments in exchange rates.[13] Recent increases in oil prices have and will continue to have great consequences to countries more dependent on imports than the United States, particularly those less developed countries with few resources. Sudden currency adjustments can have disruptive consequences that cannot be anticipated or provided for by private firms. There may then be some justification for government expenditures to improve the U.S. balance of trade or of international payments. But reducing imports of fossil fuel is only one way to improve our payments position. If energy R&D is justified on such grounds, federal support for the improvement of hothouse technology to reduce our dependence on imports of bananas and coffee is likewise justified. However, in the case of energy, reducing imports of oil in the face of high OPEC prices may be justified in order to reduce the risk of disruption, to pressure for lower prices, or as an attempt to alleviate a major world wide monetary crisis. In short, the advantage to be gained by investments in energy R&D must be compared against all other possible investments that would increase exports or reduce imports, which, in turn, must be compared to the social costs (and benefits) of simply allowing the currency exchange rate to change. Indeed, most economists believe the latter course to be the least costly.

### The Need to "Save Energy"

When there is a rapidly rising demand in the face of a short-run inelasticity of supply, the result is a sharp rise in price. The uneven incidence of price increases may raise serious questions of equity and potential social disruption. A comparison of the various options for ameliorating these problems may indicate that direct public support for energy conservation or rationing are among the most effective methods for reducing the social costs, at least until the energy system can respond. In the long run, however, the benefits of these measures may be more than offset by the distortions in the allocation of resources resulting from these very same measures. Energy though basic to the economy is a commodity like any other, and if there is no divergence between private and social costs and benefits, this product should be utilized no more or no less than any other product. Indeed, adopting energy conservation as an explicit goal for federal support of R&D would result in resources being employed for finding ways of reducing energy use that could be more productively employed elsewhere. Energy would be conserved, but the overall efficiency of the economy would be reduced.

The situation changes when all costs and benefits related to energy are either not fully perceived or not fully captured by the relevant decision-making units. Unless some way is found to internalize these external costs and benefits, society will either overutilize or underutilize energy. But this internalization can be accomplished in many ways. The most efficient way is to impose these costs on the suppliers of various forms of energy so that the price paid by the user reflects all relevant costs, and to ensure that the market process allows the buyer to perceive these costs. The user can then decide on the basis of his perceived prices the value of alternative supplies and uses of energy. If this were done, and if heavy energy-using industries, such as aluminum, continued to use very energy-intensive production processes, it would be because society valued the product of this industry (including the energy embodied therein) more than it valued other products (including the energy embodied in their manufacture). The pressure on firms to reduce operating costs would induce them to reduce their utilization of energy, as long as by doing so they did not increase their utilization of other resources to a point where the savings were negated. No appeal to "social responsibility" or a "conservation ethic" would be necessary. Nor would federal expenditures for developing energy-saving processes be required.

### Certain Research "Ought" to Be Done

Allegations made of the failure of the energy supply and use system to rationally allocate resources for R&D may be well founded. If so, a necessary—but not a sufficient—condition for government support for R&D is fulfilled. However, it may be that the system is actually working quite well, and that the problem is that certain groups in society who wish to achieve special goals are not satisfied.

The mere fact that not all perceived needs in the economy are being met is *not* a sign that is rational allocation decisions are being made, or that government intervention is called for. On the contrary, it is the function of prices to allocate limited resources among unlimited needs. Markets fail only if signals have been generated leading to the fulfillment of the *wrong* needs.

When some group dissatisfied with the pace of technological change seeks federal support for R&D on the grounds that "national needs" are not being met, there are several possible explanations. In certain cases the claim of failure is well founded. In other cases, markets may be reacting appropriately to the perceived signals, but the signals themselves may be distorted as a result of previous governmental intervention. Although in some instances the government may attempt an exactly offsetting counter-distortion, a better solution would be to eliminate the cause of the original distortion. (Deregulation of the field price of natural gas is an example.) In yet other cases, groups of firms may be appropriating inadequate resources because of collusion. Finally, the market may be working perfectly, the only problem being that certain groups in society do not like the consequences and wish to alter them by political action.

## PRINCIPLES OF EFFECTIVE GOVERNMENT INVOLVEMENT

We have argued that government involvement in the energy supply system should be governed by two principles:

1.  With respect to resources it owns, or energy it consumes, the government should behave as any socially responsible, rational economic actor and maximize benefits or minimize costs.
2.  As monitor and moderator of the energy-market system, it should correct its deficiencies and impose restrictions, subsidies or regulations to meet the needs of society as a whole.

A number of propositions regarding government involvement in energy R&D follow from these two principles.

The first is that the government should not seek general justifications to support energy R&D or pursue innovation for its own sake. R&D expenditures may be an important means of government action to carry out its responsibilities, but R&D itself is never the ultimate objective. More importantly, R&D is only one—and not always the limiting—factor in the process of technological innovation.

Second, the perspective of government should focus on the *incentives* within which decisions are made in the energy system. If there are obvious deficiencies, the government could intervene to redress the balance of incentives so that it would be rational for the firms to allocate more funds for R&D.

Third, any action taken by the government may, in its turn, introduce distortions in the system. The choice of mechanisms for government intervention should be made in a manner that minimizes secondary impacts. For example, in funding R&D directly on joint ventures, the government should be concerned not to increase concentration and monopoly by its actions.

## SUMMARY

The government's basic role should be to assure that the energy supply system operates as efficiently as possible to deliver goods and services, subject to various nonmarket social goals being taken into account. Stated somewhat more technically, the federal R&D policy can only be rationalized in terms of the government's role in correcting "failures" of the energy supply and utilization system, or providing for a public good. For example, it may be correct for the government to support an R&D program, whose initial benefits no single firm could appropriate if it undertook such research with corporate funds. Economists refer to this as the problem of "nonappropriability." However, it is very important to guard against financing each and every project that might be proposed. Such protection is available in an adversary procedure where the proponents and opponents of the projects argue their respective cases before the financing body. We will discuss this procedure later.

A second but no less important role of government should be to moderate those consequences of the operation of the energy system that produce significant social costs. To use technical language, it is a proper government function to ensure that "external costs" are "internalized" by an industry. Research and development programs may become necessary to accomplish this objective. Decisions to moderate such social costs of the energy system should be made by the political process. Some of the social costs that have been identified are:

1. Operation of the system may lead to unacceptable consequences on the physical environment in the absence of positive government action of some sort.
2. Certain operations of the system may be subject to failure, leading to damage or loss of life.
3. The system may be subject to shocks, beyond the control of any part of the system, which would intolerably impair its ability to deliver energy to society or produce short-term unacceptable social costs.

Much of the current controversy about the energy system derives from the inadequacy of its procedure to deal with the moderation of these social costs and their consequences. To deal with these issues requires both a set of explicit policies and effective vehicles of implementation. The government must assume responsibility, and hence be organized to facilitate, the balancing of the benefits of moderating externalities or correcting market failure against the increased cost of energy resulting from such activities.

There are many groups in society that are dissatisfied with various features of the present energy supply system. Many have turned to government—and more can be expected to turn to any new energy agency in the future—for aid, citing failure of the energy system as justification for their claims for support. Among the specific "failures" alleged are:

1. Fragmented decision-making authority or fragmented markets.
2. Capital requirements for development beyond the capability of a single firm.
3. The existence of national benefits that are not perceivable or appropriable by private firms.
4. Long pay-off times for a new technology coupled with a high degree of technical and marketing uncertainty.

Each of these potential failures must be carefully analyzed in each case, but even if true, they do not necessarily constitute sufficient justification for government support of energy R&D.

# Chapter Three

# The Organization of Government

Certain principles that should govern federal involvement in energy R&D have been discussed thus far. The organizational structure of government has an important, even decisive, impact upon the way these principles get put into practice and on the final allocation of resources in the energy system. It is likely that allegations of failure of the energy supply and use system will continue and intensity, together with pleas for government support of particular energy R&D programs. As a result, the danger to be avoided is that the structure of government will tend to promote programs which are unrelated either to the needs of suppliers and users of energy or to the need for moderation of the social consequences of the operation of the energy system. The government should therefore be organized to minimize such dangers.

Since R&D is not an end in itself, responsibility and support for R&D should not be organized separately from other government activities related to energy. The principle of performing research at the level closest to its ultimate use is widely accepted in industry[1] and has become national policy in most industrialized nations.[2] Except for radically new technologies that arise from inventions or scientific discoveries new to any existing firm, R&D is demonstrably most effective when performed in close connection with the organizations that will put the results to use. At the same time, research of general interest to a broad sector of industry, or research of a highly speculative nature which might lead to a basically new technology, should be supported at a sufficiently high level so that it does not have to be justified solely by its contribution to a single firm or even to an industry. Indeed, in such cases isolation from short-range needs is necessary in order to focus upon radically new technologies whose consequences cannot yet be perceived or evaluated by existing firms or by existing government programs.

Direct support for R&D is, furthermore, only one of many mechanisms for encouraging innovation; other ways are by tax incentives, procurement

*25*

schemes, and other techniques, and direct support should be compared with these for cost effectiveness. However described, government support for R&D for industrial improvement is usually a subsidy from the taxpayer to the private sector of the economy.

Even in the case of energy, which is so widely used, there is good reason to try to include all costs in the price paid by the user in order to avoid distortion in the allocation of resources. Federal support of R&D solely for the benefit of a specific system of energy supply or a class of users encourages energy suppliers to produce more, or it encourages a class of users to consume more than they would in the absence of the subsidy.

The federal government should avoid whenever possible the temptation to become directly involved in energy R&D. The historical evidence is that direct involvement by the federal government in private industry programs, where the government absorbs the risks, may become ineffective if the program loses sight of its original objectives.[3] The supersonic transport program[4] is an example of a major federal development activity that became disconnected from its goals, and in which market considerations tended to be ignored. An even more dramatic case is that of the joint Anglo-French development of the Concorde which now appears to be an economic disaster.

Decisions by the government about energy R&D should be made by a process of incremental mutual adjustment as opposed to centralized coordination. That is, the structure of the decision-making organizations of the federal government should be designed to encourage the formation of interest groups to advocate their views at the various centers of decision-making. The agencies involved would then be responsive to alternative points of view about the causes and extent of market failures before deciding on ways of mitigating the situation—and in particular before deciding if additional R&D is required.

Each office or agency concerned with a particular area should be responsible for calculating the impact of actions taken by others on its functioning and its constituency; it should present this information in the decision-making process. The agency responsible for overseeing fossil-fuel electric-power generation, for example, should examine the effect on the industry of standards proposed by the Environmental Protection Agency. On the other hand, agencies of the government responsible for development and promotion of an area should not also be responsible for regulation of the same area.

In virtually all of these respects the present organizational structure of the federal government is grossly deficient. There are only a few sectors of the energy supply system where government agencies are in a position to carry out their appropriate roles. Moreover, even when particular agencies are capable of providing the necessary function of overseeing a specific sector, they are usually unable to compare the costs and benefits of alternative courses of action. For example, the dominant federal R&D programs related to the energy system have aimed to develop new types of nuclear reactors—only one of several methods of generating electric power and one primarily aimed at reducing the future cost of electricity. Mechanisms to contrast the potential value of alternative R&D programs—such as comparing programs designed to improve the supply of electricity from fossil fuels with nuclear fuels—are not available; nor are mechanisms for comparing programs seeking to reduce transmission loss of electricity, or of utilizing it more effectively, with various alternative methods of generation.

The incomplete and fragmented federal organizational structure has in the past not only led to the concentration of R&D in certain fields but also to the complete absence of technical activities in others. Furthermore, the R&D functions are seldom connected with the agencies of the government that are responsible for the relevant aspects of the energy system. Solar energy R&D, for example, has been supported by the National Science Foundation, where there is little knowledge of the requirements for electric power or of the technology of power production and little connection with the related industries.

The absence of agencies responsible for overseeing the various elements of the energy system prevents the determination of areas of technology that would benefit the whole system (and which are not appropriable by parts of it). There has been no activity with respect to the energy supply system analogous to that of the Advanced Research Projects Agency (ARPA) in the Department of Defense, which supports the development of a technology broadly applicable to the defense mission but not specific to any single service. Nor is there an agency with the responsibility for estimating the future need for specially trained manpower or the need for supporting science that will benefit the future supply or use of energy in some as yet undefined way. The broad national requirements for energy supply can and should justify these activities.

When the air-pollution regulations, particularly those having to do with sulfur oxide emissions, were being considered,[5] no agency of the government had the responsibility or the information for estimating their potential impact on the supply of energy. Until recently there has been little assessment of the impact of these regulations on the supply, use or cost of energy.

Often there is a need to encourage the formation of groups of firms with similar interests in order to support R&D that is valuable to the group, but which no single firm could justify undertaking by itself. The present organization of government lacks agencies with the responsibility for assessing the various sectors of industry to determine whether or not there is a need for collective technical work. The government has not often initiated or encouraged organizations such has the Electric Power Research Institute (EPRI). Such associations can carry out work whose results can be appropriated by the group of member firms. No agency of government is able to monitor and oversee the activities of the associations that now exist or which may be established. It is worth observing that almost every other industrial nation provides some financial support to industrial associations to encourage collective work.[6]

Representatives of these governments participate in their deliberations and make sure that the public interest is considered. In this country real or imaginary fears of possible collusion have limited encouraging the formation and growth of associations or groups of firms that perform technical work for the benefit of similar firms.

The effective operation of a market system requires, among other things, that the buyer have adequate information upon which he can make rational economic choices. In most instances, firms (at least the large ones) can afford to obtain this information themselves, while the cost to an individual consumer of equivalent information is far too great. It is not easy for the individual consumer to perform the necessary technical work to determine the life cycle costs (including energy) of consumer durables or other products that require a large use of energy in their operation. Nor are his interests represented in the complex of government agencies that oversees or regulates portions of the energy system or regulate industry generally.

Although responsibility for the management of public lands and the purchasing of goods for the government has been clearly delineated, the agencies responsible have seldom supported the technical work needed to carry out effectively their respective functions. The General Services Administration, for example, has not supported sufficient R&D to set performance specifications for purchase (or lease) of buildings, vehicles and devices in order to minimize life cycle costs. In general the owners of federal resources have neither supported the work necessary to determine their potential value nor obtained information on the environmental consequences of their exploitation.

## PROPOSED ORGANIZATIONAL CHANGES

There have been several reorganizations and proposals for changing the federal energy policy machinery to meet deficiencies such as those described above.[7] During the period of this study there have been numerous changes in the various proposals, and some new legislative and executive arrangements have been made. (See Appendix B for a summary of key proposals and their status.) Senator Jackson introduced a bill, passed by the Senate in December 1973, that would authorize an organizational structure to reduce anticipated requirements for imported fuels by supporting a technology required to provide domestic substitutes. It proposes a management project to coordinate and fund a broad range of energy R&D efforts. It authorizes temporary government-industry corporations to undertake commercial development. It allows for federal loans and federal guarantees for the price of products. The fundamental purpose of Senator Jackson's proposed legislation is to make the United States self-sufficient in energy supplies within ten years. The difficulty with Senator Jackson's proposals is that they do not effectively relate the R&D functions to the needs of the industrial energy supply system. One infers that the Jackson bill assumes that

R&D and pilot plant construction are the only barriers to self-sufficiency. The requirement for partial funding by industry presumes that industrial firms would benefit from the corporations' activities even if they resulted in products whose costs were higher than existing or anticipated market prices.

The creation of quasi-public corporations implies that existing industrial firms are either not capable of carrying out the work, or would not perform the work effectively even if supported. We argue that this may not necessarily be the case. The bill was originally drafted before the recent rise in energy prices. The reluctance of private industry to invest in shale or coal-conversion seems to have substantially diminished. Since the patent rights of the developments by the proposed corporations would be in the public domain, there would be little competitive advantage for industrial firms to invest in the work that led to them.

The Former President Nixon proposed the creation of an Energy Research and Development Agency (ERDA) as the central executive agency to support R&D pertinent to the failures of the energy supply system. The overall reorganization plan, of which ERDA is a part, includes four principal elements:

1. A Federal Energy Administration (FEA) to coordinate at the presidential level all national policies affecting energy.
2. A cabinet-level Department of Energy and Natural Resources (DENR) to centralize the resource allocation activities now scattered throughout the executive branch.
3. An Energy Research and Development Agency (ERDA) to combine the activities of the Office of Coal Research with the promotional activities of the Atomic Energy Commission.
4. A new independent regulatory agency, the Nuclear Energy Commission (NEC), to licence civilian nuclear facilities.

Although the Federal Energy Administration has been signed into law, it is problematical at best whether the FEA will be able materially to affect policies and programs rooted in the entrenched relationships among various executive agencies and bureaus, their private-sector clients, and the pertinent congressional committees and subcommittees. The ability of such relationships to resist executive-level control is too common a theme of American political and economic history to require much elaboration here.[8]

With respect to the implications of the proposal for energy R&D, we are skeptical about the wisdom of separating the management of R&D from the executive energy-related programs. The creation of ERDA as a separate energy agency permits policy decisions about R&D to be made without direct connection with the energy industry it is intended to serve. Perhaps even more questionable is the inclusion of the military weapons program of the AEC within the scope of this organization. Attention to it will tend to distort the attention of the ERDA administration from civil problems. Separate agencies generally mean separate constituencies, which mean political independence. We have argued that federal programs on energy must be consistently related to the needs of the energy supply and use system. To separate R&D from other government resource allocation activities seems to be a giant step in the wrong direction. This is especially the case if ERDA itself develops into little more than a revitalized Atomic Energy Commission to which the Office of Coal Research and a few other technical programs have been grafted, while still including a major defense program.

## A PROPOSED ORGANIZATION

In order to illustrate a more effective governmental decision-making process, particularly concerning R&D, we suggest a possible way of organizing the government's energy activities. The present composition of the Congress and the interests of various committees may make it very difficult to establish. However, a discussion of an "ideal" organization does illustrate how the decision-making processes work.

Instead of the plethora of separate agencies, the responsibility for overseeing the energy system could be assigned to a single cabinet-level department as in the case of transportation, health and education. Within that department the major lines of responsibility should correspond to the structure of the energy industry. Such an organization would go far toward emphasizing the connection between the government's R&D activities and the needs of specific sectors—electric-power generation, transportation, residential/commercial, and industrial—resulting from failures of the market mechanism. This would facilitate the transfer of the results of public R&D programs into the market. It would also facilitate the direct comparison of the contributions to energy supply made by different technologies.

The present imbalance in the federal allocation of R&D funds and manpower among the alternative energy supply technologies is one of the situations the new executive machinery must redress. Organizations solely devoted to research and development seldom consider means other than R&D for accomplishing the ends that their programs aim to accomplish: they give the impression that real problems are being attacked simply because R&D programs exist. It is also generally sound practice to structure an agency in such a way that initial decisions must be made on the allocation of funds among competitive technologies at the lowest possible operating unit with the agency management maintaining acceptable balance between the projects.

Organizing a new energy agency by industrial sectors does have one important flaw. Each of the principal divisions would have a separate and largely independent constituency. Barriers to communication are likely to develop within such an agency, since each of these units tends to become autonomous.

This, of course, is the classic pattern of autonomous bureaus operating within executive departments effectively independent from the central administration.

In the case of energy, particularly energy R&D, however, this risk is probably one worth taking. *This is because energy R&D has no economic or social end in itself.* Moreover, the existence in the private sector of "energy companies," with interests in several aspects of energy supply, will reduce the tendency toward isolation. For these reasons we propose the organizational structure illustrated in Figure 3–1 for a federal energy department. The major activities of this organization would be within the unit called "The Energy System," which would have the responsibility to oversee the pertinent parts of that system. It should be organized along the lines suggested in Figure 3–1, with each major subdivision having the responsibility for an R&D program. Thus various R&D programs can be compared with others, and no single group is likely to dominate the entire program.

Certain technologies have been and will be identified that are broadly applicable to the entire energy system. Improvements in these technologies and their more effective use would benefit the entire energy system. A separate organizational entity, perhaps modeled along the lines of ARPA in the Department of Defense, is needed to identify such opportunities, to determine how they should be supported, and to be responsible for them.

Unlike any but the largest of the diversified firms, the government supports science to provide for new and unanticipated activities in understanding and discovery. A separate operation for this purpose should also be established within any new executive machinery. The analogy here is with the old Office of Naval Research. This same operation should assume the responsibility of collecting information, from those who oversee the energy system, on the needs for specialized manpower and encouraging or supporting training and education if required.

Opportunities for radically new devices or processes will arise, either from advances in science and technology, or as a result of the changing requirements of the market or of political decisions affecting the system. Frequently, insufficient data is available for private firms to evaluate the possibilities of new devices or processes. Decisions on whether or not to support work of this type are difficult, since scientific and technical experts with a vested interest frequently claim that industry has failed to exploit a new idea when it is in fact simply not worthwhile. A new federal organization should explicitly provide for the evaluation of new technologies in advance of the ability of industry to commit major resources to them. Again, a separate organizational unit within the energy system administration should be created for this purpose.

Those reponsible for overseeing and monitoring the energy system will obtain data related to industry performance as well as supply and demand. Since energy generated from different sources is partly substitutable, a mechanism of integrating and coordinating the description and forecasting of the

**Figure 3–1.** Proposed Federal Energy Administration

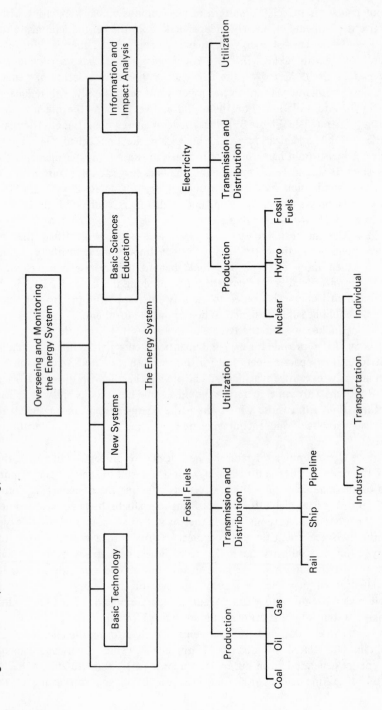

performance of the system is also required. The unit assigned this responsibility (which we call in Figure 3–1 Information and Impact Analysis) should also be capable of estimating the impact of various political decisions—such as environmental regulations—on the operation of the industry system and the consequences of changing supply and use on the environment.

There is an additional need for a means to represent the consumer of energy and to represent the potential for energy conservation, particularly in regulatory proceedings. To achieve this, Congress could declare conservation to be a national goal, and require the filing of impact statements regarding energy by agencies like the Federal Power Commission, the Civil Aeronautics Board and the Federal Housing Administration.

A possible way of making decision-makers more conscious about the existence of indirect yet important impacts of regulatory policy on energy usage would be to create an agency whose mission would be energy conservation, or more broadly stated, efficient utilization of energy (and materials) resources which gives due account to the social and private costs and benefits of energy use. This Conservation and Utilization Agency (CUA) could be given the power to intervene in selected proceedings, to point out the consequences of proposed regulatory actions on energy supply and demand. The agency's powers could be limited to *generating information,* the choice of how to weigh this information being left to the agency responsible for making the policy decision (for example the Civil Aeronautic Board in the case of airline fares).

Given this limitation, the Conservation and Utilization Agency could become expert in writing energy impact statements but would very likely have little continuing impact on energy use. However, combined with a requirement made binding by Congress on all federal, state and local agencies that energy impact statements be given weight in decisions, the CUA could prove a powerful force for the recognition of the impact of agency decisions on energy use and supply. A mechanism could be created, therefore, not to "coordinate" all policies related to energy, but to increase the awareness of government that virtually any of its actions may have a significant impact on energy usage or supply.

The study of the regulatory process tells us that regulatory agencies are likely to respond only to interests that are represented and perceived by the agency to have some power. There are numerous examples of regulatory agencies acting contrary to the public interest and in the interest of those being regulated. Consequently, regulatory agencies—even ones like the Environmental Protection Agency—are unlikely to consider the impact of their decisions upon energy use or supply unless some party in their proceedings has both an interest in presenting this information and some perceived political influence to affect the agency should it choose to ignore the information presented.

Another important role for a Conservation and Utilization Agency would be to support research on energy utilization that is not appropriable by individual consumers. It is clear that a Conservation and Utilization Agency would have to be independent of those agencies whose perceived mission is to fund R&D directed at increasing energy supply. To include such an agency in the proposed ERDA or DENR might render it ineffective, for there would be no way for it to establish the necessary connections with Congress and public-interest groups (such as consumer groups), which would assure its continuing effectiveness. The statute establishing such an agency would have to state clearly that Congress considers the efficient utilization of the nation's resources to be a goal that should be given due attention by all agencies of government in carrying out their specified duties.

In all these cases the actual R&D work should be done where it can be conducted most efficiently and most effectively translated into practice: in universities, government laboratories, associations of firms, or individual companies.

## CRITERIA FOR PROGRAMS TO STIMULATE
## TECHNOLOGICAL CHANGE

This brings us to a separate, yet crucial, issue: What are the appropriate criteria for selecting and evaluating alternative mechanisms for encouraging techno-logical innovations? There are many alternative mechanisms available to it to stimulate technical innovation independently of the particular governmental organizational structure. Up to now, selection between alternative mechanisms has been a haphazard process, largely determined by expediency or tradition.

The government's primary goal in stimulating technological innova-tion in the energy field is that the new technologies be *used* to improve the supply, conversion, transportation or use of a significant amount of the nation's energy. Except in special cases, the success of a federal R&D program should be measured in terms of actual implementation of the technology.

We believe certain general propositions are important as guides to how government should affect technological innovation:

1. Operating close to the user of the technology is usually more effective than mechanisms several steps removed from him.
2. Mechanisms that require minimum interference with market forces should generally be selected over those that involve long-term disruptions.
3. Time is valuable, but early milestones in the R&D process, although indica-tive of progress, should not be considered ends in themselves.
4. Competition is an essential element in our system. Hence mechanisms that preserve and enhance competition between new and existing technologies, between segments of the energy system, or between individual firms gener-ally produce positive benefits.
5. The day-to-day incentives for those making programmatic decisions should

be designed to ensure that final beneficial use, rather than technological perfection, is kept clearly in sight as the goal of the R&D program.
6. Because adapting technological innovations in energy takes several years, such programs must have long-term stability.

There is also a set of secondary criteria which, if not met, will result in adverse public relations and a high probability of failure:

1. The accrual of windfall profits to particular firms or individuals should be minimized. Reasonable rewards for innovation and risk-taking are, however, necessary.
2. Government outlays and tax losses must be controllable.
3. The R&D mechanism must be flexible enough to allow for major changes in public policy, but stable enough to resist the whims of public opinion.
4. The mechanism should not decrease private incentives to undertake related technological innovation.

Finally, there is the question of the degree of technical control exercised by the government. When supporting R&D for military and space requirements, where the government is the ultimate consumer of the technology, technological control should obviously rest in large measure with the government unless there are compelling reasons to the contrary. With respect to energy, where the government is acting as a surrogate for the ultimate consumers of the technology, the opposite presumption should hold. When decisions relative to industrial and economic developments are supported, organized, or operated by government agencies rather than by the users themselves, a sort of technical and economic unreality prevails. When health, safety, or environmental protection are involved, and the incentives for industries are insufficient to ensure that they will give these matters sufficient attention and control, management by the government may be necessary. In general, the burden of proof should be on the government to justify the need for technical control.

The following is a review of the pros and cons of the various mechanisms available to the government to stimulate energy R&D.

### Direct Government R&D

It is clear that activities to improve government services (such as weather forecasting), or to improve products it buys, or to lay the basis for regulation, all require direct support for R&D and *control* of its direction and application.

R&D can be done by government laboratories, such as those of the Bureau of Mines, or by special contractor organizations, such as the AEC laboratories. Both of these organizations were established when there was little or no industrial capability to undertake high-technology efforts that cut across several disciplines or areas of expertise. The technique has generally been used to develop technology in which the government had a direct role—military weapons and coal mine safety, for example.

It is believed by some that the apparent success of these activities justifies the performance of R&D to support industry in government laboratories. For example, programs continue in the Atomic Energy Commission's National Laboratories aimed at improving the energy supply system, and there are proposals that the National Aeronautics and Space Administration laboratories engage in similar work. In our view, R&D aimed at improvements in energy supply and use done at these institutions presents at least as many difficulties as opportunities. It is true that these institutions have multidisciplinary staffs with recognized expertise in some of the relevant fields, and that there are large investments in sophisticated facilities. But performing work to benefit the energy supply and use system in these organizations should be analyzed using the various criteria described above. The National Laboratories are not directly connected with those that will develop, manufacture, or use the possible results of the work. They typically will respond to the interests and incentives of their own administrators and scientists. Hence the link between laboratory programs (and hence public funds) and the needs of industry tend to be weak. There have rarely been effective mechanisms to question independently the extent, scope, or direction of laboratory programs or of their applicability to industrial needs. There is a very real danger that one outcome of the current policy debate will be a strengthening of an R&D system that may not be able to define and carry out programs related to the needs of the energy supply and utilization system, whose welfare its activities are intended to promote.

### Government Contract R&D

The government has attempted to reduce costs and risks of R&D to industry by paying someone—a university, a private R&D firm, or some other private corporation—to perform the needed R&D and then making the results available to industry for implementation. At one extreme are grants to universities or nonprofit R&D organizations far removed from the marketplace. When the individual project is in the research or bench-scale development stage, this may be the expedient or the only possible decision. This choice would be particularly appropriate if such organizations do similar work for the same industrial clients to whom the innovations are ultimately directed. At the other extreme, contracts can be made with the industrial firms that would eventually be responsible for implementing the innovations—the user industry or the equipment supplier. In this case the particular firm may thereby obtain a real advantage over all competitors.

There is good evidence that new firms, or firms outside an industry, are often more likely to be innovative than established firms within an industry.[9] Development may be supported to provide new entries into the system.

The point we emphasize is that the use of direct contracting requires an analysis of the target industry and its mechanisms for innovation.

On the positive side, contracting is a relatively simple, flexible means for buying R&D. A very broad range of entities and skills can be drawn upon, and if very good choices are made as to the contractors, the R&D may be conducted in reasonable proximity to market forces. Contracts with particular firms that have a stake in the industry *could* trigger comparable efforts by their competitors. Nonetheless, it is frequently the case that some contractor organizations depend primarily on government-funded R&D for their revenues, and are therefore insulated from the final users. Government controls—technical and fiscal—are required to protect the public interest. This may be simple if definite specifications and performance criteria can be developed in advance, but difficult for R&D in technically risky areas.

### Reimbursable Subsidies

Another approach involves direct government payments to underwrite the cost and risk of the development. The arrangement provides for a prenegotiated repayment in the event the development is successful. The payment can be treated as a loan repayable with interest following the achievement of some measurable success.[10] It could also be treated as an investment in which the government receives a fraction of the net revenues in proportion to its contribution. The advantage of this mechanism is that the work is very closely tied to market forces and places high incentive for market success on management and others in the firm. Accordingly, it should reduce the time for the R&D to have an impact on the market. The disadvantages are that it favors one firm, unless the program has sufficient funds to support competitors. (As a practical matter, this is probably unlikely in most instances.) It may be difficult to change direction or content once a program has begun. There is obvious potential for high profits at government expense. And finally, it raises questions of open-ended risk. Who pays if costs exceed estimates?

### Purchase of Products

Another way to accomplish innovation and to stimulate R&D is to arrange for the procurement of a product or service that can only be provided through the introduction of new technology or the adaptation of old technology to a new use. This method operates by providing a *market* for the desired product or system which it is deemed necessary to develop and leaves the detailed decisions about technology in the hands of the industry rather than the government. Perhaps the most effective application of this principle was the support by the U.S. Air Force of the purchase of computer-controlled machines for its industrial suppliers in the late 1950s. Clearly the purchase of computers and aircraft for government use for defense and space subsidized and stimulated the development and production of similar devices for civilian use.

When the government itself is a large buyer of the product, performance specifications can be established which require innovation, and the R&D can be paid for in the price paid for the product. The first introduction of safety devices on American automobiles resulted from purchasing standards by the General Services Administration. The General Services Administration could similarly purchase buildings where life-cycle costs—including energy use—were minimized. Oil made by synthetic processes could be purchased by the Defense Department.

Even where the government is not a direct purchaser it can frequently influence the market by setting standards for its various loan programs (e.g., Federal Housing Authority). In some instances the federal government through cooperation with private firms could arrange for the purchase of new products having improved performance. In the "first round" of its Cooperative Power Reactor Demonstration Program, the AEC stimulated the introduction of light water reactors by assisting investor-owned utilities to purchase reactors designed and developed primarily by private industry.

### Guaranteed Prices

In some cases, the policy may be to encourage industry to develop a new supply that is not profitable but meets some other national need; it may be deemed desirable to develop a supply of synthetic crude oil (syncrude), for example, to increase reliable supply. Industrial firms may not undertake the necessary work either because the estimated cost will be higher than the prices anticipated in the future or because other domestic energy supplies are inherently cheaper.

The government may agree to purchase a certain amount of synthetic fuel over a number of years. The bid price must take into account all the R&D necessary to develop the process and build the plant. Or if there is fear of a decline in price in the future, the government can guarantee a price floor (for the output of a particular plant) to reduce risk and encourage both the R&D and, more importantly, the production of oil using that process.

### SUMMARY

In this chapter we have reviewed the problems and inadequacies of the present government organization with respect to energy, the various proposals for reforming that organization, and summarized our own views by presenting an idealized form of government organization for dealing with energy R&D.

Four major principles that have governed our recommendations are:

1. Research and development is not an end in itself; therefore, its support should not be separated from government's more general objectives within the energy system.

**Figure 3–2.**   Chart Summarizing Pros and Cons of Various Mechanisms of Governmental R & D Support

| Criteria | Direct | Contract | Direct Fund | Procurement | Price Support |
|---|---|---|---|---|---|
| I.   To Estimate Potential for Success | | | | | |
| 1.   Proximity to market forces | very low | moderate | high | high | high |
| 2.   Degree of interference in market | high | high | medium | low | medium |
| 3.   Time to market impact | long | moderate | short | short | short |
| 4.   Effect on competition | neutral | may be adverse | may be adverse | neutral | may be adverse |
| 5.   Local incentives on program decisions (market orientation) | non-market | varies | high market orientation | high market orientation | high |
| II.   Minimum Standards for Public Acceptance | | | | | |
| 1.   Potential for unearned windfalls | none | low | moderate | low | moderate |
| 2.   Government financial commitments control | level but not duration | | depends on risk assignment | differs | high |
| 3.   Flexibility and stability | low flexibility | very flexible | moderate flexibility | very flexible | very flexible |
| 4.   Effect on private incentives to innovate | negative | moderate | | positive | positive |
| III.   Potential for Government Technical Control | all government | may be either | industry | industry | |

2. Because R&D itself is never the final objective, government organizations must permit the comparison between R&D and other means (e.g., tax credits, regulations, tariffs) for obtaining the same objectives).

3. Government organization must also facilitate comparisons between different R&D projects having similar objectives.

4. Once it has been determined to support a particular technological development, there remains a choice of mechanisms (e.g., direct, contract, joint-venture, procurement) for accomplishing the objective. As a mechanism, procurement offers several advantages; in particular, leaving the detailed technical choices to the firm that must ultimately bear responsibility for implementation.

In the following chapter we suggest a number of R&D projects and their organization that are derived from the principles enunciated in Chapters 2 and 3.

# Chapter Four

# Energy System Deficiencies
# and their Implications for R & D

In the preceding chapter we outlined our views on how the federal government might ideally be organized to determine the deficiencies in the energy system. Such an organization would assess the operating system of supply and use, determine what actions need to be taken to correct inherent deficiencies in the system in the public interest, and manage programs that would accomplish its aims. Research and development would be supported and encouraged only when it was the most appropriate means of accomplishing the specified ends.

We have been able to identify certain actions related to R&D and technology which we believe should be taken. It should be clear in what is to follow that the programs we recommend are related to the organizational concepts of the preceding chapter and focus on government actions necessary in its role as overseer of the system, as the corrector of deficiencies, and as a participant in the system.

## RESEARCH REQUIRED TO MONITOR
## THE SYSTEM

There is a serious lack of basic data, analysis, and information necessary to access the present energy system. Our own deliberations were handicapped by the paucity of knowledge. Thus, in its role as overseer and monitor of the energy system, the federal government must support significant research activities to describe and understand the energy system. This information is required to provide the basis for *intelligent decisions* by the government.

The research program should cover the following areas:

1. Building econometric models of future energy supply and demand in the United States.

2. Estimating the nature and extent of energy-related R&D conducted by the private sector.
3. Assessing the potential of various energy R&D projects.
4. Estimating the requirements for capital if the R&D schemes were to be put to commercial use.
5. Studying the impact of actions of various government regulatory agencies on the energy-industry-market system (e.g., analyzing the impact of regulations imposed by the EPA and the AEC).
6. Estimating the overall effects of the energy system on health and safety, the extent of pollution, etc.; and locational consequences—the effects on the system of demographic changes.

During the past ten years, the lack of this kind of information and analysis has meant that neither the government nor the public has been able to assess the consequences of major policy actions. In a period of growing economic distortion within the energy system, and growing concern for the environmental effects of energy production, the need to collect and process this information is urgent.

## R&D NOT APPROPRIABLE BY A FIRM

There are three broad categories of technical work on activities that meet this criterion. One consists of basic technology so broadly applicable to the various elements of the energy system that no firm can appropriate the results; another consists of basic scientific knowledge and trained people, which may be useful to the system in the future; and the third is related to environmental quality, health, and safety.

In some cases a technology has such broad application to large segments of the energy system that the benefits of investment in R&D cannot be fully realized by a single firm or group of similar firms. In these cases there will be underinvestment in R&D and the government should take action to increase the support. We have identified several such areas.

### Construction Technology

Over the period 1973–1985, it is estimated that the consumption of energy in the United States will expand from $77 \times 10^{15}$ Btu to between $90 \times 10^{15}$ and $120 \times 10^{15}$ Btu.

Regardless of whether this increased demand is met by nuclear power, synthetic fossil fuels, increased domestic fossil-fuel production, or imports, substantial construction expenditures will be required for additional facilities in the form of nuclear power plants, coal mines, refineries, super ports, shale-retorting plants, coal, gas and liquid plants, and so on. These requirements will have to be met by expanding the capacity of the construction industry. This industry will be required to build facilities such as shale plants and coal liquefication plants, for which no experience exists, while simultaneously expanding its capacity to handle orders for nuclear reactors and petroleum refineries. Because construction technology is important to all sectors of the energy system and is thus not appropriable by a single industry group, the government should support R&D in this area.

The following figures give some idea of the magnitude of construction necessary between now and 1985. At the end of 1973, the total nuclear electricity generating capacity of the United States was about 25,000 MWe; while some 170,000 MWe capacity had been ordered or was under construction. If present difficulties incurred in licensing procedures can be resolved during the next few years, an additional 100,000 MWe (or 100 new plants of 1,000 MWe capacity) may be built by 1985. Assuming an average cost of $700/kW (in 1974 dollars) over this period, the capital cost for this new capacity could reach $70 billion.

Assuming that the total electric supply system will have to expand from 473,000 MWe in 1973 to some 980,000 MWe by 1985, between $250 and $345 billion will have to be raised to meet construction costs.[1] As much as $160 to $200 billion will have to be invested in the oil and gas industry over the same period, and between $40 to $50 billion in facilities for the coal industry.

With capital costs for new energy-producing capacities ranging from $400–600 billion through 1985, improving construction technology will result in significant savings. At present, costs are rising incredibly fast; the capital cost for a 1,000 MWe nuclear plant increased from $165 million to $700 million between 1968 and 1973. The latter figure, when amortized, represents four to five times the nuclear fuel costs. One possible way of reducing costs is by standardizing plant design. This apparently straightforward solution may turn out to be difficult and unfeasible because agreement among different parties on nuclear safety questions may be impossible to reach.

An R&D program on construction should include work on the following areas:

1. Technology of on-site scheduling.
2. Quality control and reliability.
3. Standardization of parts.
4. Research on construction materials.
5. Research on soil mechanics.
6. Tunnelling.
7. Devising ways of testing reliability of plants once installed.

This research is mainly on construction software and does not require a large amount of money. The payoff, however, may be very great.

There is a second kind of construction technology that deserves equal consideration—techniques of residential and commercial construction which lead to reduced energy consumption for space heating. Individual architects cannot appropriate the benefits of research on questions such as the effect of building layout on energy consumption, or the effect of lamp location on lighting costs. The government should, therefore, stimulate research on these questions and disseminate the results.

### Combustion

Most processes involving energy are based on combustion. Combustion is central to such diverse fields as the internal-combustion engine, space conditioning, and industrial processes. Like construction technology, R&D on any combustion process serves many industries. Here again the benefits of such research cannot be appropriated even at the industry level, and public support is justified.

Among the key problems in combustion are:

1. Reduction of nitrogen oxides ($NO_x$) emissions.
2. Efficiency of fuel use.
3. Convection and heat transfer.

### Catalysis

Catalysis of hydrocarbon reactions are crucial throughout the energy system. Fuel cells, catalytic reactors for automobiles, coal gasification, and refining all depend on catalysts. There are some forms of basic catalysis technology which cannot be appropriated by any single firm, nor by any single industry group.

### Basic Science Research and Education

The potential applications and payoffs of basic scientific research cannot be foreseen, nor is the payoff appropriable, since it is generally not patentable. The government, therefore, should support such research. A major example of basic scientific research pertinent to the energy system—and which is currently being supported—is thermonuclear fusion. The government should continue to support research on plasma physics and on containment techniques in order to demonstrate scientific feasibility of fusion. No presumption should be made at this stage on whether fusion may or may not be an economic or environmentally acceptable way to produce electricity eventually.

Many other areas of basic scientific research may be applicable to the energy system. Among these are the areas of photo-voltaic semi-conductors, radiation effects on materials, surface physics (catalysis, new materials), fluid dynamics (combustion and heat transfer involve turbulence, often in two-phase systems), geophysics (relevant to geothermal power). The government should consider funding such research as part of its support for energy R&D.

The benefits of technical training in a highly mobile labor force cannot be appropriated by a single firm. For this reason, industry associations should support educational programs where the benefits from them accrue wholly to the industry concerned, and the federal government should support educational programs where benefits are more widespread. For example, the Electric Power Research Institute, along with individual firms, could support the education of electric utility employees who are preparing themselves to operate new nuclear power facilities. The federal government could also provide graduate fellowships for students interested in advanced construction techniques for nuclear reactors, refineries, super ports, and so on. In the first case, the electric utility industry can appropriate the benefits of training because nuclear power plant operators are being trained. In the second case, however, students are being educated in advanced construction technology, and no particular industry can reap all the benefits of this training.

## R&D RELATED TO ENVIRONMENTAL QUALITY AND PUBLIC HEALTH AND SAFETY

Environmental deterioration is an external cost the energy system imposes on society, and the government is justified in imposing regulations to reduce it. The energy system also takes its toll of human life in the shape of diseases and accident fatalities. The government must, therefore, set safety standards. To do this job, it must determine desirable levels of environmental quality, public health, and safety from society's point of view, and set standards, estimate the costs of meeting these standards, and enforce them. Designing procedures for meeting the standards is not necessarily a function of the government.

To make this process work properly, it must proceed through several iterations. It may not be possible to know the costs of the standards until industry has first worked out ways of meeting them. Then the government should be ready to adjust the standards according to the preferences of society as a whole, that is, to trade off costs and benefits. One important research task is to investigate closely just how certain pollutants affect human health. This would be a great step forward in setting rational standards.

Some research and development are needed include: areas where strip-mining and reclamation, plant siting, ecological disturbances of oil spills, the disposal of shale-fines from shale-oil refining, nuclear plant safety, pipeline safety, radioactive waste disposal, and mining safety.

In the nuclear area, the government has to conduct R&D on waste disposal and on thermal pollution (see Appendix C), as well as on safety. Examples of the last include setting process standards for plant construction and experiments on Loss-of-Fluid-Test (LOFT). Some aspects of the government's breeder program (those relating to safety) are fully justifiable according to this criterion.

## R&D TO PERMIT PRIVATE DECISIONS
## ON NEW TECHNOLOGY

In some cases, sufficient information about a new technology to determine the probable costs and benefits of its development—and who should bear the costs, or who should appropriate the benefits—is lacking. In these cases, the government has a proper role in performing or contracting research necessary to determine probable costs and benefits. This category differs from the first few cases discussed in that here the costs and benefits of a new technology may well be appropriable by a single firm once there is enough information about those costs and benefits. In the previous instance, a firm may know the costs and benefits but cannot appropriate them. Here the problem is that there is not enough information to make a sound judgment on whether the benefits of investment in R&D are appropriable or not. Ideally, the government would conduct research sufficient to provide the necessary information.

Some specific guidelines are required for federal R&D spending under these criteria. The extent to which government supports a specific R&D program should be in proportion to the benefits from that program if it were successful. As there is no objective measure of potential benefits, an adversary procedure, where partisans of different R&D schemes argue their cases, may be used to compare projects for federal support. The potential benefits of a technology may change in the future, so that a decision to support it or not to support it must be constantly reassessed. Examples of research the government might support under the appropriability criterion are solar central station conversion and "hot-rock" geothermal power.

### Solar Energy

Significant technical roadblocks remain before large quantities of power can be obtained from solar energy. A problem with one of the solar technologies is the immense area of collector plates necessary to support a central system of any significant generating capacity. Producing these collectors economically is not now possible and justifies R&D support. Other proposals for producing solar central station power include orbiting space collectors, ground collectors, and ocean thermal gradients. At present it is impossible even to identify the firms that would enter the business if solar central station technology seemed a profitable investment.

### Geothermal Energy

An interesting example of where research should and should not be provided under this criterion is geothermal energy. The process of obtaining electric power by piping dry natural steam to turbine generators already provides 330 MWe at "The Geysers" in California. Further government R&D funds might be spent, however, on obtaining geothermal energy from "hot rocks." This process, as yet unproven technically, involves circulating water through dry hot spots in the earth's crust to transfer the heat out as steam. Problems here involve drilling techniques, fracturing the rock, water injection, and steam recovery.

### The Liquid Metal Fast Breeder
### Reactor (LMFBR)

The LMFBR is by far the largest energy related R&D project currently being supported by the federal government. This program, which was initially begun in the early age of nuclear research, was enhanced in the mid-1960s by the AEC, which created an atmosphere of artificial urgency to develop a commercial breeder reactor.

Breeder reactors offer the promise of very low nuclear fuel cycle costs, resulting in electricity costs that are in effect independent of the price of uranium (see Appendix C). However, because this fuel cycle cost advantage can be offset by possible additional capital costs of breeders over present Light Water Reactors, the economic case for breeder development is at present very uncertain.

We can be confident only that breeders may become economical at some point in the future when uranium prices have risen to a large multiple (say five or six times) of present prices. Because the scientific and technical characteristics of the technology are at least partly understood, the decision to proceed with breeder development is largely an economic problem. It is therefore reasonable to allow private industry to decide whether to proceed with this development and when to do so. The electric utility industry should be capable of assembling the capital resources necessary to assume a major share of the development risks, and can also appropriate the results; yet the industry has not done so. The reluctance of reactor manufacturers and utilities to bear the major share of LMFBR development costs and risks is prima facie evidence that the case for proceeding at the current pace is not overpowering.

In our view, therefore, neither the kind nor level of present government support of the LMFBR program is justified by the criteria discussed in this report.[2]

## PROGRAMS TO REDUCE SOCIAL COSTS
## OF SUDDEN SUPPLY INTERRUPTION

Before the 1973 Arab oil embargo the United States was importing a little over a quarter of its crude oil requirements. About a third of the imports or about 8% of total requirements came from the Middle Eastern countries.

The embargo produced at least a temporary consensus that the United States should act to bring demand for energy into greater balance with secure supplies. The benefits of a secure supply accrue to the public as a whole and cannot be assigned to individuals, firms, or industries. Because the benefits of a secure supply are not appropriable, the private sector will not provide it. Some government intervention is therefore required to prevent possible future energy supply interruptions.

A broad range of options is available, including extension of offshore drilling, diversification of sources of supply, and energy conservation. Although such activities cannot be expected to change the sources of energy within the next ten years, many important new technologies—such as coal liquefaction and oil shale—provide legitimate policy options to increase long-term security of supply.

At this writing, market prices of foreign crude are $8–$9/barrel, and most of the known synthetic processes for making crude appear to be able to compete with imported crude on economic grounds. Prices in the range of $6–$8/barrel are generally considered realistic estimates of syncrude from both shale and coal.[3]

At current market prices for crude oil, therefore, some incentives exist for private companies to invest in R&D in these new technologies. However, delays in obtaining returns on such investments, and the uncertainty of long-term crude oil prices, is a matter of concern that may prevent these investments from being undertaken on an appropriate scale. If a secure domestic supply is needed it is appropriate for the government to support these technologies by ensuring against a possible decrease in prices. This can be achieved, for example, by the government offering to buy certain quantities of syncrude, even if the market price fell below its production cost.

But such a policy alone may not be enough to provide as rapid a development of these technologies as may be necessary if energy self-sufficiency (e.g., by 1985) is considered a suitable political aim. In this case, direct government R&D funding may become necessary, particularly at the pilot plant stage. Such an investment would save some critical lead time in bringing synthetic oil to the marketplace.

Developing new technologies, like coal liquefaction or oil shale, is only one way for assuring an adequate crude supply. The wisdom of government investment in these technologies must be weighed against other options. A unilateral government decision to secure oil supplies through syncrude technologies may be economically unwise, because providing incentives for developing new domestic reserves or new offshore drilling may be much less expensive. Investments to reduce the use of energy may be more effective than the equivalent investment to ensure an increase in supply.

Another entirely different type of interruption of supply of energy could occur if a nuclear power plant ever fails and releases large amounts of radiation, causing many deaths. This type of accident would almost certainly generate intense public pressure to shut down all nuclear plants. There is no apparent easy way to ensure against this event except by making reactors as failsafe as possible and developing safeguards to prevent unauthorized diversion of plutonium.

## R&D TO BETTER INFORM THE USERS
## OF ENERGY

An important role for the Conservation and Utilization Agency we have suggested would be to help correct a market failure that has been exacerbated by the
political process as it currently functions. Economists have long recognized that
society tends to underinvest in research and development because the benefits of
research, particularly the benefits of basic research, cannot be either fully
perceived or fully captured by those undertaking the research. This is particularly a problem where the units that would benefit from the research are highly
fragmented. Research directed toward improved energy utilization (such as
through the development of more efficient air conditioners) is likely to be
underfinanced by the private sector, compared to private financing of research
aimed at new forms of energy generation (such as nuclear power plants), since
the users of energy are generally more fragmented than the producers of energy.
This would indicate a need for government action, but a look at where government money is spent today on energy R&D shows an overriding concentration
on projects designed to tap new sources of energy. In our view, this is because
the producers of energy are more concentrated, and hence have more clearly
identifiable interest in obtaining federal research support.

A Conservation and Utilization Agency mentioned earlier could
commission and publicize studies demonstrating the relative payoff in terms of
resources and from improved energy utilization as opposed to new means of
energy generation. It should have its own research budget to fund demonstration
projects, such as the construction of a more efficient refrigerator. It might
persuade the GSA to offer to purchase a given number of improved appliances
for installation in its buildings, provided they could be produced at less than a
given price, thereby providing a substantial market for such products. It could
provide information about consumer durables, stating their energy consumption
so that consumers wishing to take a life-cycle approach to the purchase of such
products would have the information they need to make the necessary comparisons. It also could conduct (or commission) the tests required to show how such
labeling requirements could be met in a way that would provide the most useful
information to the consumer. It could suggest techniques for government
encouragement of the use of solar heating for homes.

## R&D OF THE GOVERNMENT AS RESPONSIBLE
## OWNER

The federal government owns substantial coal, oil, gas, shale, and geothermal
reserves. As a responsible owner and custodian of these public lands, the government should seek to maximize returns from its holdings.

Historically the government has either sold or leased public lands for
development by the private sector, and this process continues today. Before sale,

the government may, consistent with its role as owner, participate in R&D that will improve the value of its property. This R&D may take the form of surveys for accurately determining the value of resources, or development of new processes like coal gasification, liquefaction, and oil from shale for enhancing the value of publicly owned resources. Of course, these R&D investments must be measured against the potential payoffs in increased value of public lands.

## R&D OF THE GOVERNMENT AS RESPONSIBLE BUYER

In its role as a consumer of large quantities of goods and services, the federal government may support R&D to improve its purchase decisions and in turn the products and services it purchases. As a large purchaser, the government has capabilities that individuals do not have. It can gather information about alternative products, test these alternatives, and make purchase decisions. Because of the size of its purchases it can command special treatment from a seller. It can lead the formation of new product markets by acting as a nucleus around which disaggregated individual demand can cluster.

Two specific areas where R&D expenditures to help purchase decisions can lead to considerable savings are in buildings and automobiles. The federal government, in ordering buildings, should estimate total life-cycle costs of buildings and take into account the expected rise in the price of energy in these calculations. Similar calculations should be made for automobiles.

Some research and development may be needed for the government to act most intelligently as a purchaser. Expenditures for the development of performance standards, methods of testing, general design criteria, and so on can enable the government to save money in the long run.

## A FINAL WORD ON R&D

Throughout the foregoing discussion we have stressed our belief that R&D is not an end in itself. There is, of course, widespread conviction (though little firm evidence) that R&D activities lead directly or indirectly to the accomplishment of important national goals, especially economic growth. This may well be the case. But if so, it has nothing to do with the purpose of this report. Our objective has been to identify the specific failures of the predominantly private energy supply system *as they relate to the allocation of public administrative and fiscal resources for research and development.* If the political system demands public support for *basic research* as an end in itself, or as a means of other national goals—such as an educated populace—nothing in this report should be construed as arguments against such action. Quite to the contrary, we are inclined to be sympathetic to the conviction that *basic research* is a good thing and that some significant fraction of our national income should be devoted to it, regardless of other considerations.

But that is a separate matter. Our chief concern in this report has been to establish the fact that the currently apparent failures of the energy supply and consumption system are only *in small part* matters for which a technological fix is appropriate. The analogy with the Manhattan Project and the Apollo programs are completely misleading. Of course, R&D is relevant, and over the very long run may even be crucial, for it is undeniable that resource supplies are finite. But for the foreseeable future, that is not the point. As Harvey Brooks has noted, the "spaceship earth" metaphor is inappropriate.[4] The supply functions of a spaceship have zero elasticity. This is not the case with terrestrial resources. For the purposes of formulating public policy, the future effects of cost and price changes cannot be ignored.

We are aware that the emphasis this report has placed on concepts drawn from neoclassical economics inevitably contributes a tone of conservatism to our discussion. We believe this conservatism to be justified by what we see as the very real danger that new federal energy programs will introduce additional distortions into the supply and consumption system while trying to correct failures or moderate social costs. Obviously the marketplace never works perfectly, but it generally does work.

What the designers of new federal administrative machinery and programs must do is to assure themselves that the distortions caused by their actions represent a net improvement over the existing situation. This will be extremely difficult. Anticipation of second- and third-order effects is never easy. Yet the evidence of past experience is unambiguous; such effects of government R&D and regulatory policies do exist and often swamp the direct effects of given programs. The basis for the conservative approach we recommend is not that the market system is perfect, or perhaps even close to it, but that it is possible through misguided government action to make the system worse than it currently is.

Actually the choice is not between government action as opposed to private action or between action and inaction, but between intelligent rational action and unintelligent action. To assure rational action it is better to take small ameliorative steps, the consequences of which can be calculated, rather than massive revolutionary steps (such as restructuring the entire energy economy), since the consequences of the latter will be largely unknown. A policy of gradualism also allows corrective action without much loss,[5] in the event of any unanticipated adverse consequences of the adopted policy.

# Appendix A

# Summary of Certain Government Responsibilities in the Energy Market System

At the federal level, policies and actions that affect energy supply and demand originate in numerous agencies, departments and bureaus. These activities can generally be grouped under three headings: (1) regulation; (2) promotion; and (3) ownership and management.

Of the three, ownership and management has historically been the most important. The leasing and sale of public land for resource exploitation has been the principal federal government activity with respect to energy for more than half of the nation's history. Though still significant, this function is less important today. Now the government *directly* influences resource development and conservation, principally as a regulator and promoter.

The Federal Power Commission holds broad regulatory authority over the rate structure, general business practices and interconnection of the electric and gas utilities that engage in the interstate transmission of energy. The Interstate Commerce Commission (ICC), the Federal Trade Commission (FTC), and the Securities and Exchange Commission (SEC) are all charged with protecting the public interest against unfair commercial practices. The ICC has jurisdiction over petroleum pipelines as "common carriers," just as it has regulatory powers over other modes of transportation. In general, all these regulatory agencies exercise their power through the closely related activities of rate-setting and the granting (or withholding) of franchises. The success of these techniques and the nature of their impact upon commercial practice is sharply disputed.

More recently the government has been asked to regulate the actions of private industry in order to protect third parties or the environment from the harmful effects (potential or actual) of business activity. The AEC's elaborate procedures for licensing reactors producing electric power is perhaps the principal example of this sort of activity. Until recently, the Bureau of Mines had the responsibility for improving the health and safety aspect of mining practices. Health and safety authority for mines now resides in an office reporting directly to the assistant secretary of the interior for mineral resources. Finally, the regulatory activities of the Environmental Protection Agency will clearly have a growing impact upon energy supply industries as well as patterns of energy demand.

The government's role as a developer or promoter of energy-producing resources and technologies has also been, until recently, fairly narrow. The reluctance of investor-owned electric utilities to extend services to sparsely populated areas led to the creation of the Rural Electrification Administration (REA) in 1934. By providing funds, the REA encouraged municipal and cooperative utilities to establish electrical systems in rural areas.

In 1946, the Atomic Energy Act established federal control over nuclear energy development. In the ensuing years, the AEC experimented with a variety of techniques for encouraging the development of an industry based upon this new technology.

As with regulation for safety and environmental protection, there is evidence that governmental activities to promote new technologies will grow substantially in the coming years. A more detailed description of the nature of government involvement in the energy system is available in tabular form in Figure A–1.

**Figure A–1.** Tabulation of Federal Energy Agencies

The following tables display the Federal agencies which have been found to have specific energy policy roles. *Table A* includes agencies which administer specific energy policies or programs as defined at the head of the table. *Table B* includes agencies which administer policies or programs which are not specifically energy oriented but which have unique impacts on the energy system.

Each table, in the column headed "classification," includes a code showing the types of energy policy activities it performs. The key to the classification is set forth below. The remaining columns indicate that the agency has been identified as an "energy" agency in the other sources set out in the tables.

CLASSIFICATION OF ENERGY POLICY ACTIVITIES OF FEDERAL AGENCIES

A.  Specific Energy Activities
   1.  Policy Formation
      a.  Planning and Forecasting
      b.  Formulation of Standards, Rules, Regulations, and Rates
      c.  Preparation or Review of Proposed Legislation
   2.  Policy Implementation
      a.  Operations of energy facilities or production or marketing of energy or energy resources (including financial assistance for such activities by non-Federal entities).
      b.  Management of Energy Resources (including purchasing in quantities large enough to affect regional or national supplies).
      c.  Enforcement of Rules and Regulations
      d.  Research and Development, Data Collection, and Technical Assistance.

**Figure A–1. (cont.)**

B. Activities Having Unique Impacts Upon the Energy System

   1. Policy Formation

      a. Planning and Forecasting

      b. Formulation of Standards, Rules, Regulations and Rates

      c. Preparation or Review of Proposed Legislation

   2. Policy Implementations

      a. Operation of facilities or production of resources having unique impacts upon the energy system.

      b. Management of Resources

      c. Enforcement of Rules and Regulations

      d. Research and Development, Data Collection, and Technical Assistance.

Source: U.S. Senate, Committee on Interior and Insular Affairs, *Federal Energy Organization: A Staff Analysis* (93rd Congress, 1st Session, 1973).

**TABLE A.**  FEDERAL AGENCIES WHICH ADMINISTER ENERGY, POLICY OR PROGRAMS

Category A—Agencies which administer programs or develop or implement policies which have been specifically initiated for their particular impacts upon the Nation's energy system]

| Agency | Classification | | | | | | |
| --- | --- | --- | --- | --- | --- | --- | --- |
| | 1 | 2 | 3 | 4 | 5 | 6 | 7 |
| Executive office of the President: | | | | | | | |
| Domestic Council | A.1.a.c. | | | | | | |
| Office of Emergency Preparedness | A.1.a.b.; A.2.a.b.c. | X | | X | | | X |
| Office of Management and Budget | | | | | X | | X |
| Natural Resources Programs Division | A.1.a.b.c. | | | | | | |
| Office of Science and Technology | A.1.a.; A.2.d. | | | X | | | |
| Federal Council for Science and Technology. | A.1.a.; A.2.d. | X | | X | | | |
| Oil Policy Committee | A.1.a.b. | | | | | | |
| Oil Import Appeals Board | A.2.c. | | | | | | |
| Joint Board on Fuel Supply and Transport. | A.1.a. | | | | | | |
| Department of Agriculture: | | | | | | | |
| Forest Service | A.2.b. | X | | | X | | |
| Rural Electrification Administration | A.2.a. | X | X | | X | | X |
| Department of Commerce | | | | | | | |
| Bureau of Domestic Commerce | A.1.a.; A.2.d.; B.2.d. | | | X | X | | |
| Office of Import Programs | A.1.a.; A.2.c. | X | | | | | |
| Department of Defense | | | | | | | |
| Army—Corps of Engineers—civil | A.1.a.; A.2.a.b.c. | X | X | | | | X |
| Office of Naval Petroleum and Oil Shale Reserves. | A.1.a.b.; A.2.b.c.d. | | | | | | X |

**Figure A–1. (cont.)   TABLE A.   FEDERAL AGENCIES WHICH ADMINISTER ENERGY, POLICY OR PROGRAMS**

| Agency | 1 | Classification | | | | | |
|---|---|---|---|---|---|---|---|
| | | 2 | 3 | 4 | 5 | 6 | 7 |
| **Department of the Interior:** | | | | | | | |
| Alaska Power Administration | A.1.a.b.c.; A.2.a.b.d. | X | | | X | | X |
| Bonneville Power Administration | A.1.a.b.c.; A.2.a.b.d. | X | | | X | | X |
| Bureau of Land Management | A.1.a.b.c.; A.2.a.b.c. | X | X | X | X | | |
| Bureau of Mines | A.1.a.b.c.; A.2.a.b.c. | X | X | X | X | | X |
| Bureau of Reclamation | A.1.a.b.c.; A.2.a.b.c. | X | X | X | X | | X |
| Defense Electric Power Administration | A.1.a. | X | | X | X | | |
| Geological Survey | A.1.c.; A.2.d. | X | X | X | X | X | X |
| Office of Coal Research | A.1.a.; A.2.d. | X | X | X | X | | |
| Office of Oil and Gas | A.1.a.; A.2.d. | X | X | | X | | |
| Oil Import Administration | A.1.a.b.; A.2.c. | X | X | | X | | X |
| Southeastern Power Administration | A.1.a.b.; A.2.a.b. | X | X | X | X | | |
| Southwestern Power Administration | A.1.a.b.; A.2.a.b. | X | X | X | X | | X |
| **Department of Justice** | | | | | | | |
| Land and Natural Resources Division | A.1.c.; A.2.c. | | | X | | X | X |
| Antitrust Division | A.1.a.; B.2.c. | | | | | | X |
| **Department of State** | | | | | | | |
| Office of Fuels and Energy | A.1.b.; A.2.d. | X | | | X | | X |
| **Department of Transportation** | | | | | | | |
| Office of the Secretary (grants-in-aid for natural gas pipeline safety). | A.2.a. | | | | X | | X |
| Federal Highway Administration (use of trust fund derived from energy tax). | A.1.b.; B.1.a.c.; B.2.a.b.d. | | | | | | |
| **Department of the Treasury** | | | | | | | |
| General Counsel | A.1.a. | | | X | X | | X |

| | |
|---|---|
| Atomic Energy Commission | A.1.a.b.c.; A.2.a.b.c.d. |
| Environmental Protection Agency | |
| Office of Air Programs | A.1.a.b.c.; A.2.c.d. |
| Office of Radiation Programs | A.1.a.b.c.; A.2.c.d. |
| Office of Solid Waste Management Programs | A.1.a.; A.2.a.b.d. |
| Federal Maritime Commission (oil pollution financial responsibility) | A.1.b.; A.2.c. |
| Federal Power Commission | A.1.a.b.c.; A.2.b.c.d. |
| Federal Trade Commission | A.2.c. |
| General Services Administration Federal Supply Service | A.1.b.; A.2.a.c.d. |
| National Aeronautics and Space Administration Space and Power Program | A.2.d. |
| National Science Foundation | A.1.a.; A.2.d. |
| Securities and Exchange Commission | A.1.b.; A.2.c. |
| Small Business Administration | A.1.b.; A.2.a. |
| Tennessee Valley Authority | A.1.a.b.c.; A.2.a.b.c.d. |
| Water Resources Council | A.1.a.; A.2.d. |

*Table A Notes (Fig. A–1) on page 60*

**Figure A–1. (cont.)  TABLE A.  FEDERAL AGENCIES WHICH ADMINISTER ENERGY, POLICY OR PROGRAMS**

NOTES

Col. 1: Agency was classified as an energy agency in an independent survey made by the committee staff from available sources. (See the attached classification outline).

Col. 2: Agency responded affirmatively to questionnaire concerning fuels and energy goals.

Col. 3: Agency was deemed to have energy related programs in an analysis made in 1968.

Col. 4: Agency was reported to have prepared or contracted for energy related studies.

Col. 5: Agency claimed direct statutory authority in the energy field.

Col. 6: Agency claimed indirect statutory authority in the energy field.

Col. 7: Agency was listed in a 1971 compilation of agencies concerned with oil and gas matters prepared by the Office of Oil and Gas.

**TABLE B.  FEDERAL AGENCIES WHICH ADMINISTER ENERGY POLICY OR PROGRAMS**

Category B—Agencies which administer programs or develop or implement policies which were not specifically intended to have unique impacts upon the energy system but which have proven in practice to have influences upon the energy system which are significantly different than the influences they have on other industrial or social systems]

| Agency | 1 | 2 | 3 | 4 | 5 | 6 | 7 |
|---|---|---|---|---|---|---|---|
| | | | *Classification* | | | | |
| Executive Office of the President: | | | | | | | |
| Council on Environmental Quality | B.1.a.b.c. | X | | | X | | X |
| Office of Management and Budget Review Division | B.1.a.b.c. | | | X | | | |
| President's Panel on Oil Spills | B.1. | | | X | | | |
| President's Task Force on Air Pollution | B.1. | | | X | | | |
| Department of Commerce | | | | | | | |
| Bureau of Census | B.2.d. | X | | | X | X | X |
| Maritime Administration | B.2.a. | | | | | | X |

| | | | | | | | |
|---|---|---|---|---|---|---|---|
| Department of Defense<br>  Defense Supply Agency, Central<br>  Supply and Maintenance. | B.2.a.b.d. | | | X | | X | X |
| Department of Housing and Urban<br>Development:<br>  Department participation in Urban<br>  Transportation R & D. | B.2.d. | | | | | | |
| Department of the Interior:<br>  Bureau of Indian Affairs | B.2.b. | X | | X | | | X |
| Department of Transportation<br>  Office of the Secretary—<br>  Transportation Planning R & D. | B.1.a.; B.2.d. | | | X | | | X |
| Coast Guard (oil pollution)<br>  Urban Mass Transportation<br>  Administration. | B.1.b.; B.2.a.c.d.<br>B.2.d. | | | | | | X |
| Department of the Treasury<br>  Internal Revenue Service | B.1.b.c.; B.2.c. | | X | X<br>X | | | |
| Civil Aeronautics Board (subsidy of<br>Air service). | B.2.a. | | | | | | |
| Environmental Protection Agency:<br>  Office of Water Programs | B.1.a.b.c.; B.2.c.d. | X | | X | | X | |
| Interstate Commerce Commission | B.1.b.; B.2.c. | | | | | | X |
| National Aeronautics Space Administration<br>  Office of Applications | B.2.d. | | | | | X | |
| National Water Commission | B.1.a.c. | | | | | | |

*Table B Notes (Fig. A–1) on page 62*

**Figure A–1. (cont.) TABLE B.** FEDERAL AGENCIES WHICH ADMINISTER ENERGY POLICY OR PROGRAMS

**NOTES**

Col. 1: Agency was classified as an energy agency in an independent survey made by the committee staff from available sources (See the attached classification outline).

Col. 2: Agency responded affirmatively to questionnaire concerning fuels and energy goals.

Col. 3: Agency was deemed to have energy related programs in an analysis made in 1968.

Col. 4: Agency was reported to have prepared or contracted for energy related studies.

Col. 5: Agency claimed direct statutory authority in the energy field.

Col. 6: Agency claimed indirect statutory authority in the energy field.

Col. 7: Agency was listed in a 1971 compilation of agencies concerned with oil and gas matters prepared by the Office of Oil and Gas.

# Appendix B

# Summary of Key Proposals for Government Involvement in the Energy System

## ADMINISTRATION PROPOSALS FOR ENERGY

On June 29, 1973 former President Nixon announced the following measures:

A. The creation of a new office, the Energy Policy Office, under the direction of John A. Love, to be responsible for formulating and coordinating energy policies at the presidential level.

B. That he was asking Congress to create a new Department of Energy and Natural Resources (DENR) responsible for balanced utilization and conservation of America's energy and natural resources. This department would take charge of all the present activities of the Department of the Interior, except the Office of Coal Research and some other energy research and development programs, which would be transferred to a new Energy Research and Development Administration. This department would also take over energy-related functions from other federal government departments such as Agriculture and Commerce.

C. That he was asking Congress to create an Energy Research and Development Administration (ERDA) to have central responsibility for the planning management and conduct of the government's energy research and development. In order to create the new administration, the present functions of the Atomic Energy Commission, except those pertaining to licensing and related regulatory responsibilities, would be transferred to it as would most of the energy R&D programs of the Department of the Interior.

D. That the five-member organization of the AEC should be retained to provide direction for a separate and renamed Nuclear Energy Commission, which would carry on the important licensing and regulatory activities within the AEC.

## Status of Administration Proposals

Of former President Nixon's proposals, the Energy Policy Office (EPO) under John Love became the Federal Energy Office (FEO) under William Simon, who subsequently was appointed Secretary of the Treasury.

A. The FEO was succeeded by the Federal Energy Administration, set up in July 1974. The FEA took over FEO duties for fuel allocation, pricing, rationing (if put into effect), and federal-state coordination. FEA is also charged with developing a comprehensive national energy policy. The FEA is headed by an administrator and eight assistant administrators.

John Sawhill, the first FEA administrator, was asked to resign at the end of October 1974, apparently because of his strong and public advocacy of conservation measures such as an excise tax on gasoline. President Gerald Ford nominated Andrew Gibson, a former president of Interstate Oil Transport Co., to be Sawhill's successor, but criticism of potential conflict-of-interest led him to withdraw. Frank Zarb was then appointed as Administrator.

B. DENR (S. 2135, H.R. 9090). Committees in both houses held hearings on the proposed Department of Energy and Natural Resources but the bills are still pending at this writing, with no action anticipated until the new Congress convenes in 1975. DENR would incorporate most of the Interior Department's responsibilities, plus selected activities from Agriculture, Commerce, Transportation, and the Corps of Engineers. It would also absorb the FEA and the Energy Research and Development Administration (ERDA).

C. ERDA (HR 11510). This bill, passed in October 1974, became Public Law 193–438, establishing a new Energy Research and Development Administration and a new Nuclear Regulatory Commission. Congress gave ERDA federal responsibility for energy R&D, incorporating energy R&D activities of several federal agencies.

Transferred to ERDA are all AEC functions except those of a licensing or regulatory nature; fossil fuel R&D from the Office of Coal Research and the Bureau of Mines; underground electric power transmission research from the Department of Interior; projects to develop solar heating and cooling systems and geothermal power, from the National Science Foundation; and R&D on alternative automotive power systems, from the Environmental Protection Agency.

Congress also directed the ERDA administrator to conduct a study of the potential energy applications of helium, and to report within six months of enactment his recommendations on the management of federal helium programs, as they relate to energy.

ERDA is headed by an administrator, a deputy administrator, and six assistant administrators for: fossil fuels; nuclear energy; environment and safety; conservation; solar, geothermal, and advanced energy systems; and national security. These eight top officials are appointed by the President with the advice and consent of the Senate.

D.   Special Energy R&D Appropriations (H.R. 14434) was passed in June, 1974 (Public Law 93–322). It allocates $2,236,089,000 for energy R&D in FY 1975. OMB sent this budget to Congress after considering former AEC Chairman Dixy Lee Ray's report to the President on energy R&D. The amount is $32.3 million higher than the amount requested in the budget, and $889.5 million over the amount funded in the FY 1974 budget. It provides larger amounts for secondary and tertiary oil recovery, and for the Liquid Metal Fast Breeder Reactor program. Oil shale R&D was not funded.

## SENATOR JACKSON'S PROPOSALS

The Jackson bill (S. 1283), passed by both houses, went into conference. The committee of conference recommended that it be passed. An energy R&D bill, it calls for the expenditure of $20 billion over the next ten years to develop a specified series of energy production options. It is designed to create a framework for non-nuclear energy research, development, and demonstration activities. It lists specific short-, medium-, and long-term research areas, covering the whole spectrum of energy supply options. These range from improving the efficiency of conventional fossil fuels to development of renewable energy sources, such as solar and geothermal power. Included also would be projects on conservation and environmental effects. Mechanisms for accomplishing these objectives include guaranteeing prices for syncrude, setting up joint-industry-federal corporations, and conventional contracting for research services with private industry, universities, and government laboratories.

In addition, Senator Jackson supports the creation of a Department of Energy and Natural Resources assuming the functions of the Federal Energy Administration and the Energy Research and Development Administration.

## COUNCIL ON ENERGY POLICY (S. 70)
## AND MAGNUSON BILL (S. 357)

S. 70 was a bill to establish a Council on Energy Policy, which would prepare a comprehensive long-range for energy utilization, coordinate all federal energy activities, and gather and analyze statistics on production and consumption for policy formulation purposes. This bill has been dropped. Meanwhile, ERDA legislation provided that an Energy Resources Council be established in the Executive Office to provide interim coordination. This council includes the Secretary of the Interior, the Administrator of FEA, the administrator of ERDA, the Secretary of State, the director of OMB, and such other officials as the President may designate.

The Magnuson bill (S. 357), to establish a Federal Power R&D board to support R&D in supply and consumption aspects of electric power, was superseded by S. 1283. The hearings on S. 357, however, did spur industry to form the Electric Power Research Institute.

## CONCLUSION

At this point the relationship between ERDA and FEA, including the extent to which their activities will be coordinated is not yet clear.

FEA's policy responsibilities are also unclear, obscured by power struggles in the federal energy hierarchy, involving OMB director Roy Ash, Treasury Secretary William Simon, and Interior Secretary Rogers C. B. Morton.

With the establishment of ERDA, and given the passage of the Jackson bill (S. 1283), these two proposals will in effect be fused, Jackson's bill providing the substantive research program for ERDA.

Arguments against setting up such an energy R&D agency divorced from management functions were set forth in Chapter 3, but the organization of ERDA itself into six separate departments is compatible with the principles suggested in that chapter.

If DENR were to be established, management and research functions would be combined in one department, as advocated in our proposal. Although the establishment of ERDA may reduce political momentum for passage, DENR is still a possibility. Congress asked (in ERDA legislation) that the President transmit as promptly as possible any recommendations he deems advisable for organization of energy, including DENR, an Energy Policy Council, and a consolidation in whole or in part of regulatory functions concerning energy.

## SOURCES

Mike Telson, Senate Interior Committee.
Larry Weiss, Special Counsel's Office, FEO.
Steve Carhart, Energy Policy Project.
*Conservation Report,* National Wildlife Federation.
*Congressional Record.*
*Energy Users Report,* Bureau of National Affairs.

## Appendix C

## Description of Certain Energy Related Technologies

I.   *Technologies that contribute to energy supply diversification and/or provide an additional energy resource:*
     —oil shale
     —coal gasification high Btu
     —coal liquefaction
     —fusion
     —LMFBR
     —geothermal
     —solar
     —fuel cells
     —hydrogen

II.  *Technologies that contribute to a better efficiency and/or a better environment with respect to energy supply:*
     —thermal pollution control in power production
     —electric power transmission technologies
     —nuclear waste disposal
     —low Btu gas

III. *Technologies that contribute to a better efficiency and/or better environment with respect to energy consumption:*
     —conservation of energy in building design and operation
     —energy conservation techniques in the industrial sector

## TECHNOLOGIES THAT CONTRIBUTE
## TO ENERGY SUPPLY DIVERSIFICATION
## AND/OR PROVIDE AN ADDITIONAL
## ENERGY RESOURCE

### Oil Shale

1. **Current Status of the Technology.** Oil shale deposits are located in several areas of the United States but only the Green River formation in Colorado, Utah and Wyoming is considered to be commercially attractive. In this area, potential resources are estimated to be:[1]

–600 billion barrels of oil, from shale of 25 or more gallons of oil per ton.

–1,630 billion barrels of oil, from shale of 10 to 25 gallons of oil per ton.

This represents about six times the known U.S. crude oil resources in 1970.[2]

Although in the last 30 years much effort has gone into investigating the utilization of oil shale for the production of crude oil and significant advances have been made in shale oil mining technology (for the richer seams), no commercial-sized plants have yet been constructed.

These investigations (conducted both by public and private sectors) have resulted since the mid-fifties in the development of different retorting processes at the pilot plant stage:

a. The Bureau of Mines obtained the most promising results from the gas-combustion retorting process.

b. The Union Oil Company of California tested its own process on a demonstration scale of about 1,000 tons/day from 1956 to 1958.

c. Colony Development Company at first a venture of the Standard Oil Company of Ohio, the Oil Shale Corporation and the Cleveland Cliffs Iron Company) constructed a "semi-works" plant using the Tosco II retorting process.

d. Mobil Oil led a group of six companies which did research and development on the gas-combustion retorting process under a research lease from the Bureau of Mines from 1966 to 1968.

As mining and retorting make up about 60 percent of the cost of producing shale oil, techniques for recovering oil from shale in place (by fracturation and heating) also have been explored, especially by Equity Oil Company and Sinclair Oil. In situ recovery will be a breakthrough and will avoid many environmental problems associated with shale oil production, except water supply (see below). Work on this, however, has not yet progressed to a point where it is possible to pass judgment on its feasibility.[3]

Major R&D efforts are presently being done by:

a. The Colony group (now led by Atlantic Richfield, which spent some $55 million through 1972 investigating economical engineering and environmental aspects of a commercial oil shale plant).[4]

b. The Bureau of Mines, acting through the Laramie Energy Research Center, which has mainly concentrated its effort on the recovery of oil shale by in situ methods (the total program in FY 1972 was $2.5 million and in FY 1973 was $2.3 million).

c. Development Engineering, Inc., which is presently carrying out a five-year R&D program of $2.5 millions on retorting and related environmental considerations.[5]

Although the surface retorting process has progressed to the point where commercial scale plants can be constructed, the excavation and disposal of the huge amount of rock involved present technical and environmental problems of great magnitude. Five hundred million tons of rock a year (almost equal in tonnage to the entire 1973 U.S. production of coal) must be mined in order to produce 1 million barrels/day of syncrude.[6]

**2. Future Prospects.** Estimates of costs of producing syncrude from shale in plants whose construction is started now range from $6 to $8 per barrel. This makes shale oil competitive with crude oil given the present prices of imported crude. Two new industrial semicommercial plants have already been announced to be on line by 1979.[7]

Forecasts of the possible capacity of the shale oil industry in 1985 differ greatly. The recent National Academy of Engineering (NAE) report forecasts a maximum production of 0.5 million barrels/day in 1985, requiring an investment of up to $4 billion.[8] The Department of the Interior suggested a possible production capacity of 0.8 to 1.3 million barrels/day in 1985, and the Shell Oil Company estimated possible production to be 1.5 million barrels.[9] The upper limit on production from a strictly technical point of view, however, seems to be two or three times this figure. If we assume that the cost of a 100,000-barrel/day plant[10] will be about $800 $\times$ $10^6$ it will be necessary—in order to produce 1.5 million barrels/day—to attract $12 billion by 1985 into the oil shale business in competition with other investment opportunities. These high capital requirements probably constitute—besides environmental considerations and a shortage of skilled personnel—the major limitation to massive shale oil production in 1985. However, economies of scale may eventually reduce these figures.

**3. Externalities.** Shale oil costs still remain uncertain because the environment-protection costs are not clear; they vary with the process used, and the mining site, and till now proper standards have not been defined.

a. Mining the shale: A federal decision is needed on mining practices. In the absence of clear regulation, the highest-grade shale would be mined by room and pillar techniques, leading to beneficial use (perhaps) of only one-third of the resources; the remainder would either support the strata above, or be otherwise unavailable.
b. Water supply appears as a major problem in oil shale production. Adequate water for massive production has to be provided in Colorado (as the shale cannot be carried far economically), a water-scarce area. A production of even 2 million barrels/day will need massive quantities of water brought from outside.[11] Pollution from effluents will also have to be prevented.
c. Disposal of waste: The tailings from even one 100,000-barrel/day plant will accumulate at the rate of 40–50 acre-feet per day. The split shale has more volume than the original rock and a little more than half can be dumped in remote canyons near the mines. But rainfall leaching could affect the quality of water runoff in rivers downslope unless preventive measures are taken. Furthermore, some of the shale is fine and transportable by the wind. Since no great amount of spent shale has yet accumulated, the total range of problems is not yet well defined.[12]

**4. R&D Requirements.** The major R&D programs necessary to improve and develop oil shale technology are the following:

a. Demonstration of the economics of a commercial-size oil shale plant based on currently experimental retorting techniques.
b. Obtaining information on which the development of methods for maximally efficient use of the oil shale resources can be based (R&D on physical and chemical properties of oil shale, fundamentals of catalytic, thermal and chemical treatment of the oil shale, etc.)
c. Assessment of the nature and extent of environmental effects and the determination of the costs of environmental protection.
d. Acquisition of knowledge and skills of monitoring and control.
e. Performing in situ retorting techniques that will have less effect on the environment.
f. Improvement of shale mining techniques, particularly investigating how to best extract the very thick 2,000-foot deposits where shale occurs in varying thickness and quality at different depths.
g. Work on by-product recovery.
h. Investigation of lower-cost methods of recovering oil from low-grade shale.

Over the period 1975–1979 the government plans to spend a total of $127.8 million in order to test in situ retorting of oil shale, using a combination of several different fracturing techniques and retorting conditions.[13]

### Coal Gasification (Pipeline Quality Gas—High Btu)

**1. Current State of the Technology.** The concept of converting the nation's vast uses of coal to gaseous fuel is not a new idea. In many areas coal gas was used before natural gas became available, even though it was a product with a lower Btu content and relatively expensive.

The basic principle of coal gasification consists of heating coal to an elevated temperature and then treating it with steam; under these circumstances carbon monoxide and hydrogen (possibly along with some methane) are formed, and this mixture of gases has to be converted to methane.

At present, with the improvement of new gasification techniques, coal gasification is a promising technique for developing substitute natural gas supplies. During the last few years the government and the gas industry have confirmed the technical feasibility of gasification methods and are now working on the initial stages of confirming its commercial feasibility. Research done throughout 1970 by industry and the Department of the Interior laid the foundation in 1971 for the Department of the Interior-American Gas Association Joint Program, which seeks to evaluate the known coal-gasification processes through the pilot plant stage.[14] The new plan for energy R&D drawn up by the federal government calls for a speeding up of this program.[15]

There are different types of gasification techniques. The gasifier can be of the fixed-bed, fluidized-bed, or moving-bed types, with each of these having numerous possible configurations. Two pilot plants are already in operation. One uses the $CO_2$ acceptor process, in which the initial heat is produced by the use of dolomite. The other, the HYGAS process, utilizes a hydrogasifier that produces substantially more methane in gasification than any other known process (which increases efficiency and reduces the amount of methanation required). But before full-scale plants can be constructed, these processes will have to be put through the demonstration plant stage, and this will take four to five years.

The Lurgi process, which has been successfully tested on the commercial level in different countries, produces low Btu gas and could be modified to produce high Btu gas.

**2. Future Prospects.** The development of a commercial capability to gasify coal could have a significant impact on the energy economy of the nation in that it will allow the increased utilization of the plentiful coal resources in an environmentally acceptable fashion. In a period of escalating imbalance between availability of new natural gas reserves and the growing consumer demand, synthetic gas could make a significant contribution to the gas supply system.

This contribution, however, depends strongly on the production costs of synthetic gas. Although FMC Corp. announced costs to be between 75¢ and 90¢/MBtu for its first plan, using their COGAS process (producing both synthetic oil and gas), and scheduled to operate by 1976;[16] but a range of $1 to $1.25/MBtu appears more likely.[17] Several studies indicate that the new processes will be only slightly cheaper (to start with) than the Lurgi process (at most by 10–15 percent).[18]

A major constraint for the development of a synthetic gas industry concerns capital requirements, which are estimated to be some $300 million for a plant of 250 million standard cubic feet (scf)/day capacity and an additional $60–80 million for the corresponding coal mine.[19]

**3. Externalities.** Synthetic fuels, especially gas from coal, can be made relatively free of ash and sulfur; they may become significant sources of primary energy for steam generation in areas of serious air pollution problems.

As high-Btu gas can be carried through the existing gas pipeline system, gasification techniques will draw midwest and southwest coal reserves nearer to the consumption centers. However, the present national pipeline network is not located ideally for that service.

The establishment of a domestic coal gasification industry would have the additional advantage of creating economic growth in many rural areas of the country.

The major environmental intrusion of coal gasification techniques concerns their important water-supply requirements, plus the problem of mining the coal with minimum environmental impact.

**4. R&D Requirements.** Two of the three pilot plants scheduled in the first phase of the Interior-AGA R&D program are already in operation (the $CO_2$ acceptor process and the HYGAS process), and the third one, using the BCR BI-GAS process is to be built at Homer City, Pa.

Two private organizations (El Paso Natural Gas Company and a venture composed of Texas Eastern Transmission Corporation, Pacific Lighting Service Company, and Utah International, Inc.) are presently developing the Lurgi process, and plan to put into operation by 1975–1976 two 250-million scf/day plants.[20] However, results obtained from the Interior-AGA pilot plant program could significantly modify this early scheduled commitment.

The Perry report suggests an annual R&D expenditure of $140 million in order to achieve commercial development by 1980.[21] According to recently formulated government plans, a total of $340 million will be spent over 1975–1979 for investigation of the feasibility of several gasification processes and for building a demonstration plant. If successful, several full-scale plants could be operating by 1980.[22]

Major technical problems that are yet to be solved in coal gasification concern:

a. Coal feeding.
b. Gasification.
c. Gas clean-up.
d. Methanation

**Coal Liquefaction**

**1. Current Status of the Technology.** Conversion of coal into liquid fuel is an important part of the Office of Coal Research (OCR) program, but it has not received as much emphasis as coal gasification. There has been no major improvement in this area beyond that achieved by the Germans in World War II. The United States has had no experience in this field, and every pilot plant built in this country has run into major equipment failures where least expected because of lack of experience.

Coal can be converted to low-sulfur liquid fuel by direct hydrogenation, by extraction with subsequent hydrogenation of the extract, or by carbonization followed by hydrogenation of the tar produced. Three pilot plants have been built in cooperation between OCR and private industry:

a. The Cresap, W. Va. pilot plant of "Project Gasoline," now shut down, which was operated by Consolidated Coal Company through a $20 million contract between 1963 and 1972.
b. The COED (Char Oil Energy Development) pilot plant in Princeton, N.J., built by FMC Coal, has demonstrated during the past two years—at design capacity—the conversion of coal to synthetic crude oil, gas, and char. It converts coal through fluidized-bed pyrolisis, followed by hydrotreating of the coal oil to yield synthetic crude oil. Some $20 million will have been spent on this contract by the end of 1974.[23]
c. Construction of the Solvent Refined Coal (SRC) pilot plant at Fort Lewis near Tacoma, Wash., was started in 1972. The total cost of the pilot plant is about $17.4 million.[24]

**2. Future Prospects.** The development of a commercial coal liquefaction capability would allow increased utilization of our coal resources and avoid most of the environmental problems associated with direct combustion of coal (such as higher levels of sulfur oxide and particulate emissions). A viable coal liquefaction industry could also have considerable effect on future U.S. policy on liquid fuel imports.

Although somewhat uncertain, production costs in future plants of 100,000-barrel/day capacity are estimated to be $6 to $8/barrel, with the higher figure being more probable.[25] Investment costs for such plants should be around $500 million. It should be noted that coal liquefaction is generally estimated today to be more costly than producing syncrude from shale,[26] although the range of costs is similar for both.[27] The recent rise of imported oil prices has made synthetic oil more attractive, and it is necessary to have a systematic improvement of the different coal-conversion processes. The most economical results would probably be obtained in mixed production units combining coal gasification and liquefaction processes.

**3. Externalities.** Synthetic oil is a clean fuel; it has been recently demonstrated that a 3 percent sulfur coal can give a 0.3 percent sulfur fuel oil.

One to three barrels of oil can be produced from a ton of coal, depending on the process used, and the major externalities would be associated with coal mining in the event of a large-scale development of synthetic oil; for example the development of a capacity of 3.6 million barrels/day, which is equivalent to our oil imports in 1970, would require a doubling of our present coal production. Water requirements for liquefaction would also be important though less critical than for gasification.

**4. R&D Requirements.** Most of the alternative processes have been tested only at the laboratory level. The next steps involve demonstrating their feasibility at the pilot plant scale and then at the demonstration plant scale. Each demonstration plant is expected to cost $75 to $125 million.[28]

According to the recent announced plans, the government intends to investigate several processes for liquefying coal in order to select the most promising of these for further testing in pilot plant scale. Up to $375 million has been budgeted for coal liquefaction over 1975–1979.[29]

The major problems that have to be solved concern:

a. Low-temperature catalysts and ones less sensitive to contamination from gases.
b. Material handling and equipment problems.
c. Simplification of processes in order to achieve lower costs.

**Nuclear Fusion**

**1. Current Status of the Technology—a. Technology Description.** Confinement of heavy isotopes of hydrogen (deuterium and/or tritium) at sufficiently high temperature and density for a long enough time will result in the fusion of these isotopes to produce a heavier element, resulting in the release of a large amount of energy. Conversion of this energy to electricity is the method of power production by means of a nuclear fusion reaction.

The fuel required for the fusion reaction (deuterium) is naturally abundant in sea water. If a deuterium-tritium reaction is used, the tritium must be obtained by a subsidiary breeding reaction, using lithium, which is also in plentiful supply for this purpose.

**b. Project Developers and Current R&D.** Technical feasibility of controlled nuclear fusion has not yet been demonstrated. Significant progress has been made during the past few years in confining the plasma by intense magnetic fields (Tokamak techniques) and in understanding the physics of compression and inertial confinement with lasers.

Some $600 million has already been spent on nuclear fusion, most of it by the AEC. The annual expenditure in FY 1973 was $74.8 million ($39.7 million for magnetic confinement and $35.1 million for laser-induced). This is expected to be increased to $98.7 million in FY 1974 ($55.8 million for magnetic confinement and $42.9 million for laser-induced), and rise to $102 million for magnetic confinement and $66 million for laser-induced fusion in FY 1975.[30]

Private support to Fusion Research, which is provided by Gulf General Atomics, Exxon, Edison Electric Institute, several utility groups, and Texas Atomic Energy Research Foundation, represent only about 3–4 percent of government support.

**2. Future Prospects.** Several scientific groups now think that "in a few years" they will be able to demonstrate experimentally that adequate plasma confinement can be achieved so that building a nuclear fusion reactor is feasible. However, beyond the scientific feasibility lies the even more challenging barriers of engineering "breakeven," i.e., getting more energy out of the device than is put in, and economic "breakeven," i.e., producing enough net energy at sufficiently low cost to be competitive with alternate sources of energy. While good hope exists for successful completing of this stage, no guarantee exists today that they will be reached. Fusion using lasers is at an earlier stage of development. Lasers large enough to produce sufficient energy for a possible technical "breakeven" have not yet been constructed.

**3. Externalities.** Fusion power, like fission power, would produce no combustion products. The main radioactive by-product would be tritium, which is less hazardous than plutonium and will be recycled in the reactor as a fusion fuel. Engineering and safety problems associated with handling tritium, however, have to be solved.

Fusion plants promise to be more efficient than plants operating today if the higher temperatures involved could be used with topping cycles, but in this respect fusion is not significantly better than some other proposed cycles.

The nature of fusion process itself eliminates any possibility of nuclear disaster. Nevertheless a mechanical accident, especially to the expensive plasma-confinement system, could be economically catastrophic.

**4. R&D Requirements.** The immediate major problems that have to be solved concern:

    a. Containment of plasma for a significant time interval.
    b. High-temperature and radiation-resistant materials.
    c. Reactor design, especially in regard to large volumes of high magnetic fields.
    d. Recovery and recycling of tritium from the system.
    e. Lithium blanket design.
    f. Chemical and safety problems of handling liquid lithium.

Because of the great uncertainty in the results of research, an appraisal of the appropriate R&D expenditures and time schedule is difficult. The Perry report estimates that scientific feasibility might be demonstrated by spending $100 million a year over 1974–1982.[31] The government proposes, as part of the new energy R&D plan, to spend $1.45 billion over 1975–1979 in order to establish the feasibility of both magnetic confinement and laser-fusion power generation.[32] Estimates of the costs of the next step, showing engineering feasibility, are more speculative but will surely be several billion dollars.

Because fusion technology is still in a basic research phase, and as a consequence results obtained are difficult to appropriate, incentives for private effort are very weak.

**Breeder Reactor Technology**

**1. Current Status of the Technology.** The idea of building a "breeder reactor," that is, a reactor that produces more fissionable material than it consumes, was present in the early stages of nuclear research, when Fermi demonstrated that fast neutrons operating in a reactor fueled with a mixture of $^{238}$U and $^{239}$Pu would lead to a net gain of half an atom of $^{239}$Pu (got by transformation of $^{238}$U) per atom of $^{239}$Pu used in the fission reaction.

During the 1960s the AEC went on supporting research on the breeder concepts, and besides Argonne, the center of this effort, major AEC contracts were awarded to Atomic International, General Electric and Westinghouse, which were all associated with the breeder program.

By 1965, after some $300 million in R&D funds had been spent on different breeder concepts,[33] the government made the decision to emphasize the Liquid Metal Fast Breeder Reactor (LMFBR) concept. This appeared to be the most promising, and the government decided to build a 400 MW sodium-cooled "Fast Flux Test Facility" (scheduled to operate by 1975).

A second step in government commitment to the LMFBR program came in 1970 with the decision to build a 300 MWe "demo plant" at a scheduled cost of $700 million. A contribution of $240 million will be made by the utility industry and the Tennessee Valley Authority, and Commonwealth Edison, as future owner of the plant, will contribute between $90 and $150 million toward its funding.[34] This complicated venture arrangement, which was made after two years of difficult negotiations among AEC, utilities, and manufacturers for building this "demo plant," has not yet started to operate.

**R&D Expenditures.** For FY 1974, the government R&D expenditure on LMFBR was about $357 million,[35] and represents 40 percent of its total energy R&D funding. Total government effort from 1950 to 1973 is estimated to have been about $1.3 billion, and corresponding private effort (not including participation in "demo" programs) was between $250 and $350 million, one-third of which has come from reactor manufacturers (General Electric, Atomic International, and Westinghouse), and two-thirds from utilities.

Research on "backup breeder" concepts has been progressively downgraded since emphasis was given to the LMFBR:

|  | *AEC Funding (in $ millions)* | | |
|---|---|---|---|
|  | *FY 1969* | *FY 1972* | *FY 1974* |
| Light water breeder reactor | 13.5 | 23.8 | 17.8 |
| Gas-cooled fast breeder reactor | 1.9 | 1.0 | 1.0 |
| Molten salt breeder reactor | 5.2 | 4.8 | 0.0 |

Gulf General Atomic, supported by a group of 43 utilities, is presently studying basic problems associated with the GCFBR concept.

**2. Future Prospects.** As breeder reactors consume some one hundred times less uranium than LWRs, the kilowatt-hours they will produce will be practically independent of uranium ore cost, and so by using high-cost as well as low-cost uranium, breeder reactors would provide us with almost unlimited uranium resources. Yet, because of our very meager knowledge about uranium reserves, the urgency of the need to develop such uranium-conserving machines is today a matter of controversy. On strict economic grounds, the case for developing the breeder is also very uncertain, because their fuel cycle advantage over LWRs may be offset by possible larger capital costs.

**3. Externalities.** Like the nuclear reactors in use today, LMFBRs will "breed" highly toxic plutonium, but in much larger quantities. As a result of a large-scale LMFBR program, annual U.S. plutonium production from this type of reactor could reach some 80,000 kilograms by the year 2000. The major externalities in LMFBR development are related to plutonium handling, processing and refueling. The handling, shipment, processing and storage stages of the LMFBR fuel cycle could give rise to many possibilities for critical incidents, leaks, or miscalculations that could cause significant environmental contamination.

In addition, plutonium must not only be contained, it must be safeguarded to prevent its diversion to nonpeaceful purposes. This is a serious problem posed by the entire nuclear technology, but on a larger scale by breeders.

Besides the possible environmental intrusions, some environmental benefits are expected from the introduction of LMFBRs related to mining of uranium. Economic and societal costs of uranium mining associated with LWRs are very small compared with the costs associated with fossil fuel extraction; for the breeder, costs would become virtually negligible; in addition, the better efficiency of the LMFBR reduces thermal pollution problems presently associated with light water reactors.

**4. R&D Requirements.** The AEC plans to spend $2.5 billion over 1975–1979 on the LMFBR. This includes support of a Fast Flux Test Facility (FFTF) and an LMFBR demonstration plant. An additional $350 million is slated to be spent during the period to solve problems concerning plutonium handling, other safety questions, and to develop the technology alternative for breeder concepts such as Molten Salt Breeder Reactor (MSBR) and Gas Cooled Fast Breeder Reactor (GCFBR).[36]

Private contributions necessary to this program are difficult to estimate. Concerning utilities, it appears that their present $250 million commitment in the demo plant constitutes a limit on their immediate financial capabilities, and clearly their commitment was made with the condition they would not have to support overrun costs. This means that the government will have to support alone the huge unscheduled costs incurred by both the FFTF and the demonstration program. (Official costs of the FFTF have risen from $120 million to $600 to $800 million), and that of the demo plans to $700 million.[37]

Though private manufacturers (such as Westinghouse, GE, AI) are presently closely associated with AEC efforts, their own R&D contribution remains modest and none of them seems ready to assume a significant share of the risk associated with the LMFBR development. It is clear that despite the AEC's efforts to commit private industry to the LMFBR, this program remains mainly a governmental program chiefly dependent on AEC's funding and support.

**Geothermal Energy**

**1. Current Status of the Technology.** Even if most of the heat stored in the earth is at too great depth or too diffuse to be considered a potential resource in the near future, economically significant concentrations of geothermal energy are present in several major types of occurrences.

    a.  Local Geothermal Reservoirs:  Elevated temperatures are found in local "hot spots," impermeable rocks at less than 3 kilometers from the surface. The thermal energy is stored both in solid rock and in water- and steam-filled pores and fractures; and water or steam serves to transfer the heat to the surface. In most of the hot-water geothermal systems, the water is a dilute solution containing sodium, potassium, chloride, bicarbonate, sulfate, borate and silica. A small proportion of the local geothermal reservoirs produce superheated steam, which can be piped directly to a turbine (dry steam fields). The Geyser field in California is of this type.

    b.  Hot interstitial waters in deep sedimentary basins represent an additional large geothermal potential.

    c.  Dry anomalously hot bodies of rock (up to 380°C within 3 kilometers of the surface) may constitute, in the future, new geothermal reservoirs if economic methods can be found to circulate water through them to transfer the heat out as steam. Perhaps 1,000 such bodies are present in the western United States.

Presently identified recoverable geothermal reservoirs in this country represent some $10^{16}$ Btu; only 15 percent of them could be utilized with current technology. An additional 6 to $12 \times 10^{16}$ Btu of yet undiscovered recoverable resources are expected to be found,[38] but marginal resources are estimated to be of the magnitude of $10^{16}$ Btu.

R&D on geothermal energy has been performed by geothermal resource companies, manufacturers, utilities, and the Department of the Interior. The total expenditure on R&D up to 1973 is approximately $7 million.[39]

At the present time, generation of electricity from natural steam in the United States is limited to the Geysers region of Northern California, which had an installed capacity of 298 MW in 1972,[40] and is expected to rise to 900 MW in 1976.[41]

**2. Future Prospects.** Power from favorable geothermal systems (dry steam fields) is presently cheaper than either fossil fuel or nuclear power. Generating costs achieved in the Geysers with a load factor of 85 percent can be broken down as follows:[42]

| | |
|---|---|
| Steam delivery | 2.66 mills/kWh |
| Operating costs | 0.45 mills/kWh |
| Capital costs | 2.16 mills/kWh |
| Total Generating Costs | 5.27 mills/kWh |

However, the cost of generating power from the more abundant hot water reservoirs should be somewhat greater because of the more complex equipment required (the turbines using low-pressure steam cost more) as well as the higher reinjection costs of the large volumes of geothermal water involved.

Important uncertainties remain concerning future costs, and the projections made today foresee a moderate development of geothermal electricity generated from the most economical geothermal resources.

**3. Externalities.** Geothermal energy does not produce atmospheric pollutants such as sulfurdioxides ($SO_x$) and nitrogen dioxides ($NO_x$) which arise from fossil fuel combustion, it does not require that fuel be mined or transported. Major environmental problems of geothermal energy development concern thermal effects, low subsistence, land despoilment, and cooling water for closed geothermal systems. Careful attention must be paid to prevent release of gases such as hydrogen sulfide. The complete impact of these problems are yet to be assessed.

As the efficiency of geothermal plants is low (15 percent) because of low temperatures involved, there is a problem of waste heat, and cooling towers four times larger than those for fossil plants would be required.

**4. R&D Requirements.** Besides the necessity of a better assessment of total geothermal resources, important R&D efforts have to be made in the following areas:

a. Improvement of technologies associated with nondry steam sources (involving separation of steam from water, development of secondary fluid systems dealing with corrosion, and contamination of surface waters).

b. Construction of prototype systems for utilization of hot-water brines.

c. Demonstration of feasibility of extraction of heat from geothermal sources not containing water (including improvement of drilling and fracturing techniques of hot rocks).

d. Prototype of power systems for low-temperature sources.

e. Techniques for locating hot rocks without having to resort to expensive drilling.

f. Studies on seismic operations, subsidence, environmental pollution and disposal of effluents.

Incentives of utilities and manufacturers to develop geothermal systems are weak because of the apparent limited capacities in the immediate future (dry steam fields) and the uncertainties of the longer term market.

The government is now planning to spend $185 million over 1975–1979 in order to: (a) increase knowledge of location and extent of geothermal resources; (b) identify and resolve the environmental barriers; and (c) accelerate through demonstration plants the commercial use of geothermal energy. The government program is designed to stimulate the commercial production of at least 20,000 MWe by 1985 from various types of geothermal resources and to encourage use of geothermal energy for various nonelectric purposes such as heating and cooling.[43]

### Solar Energy

1. **Current Status of the Technology.** Although solar energy has always been considered a "free" and almost unlimited potential source of energy, its large-scale utilization was not seriously considered until recently because of the considerable technological breakthroughs needed. During the sixties, the anticipated uses of solar energy were for small-scale application in developing countries (solar cookers for India, solar engines for remote areas). Major results of research during this period was to provide high-cost photovoltaic solar-cell systems for space applications.

In the early seventies a new interest in solar energy arose, characterized by a series of proposals for large-scale use in developed countries. Solar energy "farms" on the ground or satellite central stations and large-scale cultivation of algae or trees for trapping incoming solar energy for subsequent use as fuel were envisioned.

While several of these schemes appear plausible, the technology to accomplish them is still largely speculative. Current R&D can be characterized by three major fields of interest:

   a. Economical systems for heating and cooling buildings.
   b. Economical methods for producing and converting organic materials to liquid, solid and gaseous fluids.
   c. Economical methods for generating electricity, either by utilizing photovoltaic space of terrestial collecting areas or by using heat engines that could be collectors on the ground; or in the ocean utilizing temperature differences.

On the government side, research has been supported by NASA (electric applications), the National Science Foundation (various aspects of solar energy), and more recently the National Bureau of Standards (space heating and air conditioning). The Department of Housing and Urban Development is sponsoring research in "industrialized" housing, and the U.S. Air Force has an active program in the field of selective coating materials.

Private effort is presently weak except in heating and cooling of buildings, where numerous private firms are already involved.

Figure C–1 gives the present status of research in the different fields of application of solar energy, according to the Solar Energy Panel assessment.[44]

**Figure C–1.**  Status of Solar Utilization Techniques

| Technique | Status | | | | | |
|---|---|---|---|---|---|---|
| | Research | Development | Systems Test | Full-Scale Demonstration | Model Plant | Commercial Readiness |
| **Thermal Energy for Buildings** | | | | | | |
| Water Heating | X | X | X | X | X | X |
| Building Heating | X | X | X | X | | |
| Building Cooling | X | X | | | | |
| Combined System | X | X | | | | |
| **Production of Fuels** | | | | | | |
| Combustion of Organic Matter | X | X | X | X | | |
| Bioconversion of Organic Materials to Methane | X | X | X | X | | |
| Pyrolysis of Organic Materials to Gas, Liquid, and Solid Fuels | X | X | X | X | X | |
| Chemical Reduction of Organic Materials to Oil | X | X | X | | | |
| **Electric Power Generation** | | | | | | |
| Thermal Conversion | X | | | | | |
| Photovoltaic | | | | | | |
| Residential/Commercial | X | | | | | |
| Ground Central Station | X | | | | | |
| Space Central Station | X | | | | | |
| Wind Energy Conversion | X | X | X | | | |
| Ocean Thermal Difference | X | X | X | | | |

Note: X indicates effort is under way but not necessarily complete.
Source: OST, Solar Energy Panel, *Solar Energy Utilization* (Washington, July 14, 1972), Table 3–1.

Between $50 and $100 million have already been spent on all solar energy research, including power for space.[45]

2. **Future Prospects.** The fundamental question in solar energy is simply whether the capital expenditures needed to collect and use the "free" fuel could be made low enough so that the entire system produces useful energy in an economically competitive way. This appears unlikely for central station solar power for the next 15 years, and is also doubtful for decentralized electric generation during the same period. The only significant contribution of solar energy in the near future will be for residential heating and cooling. In July 1972, however, the Solar Energy Panel estimated that by 1985 less than 1 percent of the market for thermal energy for buildings will be captured by solar conversion technology (rising to 10 percent by the year 2000).

3. **Externalities.** Solar conversion offers "free" fuel and greatly reduced environmental intrusion. Large land requirement would be, however, a severe intrusion by schemes utilizing photovoltaic cells for direct-conversion central stations. Land or water requirements would also be very critical for the development of solar renewable organic fuels.

4. **R&D Requirements.** R&D in solar energy is mainly in a basic stage. As a consequence, a major share of the results from this research is not easily appropriable and needs to be supported by some federal action. Concerning the application in residential heating and cooling, the market appears disaggregated, and there is little incentive to develop a high-capital-cost item for consumers. Figure C–2 gives a list of major problems that remain to be solved.

The government has proposed the following research program— distributing a total of $200 million—over 1975–1979:[46]

a. Determining through pilot applications the effective use of solar thermal energy for *heating and cooling of buildings* ($50 million).
b. Using solar *thermal energy* for electric power generation through operation of a pilot plant (10 MWe) ($35.5 million).
c. Using *windpower* for electric power generation by constructing and testing individual windmills (> kWe) and a windmill farm (10 MWe) ($31.7 million).
d. Determining technical feasibility of producing electric power from *ocean temperature gradients* by laboratory scale testing of prototypes and full-scale testing of necessary components ($26.6 million).
e. Determining the capability to produce economically competitive *photovoltaic cells* ($35.8 million).

**Figure C–2.**  Summary of Major Technical Problems—Solar Energy

| Techniques | Major Technical Problems to be Solved |
|---|---|
| Thermal Energy for Buildings | Development of solar air-condition and integration of heating and cooling |
| Renewable Clean Fuel Supplies Combustion of Organic Materials | Development of efficient harvesting, chipping, drying and transportation systems |
| Bioconversion of Organic Materials to Methane | Development of efficient collection of organic waste and conversion processes |
| Pyrolysis of Organic Materials to Gas, Liquid and Solid Fuels | Maximize fuel production for different feed materials |
| Chemical Reduction of Organic Materials to Oil | Optimize organic feed system and oil separation process |
| Electric Power Generation Thermal Conversion | Development of collector, heat transfer and storage units |
| Photovoltaic | Development of low-cost long-life solar array |
| Systems on Buildings | Energy storage |
| Ground Station | Energy storage |
| Space Station | Development of light-weight, long-life, low-cost solar array; transportation, construction, operation and maintenance; development and deployment of extremely large and light-weight structures |

Source:  OST, Solar Energy Panel, *Solar Energy Utilization* (Washington, July 14, 1972), Table 3–2.

      f.  Demonstrating through pilot plant the economic feasibility of *conversion of wastes* to fuels and use of biota as fuel for power plant operation ($20.4 million).

**Fuel Cells**

      **1. Current Status of the Technology.**  Fuel cells are electrochemical devices in which the chemical energy of a fuel, such as hydrogen, is converted continuously and directly to low-voltage, direct-current electricity. Theoretically, fuel cells are reliable, direct conversion devices with no moving parts, which could operate with an efficiency of 90 percent or more (although 75 percent is a better interim goal). The fact that they consume fuel only when the system delivers power makes them extremely flexible, and extensive use of them has been imagined in transportation, domestic and industrial sectors.

      The major goal of R&D activity on fuel cells, which started in 1950, was to provide economical electricity at dispersed locations by a power system in 10/20 MWe blocks, for which there existed a considerable market if competitive prices could be achieved. A strong effort was made by the Office of Coal Research, which outlined a program with the Westinghouse Research Laboratory for the development of a fuel cell using coal as a fuel, and also by the Team for Advanced Research for Gas Energy Transformation (TARGET), a team of thirty-two natural gas utilities working in conjunction with Pratt & Whitney and the Institute of Gas Technology. Up to 1972, more than $50 million has been spent by the latter group as the first half of a nine-year R&D program.

Practical feasibility of fuel cells has been clearly proved. Hydrogen-oxygen fuel cells are now used in space vehicles and satellites, and the TARGET group experimented in 1971 in Farmington, Conn., with the world's first natural gas fuel cell. Fuel cells using $CH_4$ as a basic fuel also currently operate; however, in both these cases, gases are first cracked to $H_2$ and the fuel cell as such is fueled by $H_2$. The efficiency of the whole system (including cracking) is only about 30 percent. However, after more than fifteen years of intensive research, large-scale commercial utilization of fuel cells is not yet at hand, and except for the TARGET group, there has been a decline in interest resulting from several intractable problems of producing an economic commercial-scale fuel cell.

2. **Future Prospects.** Proponents of fuel cells see in them the possibility of a revolutionary change in present methods and systems for distributing energy and one with minimum environmental problems. If used on a wide scale, they would constitute flexible power-supply sources located close to consumption sites, which would considerably reduce transmission requirements, raw fuel being transported to the fuel cell powerplants by gas or liquid pipelines or trucks. Because of their reliability and their small size, and because they do not present cooling problems, they could be located in urban areas, which would considerably increase the number of suitable sites for power plants. Fuel cells of 55 to 60 percent efficiency, located near the demand point, would reduce energy required to produce a given amount of electricity (generation and transmission losses taken into account) between one-quarter to one-third. In addition, fuel cells appear to be the best electricity generating technique associated with the hydrogen storage concept.

How practical fuel cells are, however, and when these benefits could be obtained, remains controversial. The National Petroleum Council (NPC) noted recently that unless major new developments occur in fuel cell technology, this method will have little impact on fuel utilization.[47] At present, capital costs of the only type fuel cell remaining in a major development program are seen to be no less than those of conventional generating plants, with overall efficiency not much higher.

Pratt & Whitney disagree. They consider the fuel cell as one of the few options that can be used in the near term. Operation capability of the fuel cell, it says, is being demonstrated within the company in a number of small installations, and its application within the national electric supply system could begin in less than five years if the necessary technological effort is made. One should note, however, that these fuel cells use hydrogen as a fuel (from reformed natural gas), which severely limits their scope for widespread installation.

**3.   Externalities.**   Air pollution problems could be eased by the use of fuel cells because of: (a) reduced emissions from the cells themselves; and (b) "scattered" sources of emissions. Because of probable modular construction, high reliability could be attained from these units. Siting problems could be minimized if, as predicted, fuel cells could be located in urban areas and areas where water is scarce.

**4.   R&D Requirements.**   To achieve the demonstration of fuel cells in the range of 10—20 MW in the next three to five years, Pratt & Whitney suggest three major steps: (a) support R&D to improve fuel cell technology; (b) support a demonstration power plant program; (c) operate early production power supplies. According to Pratt & Whitney, this aim will be reached only if the natural gas utilities, the electric utilities and the government are willing to spend between \$40 to \$60 million over the next three years. Thereafter, a demonstration program would require about the same amount of funds to design the first on-site, dispersed fuel cell power plants.[48]

As part of the recent five-year energy R&D program, the government proposes to study a variety of types of fuel cell. Both centralized and decentralized applications will be studied. Pilot plants of 10 kW or larger are planned. A total of \$80 million is expected to be spent over the 1975—1979 period.[49]

### Hydrogen Production and Utilization

**1.   Present Status of the Technology.**   Hydrogen can be produced today by the electrolysis of water. Large-sized plants are already in operation in various countries producing hydrogen for use in the chemical industry (mainly in ammonia production). Hydrogen is made in electrolysis cells; the passage of a direct current between two electrodes immersed in a potassium hydroxide solution leads to decomposition of water into hydrogen and oxygen. The cost of electricity strongly influences the economics of this process, representing some 84 percent of the cost of generating hydrogen when electricity is 6 mills/kWh.

A second process (thermochemical process) producing hydrogen via a complex set of reactions at up to 700°C leading to thermal decomposition of water is at an earlier stage of exploration. Production costs in advanced electrolysis plants are presently estimated to be about \$4 per Btu if the electricity price is 8 mills/kWh.[50] Although this high cost of production excludes consideration of hydrogen as an alternative fuel in the near future, a number of studies were carried out by various organizations in 1970–1971. Since 1971, the American Gas Association has sponsored a detailed study of a hydrogen energy distribution system carried out by the Institute of Gas Technology and designed to (a) investigate both proven and unproven methods of generating hydrogen from water; (b) consider materials requirements and safety factors in the transmission, distribution and end-use of hydrogen.

2. **Future Prospects.** If hydrogen appears to be readily substitutable for most other fuels and as a result is considered an ideal synthetic fuel, the large amounts of electricity required for its production could constitute a restraint on its large-scale utilization. For example, just to meet one-half of the fuel needs for transportation in the year 2000 by electrolytically produced hydrogen would require an additional generating capacity of nearly 1 million MWe, which will represent between one-third and one-half of the total electric capacity at that time. However, a very attractive feature of hydrogen is that it can be stored and electricity generated during off-peak hours from steam electric plants; or interruptive sources, such as solar, could be used to generate hydrogen that could be stored for seasonal and daily peak-load variations in energy demand. This would lead to a more efficient utilization of power generation capacity.

Because of its versatility and the environmental benefits its use could bring, hydrogen is considered by its proponents as a very tempting solution to long-term energy problems. It is produced from water by the addition of energy and can be oxidized back to water to give up this energy as heat or electric power; unlike electricity hydrogen can be economically transmitted through invisible underground installations; and hydrogen-powered vehicles might be more feasible than electric propulsion.

3. **Externalities.** Since hydrogen appears as a very clean fuel (the direct product of combustion of hydrogen is water), no permanent dislocation could occur in the environment using the hydrogen water cycle. And although safety considerations are important, they are not expected to present a serious technical obstacle to a widespread use of this technology.[51] Hydrogen production would, however, have several indirect impacts on the environment caused by the generation of the large amounts of initial electricity required.

4. **R&D Requirements.** One of the energy study panels recently set up by the Office of Science and Technology was assigned to look into synthetic nonfossil fuels, and gave the following recommendations concerning hydrogen:[52]

    a. Concerning hydrogen production, the process likely to be used for the large-scale production is electrolysis of water. With further research and development, an efficiency increase of 25 percent and plant-cost reduction of 45 percent appear possible. The thermochemical production method has not been developed beyond the laboratory stage, but could be an attractive long-range method. Radiolytic and direct thermal decomposition of water do not seem to offer commercial possibilities. Several biological production schemes should be investigated, however, to establish whether (at least) this might be a useful waste-treatment process.

b.  Concerning large-scale *storage and transportation* of hydrogen, the technology appears well developed. The use of underground aquifers or depleted gas wells for storage of hydrogen is, however, an area requiring further work. Small-scale storage, particularly for mobile energy, is one of the priority areas for further development.

c.  *Concerning hydrogen utilization as a fuel,* the need for government-supported R&D appears to be relatively small in the urban-use sector, although eventual support for demonstration and conversion efforts would require significant funding levels. Adapting hydrogen fuel to transportation uses, particularly for aircraft and automobile use, represents an area where R&D is needed.

In electrical generation, fuel cells and turbines would both benefit from the use of hydrogen, or hydrogen and oxygen, but both systems need further development. In general, the panel concluded that the main obstacle to the use of hydrogen as a universal fuel is an economic one, and that an extensive and long-range R&D program could do much to narrow the gap between its cost and the cost of fossil fuels. The panel recommended a general R&D support of about $100 million over five years by the government over the whole field of nonfossil synthetic fuels, including fuel production, use of fuels in transportation, electricity generation, and industrial and urban costs.

## TECHNOLOGIES THAT CONTRIBUTE TO ENERGY-SUPPLY DIVERSIFICATION AND/OR BETTER ENVIRONMENT WITH RESPECT TO ENERGY SUPPLY

### Thermal Pollution-Control in Power Production

1.  **Current Status of Technology.**  With the rapid increase in size of steam electric power plants during the 1950s, the effects of discharging greatly

increased amounts of waste heat into a body of water at one point became more apparent. With the rapid increase in the number of power plants (particularly nuclear plants, which are less efficient than fossil plants) in the past few years, this problem became more acute, and now constitutes an important constraint in plant siting.

Effects of steam plant thermal discharge to bodies of water are presently minimized by two principal methods: (a) use of diffusers and mixing systems to distribute the heated condenser cooling water evenly through the mass of the natural body of water and (b) use of cooling ponds and wet cooling towers.

Research efforts are presently directed chiefly toward (a) defining more accurately the thermal effects in specific situations (particularly biological effects) and establishing valid temperature limits; and (b) cooling-tower technology development and new siting approaches such as floating islands. R&D is performed by reactor manufacturers, utilities, the Environmental Protection Agency, the Geological Survey, the Bureau of Fisheries, AEC, and TVA. Up to 1972 some $30 million had been spent on R&D in this area.

**2. Future Prospects.** With the limited exception of ocean sites, once-through cooling for new plants is expected to become increasingly difficult. With more large wet-cooling towers, there may be added concern about their environmental effects. A new technological opportunity on the horizon is the dry-cooling tower, in which heat is transferred directly to the air by radiation and conduction rather than evaporation. Dry cooling, if successfully demonstrated for large-scale application, could free power plants from dependence upon large water supplies.

A particularly promising concept is to combine dry cooling with the gas turbine. A reactor manufacturer Gulf General Atomics (GGA) is presently proposing to combine such a concept with a high-temperature reactor which, if it can be successfully demonstrated, would make this type of power plant virtually independent of water resources. But new environmental intrusions are introduced with the dry cooling tower, particularly noise and esthetic considerations.

**3. R&D Requirements.** The OST report, "Electric Power and the Environment," and the report of the R&D Goals Task Force to the Electric Research Council recommend increased research to improve the technology of wet-cooling towers and development of dry-cooling tower technology to the point of a large-scale demonstration with a commercial plant. Major topics that have to be investigated in the near future concern:

   a. Advancements in cooling power technology.
   b. Design studies of large dry-cooling tower applications to power plants.

    c.  System studies and cost evaluations of the use of waste heat in sewage-treatment plants, agriculture and aquaculture.

    d.  Studies of the environmental effects of wet-cooling towers.

    e.  Studies of new siting approaches.

R&D requirements seem to be presently about $10 million per year;[53] incentives and adequate fundings seem only to exist for short-term problems. Waste-heat management is only a small part of the cost of plant, but it is important because of environmental problems. There exists a good incentive for private development in this area.

It must be noted that indirectly the development of higher power systems (HTR, LMFBR, MHD and combined gas turbine–steam turbine cycles) will contribute to easing thermal problems by reducing the amount of heat rejected per unit of electricity generated.

### Electric Power Transmission Technology

**1. Present Status of the Technology.** The cheapest method for transmission of power today is to transform to a high voltage—69 or 138 kV for short distances and up to 765 kV for long distances—and to transmit through overhead lines hung from towers. Typical costs of such lines are about $100 per million voltamperes (MVA) per mile, excluding the cost of the 100 feet or more right of way required.[54]

In urban areas, where real estate costs are prohibitive, or in scenic regions, where strong public pressure forbids overhead lines, power must be transmitted underground in buried cables (high-pressure oil-filled cables—HPOF). But HPOF cables have less power-carrying capacity and cost between ten to twenty times that of conventional overhead lines (their present capacity is limited to some twenty miles).

Several advantages are gained by conversion of the generated alternating current to direct current and "inversion" at the point of use back to alternating current. DC lines are free from the out-of-phase current effect that limits the length of underground AC lines, but the rectification and inversion equipment are expensive. Thus DC transmission is presently economically justified only in an overhead line several hundred miles long.[55]

However, because of increasing environmental constraints on the extension of overhead lines, significant attempts have been made in the last few years to improve capacity and cost of underground lines and to explore the possible use of superconductors. As temperature of metals is lowered toward absolute zero (−273°C), their resistance to the passage of electric current—the property that causes losses and results in generation of heat in power lines—diminishes. Once a certain critical temperature is reached, falling between 1° and

10° absolute, the electrical resistance of a metal drops suddenly to zero and it becomes super-conducting. In 1972, super-conducting cables were reported to have been demonstrated abroad, but not in the United States (350 MW in Moscow).[56]

Much of the present scientific base of superconductivity was established in the United States because of the AEC's need for more powerful magnets for high-energy physics, from basic work of the National Bureau of Standards, and from the Department of Defense support for the National Magnet Laboratory at MIT. The two most advanced groups in the United States are presently the Linde Division of Union Carbide, funded by Edison Electric Institute and the Department of the Interior, and the Brookhaven National Laboratory of the AEC, funded by NSF through its RANN program.

Principal responsibilities in supporting R&D for electric transmission of all types have been borne by the Electric Research Council, cable and equipment manufacturers, electric utilities, and the Department of the Interior. Some $20 million has been spent up to 1972 in this area.[57] The current funding allocation for superconducting transmission is about $1 million to $1.5 million each year.

**2. Future Prospects.** The electric power industry is experiencing two conflicting public pressures—one to increase production and distribution of power and the other to replace overhead transmission by underground transmission. Given the projected increase in power requirements two or three decades from now, the present method of transmitting power may result in transmission losses comparable to the total power produced today. It has been estimated, furthermore, that by 1990, in order to meet the nation's electrical power needs, some 10 million acres of additional land will be needed just for transmission lines.[58]

To permit the increase in power production with the ever-increasing distance between power-plant and consumer, improved and new technologies are required to reduce transmission losses and limit environmental intrusion. Despite the attractive property of superconducting cables, many engineering problems remain to be solved. No object as long and thin as a power line has yet been refrigerated at temperatures of liquid helium. Cryogenic cables, however, which operate at temperatures higher than those of superconducting but nonetheless have transmission losses less than one-sixth of that incurred by conventional underground cables, have already been successfully tested. An extensive R&D effort is needed now to test and implement available new technologies and to improve longer-range solutions to electric transmission problems.

**3. R&D Requirements.** Concerning conventional transmission techniques the Federal Power Commission lists five currently needed improvements of the technology:[59]

   a.  Improvement in equipment reliability through advances in materials technology and engineering design, and the establishment of needed testing facilities.

   b.  Continued improvement in the aesthetics of transmission-tower design.

   c.  Continued advances in extra-high voltage (EHV) transmission from 500 kV to 1,000 kV.

   d.  Continued development of new transmission techniques such as DC transmission methods and cryogenic cables.

   e.  Development of reliable, economic methods for underground high-voltage transmission lines.

Beyond these short- and medium-range improvements, superconducting techniques appear probably as the only way in the long run to transport large blocks of power underground over a distance of several hundred miles; but engineering breakthroughs have to be achieved before a superconducting cable will operate in an economical and reliable way.

As part of the recently announced energy R&D research program, the government proposes to set up prototype 1,100 kV AC overhead transmission lines and a DC terminal demonstration project. Model tests of superconducting cables are also planned. A total expenditure of $39.7 million on overhead transmission and distribution and $42.6 million on underground transmission and distribution are envisaged over 1975–1979.[60]

### Nuclear Waste Processing and Disposal

**1. Present Status of the Technology.** A current controversy affecting nuclear energy R&D policy concerns the adequacy of present technologies for the management and perpetual storage of the intensely radioactive wastes produced in a multiplicity of chemical and physical forms at every stage of the nuclear fuel cycle. Principal sources of high-level wastes are the fuel processing plants, where the uranium and plutonium in irradiated fuels are reclaimed from the other heavy elements and fission products present. As generated, these wastes are complex aqueous mixtures containing radioactive isotopes of about thirty-five fission product elements and eighteen actinide and daughter elements. Current regulation calls for these wastes to be solidified within five years of their generation and for the resultant stable solids to be shipped to a federal repository.

A major hazard associated with this long-term storage is the ingestion hazard by the general population as a consequence of a breach of containment that would result in contact between waste and ground water. The potential hazard is dominated initially by $^{90}$Sr and $^{137}$Cs, and it is only after some 350 years of storage that their activity decreases significantly (by about three orders of magnitude).

For the last 20 years the AEC has developed techniques to solidify the wastes into forms that can be safely shipped and stored for long periods. This program has been reviewed by the National Academy of Science and the National Research Council. Four processes have been developed. Among them the most experience has been achieved with the AEC's fluidized-bed waste calcining plant in Idaho, which has been working for several years.

Concerning storage, the natural salt deposits have been designated by the NAS–NRC as the best place to dispose waste because (a) salt deposits are located in stable regions; (b) at such a depth that it cannot be accidentally disinterred by natural forces operating from the surface; (c) salt is capable of rapid plastic deformation in case of fracture, maintaining the integrity of the formation. This program has been too narrow and has some serious drawbacks.[61] For instance, AEC's plans to demonstrate storage in solid form in a salt mine near Lyons, Kansas, have been upset by intense opposition and criticism during the last two years, and the AEC announced recently its intention (a) to return to the concept of long-range storage in near-surface vaults or mausolea, which was dropped earlier as a safe but temporary solution requiring active surveillance; and (b) to explore a broader range of options.

Storage of high-level liquid wastes has been practiced for many years within the AEC complex; more than 80 million gallons of acid and alkaline solutions and sludges from weapon-production processes are stored in about 200 tanks. The storage used was by no means perfect, and serious leaks have occurred which, however, have been contained within the immediate vicinity of the vessels without any direct consequences to people.[62]

Through 1969 and into 1971, some $5 million was spent each year by the AEC on disposal problems of waste from the civilian nuclear energy program, the largest single amount being related to the intermediate step of solidification, the problems surrounding which are now relatively well understood.

**2. Future Prospects.** If nuclear power is to become the major source of electricity, a safe, reliable and environmentally compatible technology for indefinite storage must be perfected and demonstrated. Proponents of nuclear power say that the amounts of waste are inconsequentially small in physical quantity (some $138 \times 10^3$ cubic feet of high-level solidified waste will be accumulated by the year 2000),[63] and while such storage would require each generation to take over the management of its ancestors, the task is "not much more difficult than guarding the gold at Fort Knox."[64]

Two experts, however, Professor M. Benedict and Professor D.J. Rose, testifying before the Task Force on Energy said there is an imperative need that AEC identify a demonstrably safe salt deposit to serve as a national waste repository, or develop a safe alternative storage concept.[65] Figure C–3 gives alternative solutions to the problem and the approximate expected cost of each.[66]

**Figure C-3.** Cost, Advantages and Disadvantages of Nuclear Waste-Disposal Options

| Waste-Disposal Options | Cost ($10^{-3}$ mills/kWhe) | Advantages | Disadvantages |
|---|---|---|---|
| (1) Salt Mine Storage | 45–50 | Most technical work to date<br>Plastic media with good thermal properties<br>Occurs in seismically stable regions | Corrosive media<br>Highly susceptible to solutioning<br>Normally associated with other valuable minerals<br>Difficult to monitor and retrieve |
| (2) Granite Geological Structure Storage | 50–55 | Crystalline rock<br>Low porosity if sound<br>Thermal properties comparable with salt<br>Retrievable maybe | Non-plastic media<br>Presence of ground water<br>Difficult to monitor |
| (3) Melt Insitu Storage (In a hole bored beneath the waste processing plant) | 11–16 | Inplace creation of insoluble rock-waste matrix<br>No transportation and reduced handling | Highly mobile wastes during 25Y boiloff<br>Presence of ground water<br>Irretrievable<br>Proliferation of disposal sites<br>Difficult to monitor |
| (4) Melt Insitu Central Repository | 31–36 | Inplace creation of insoluble rock-waste matrix<br>Short boiloff period<br>Non-proliferation of sites | Presence of ground water<br>Irretrievable<br>Difficult to monitor |
| (5) Antarctic Rocks | Unknown | Immobile water | Very narrow temperature limits<br>Not a permanent geologic feature<br>Difficult environment |

| (6) Continental Ice Sheets | Unknown | Immobile water | Cannot dispose of actinides<br>Limited amount of ice<br>Not a permanent geologic feature<br>Difficult environment |
| --- | --- | --- | --- |
| (7) Mausolea Storage | 25 for 50 years | Allow future retrieval | Temporary solution<br>Permanent surveillance needed<br>Wastes vulnerable to natural and societal hazards |

Source: A. S. Kubo and D. J. Rose, "Disposal of Nuclear Wastes," *Science* 182 (December 1974): 1205.

In addition to these options, another desirable way of reducing the long-term risks is to separate the high level of wastes into chemical components that are similar to each other in terms of heat dissipation and duration of their potential hazard. Of these homogeneous wastes, actinides could eventually be recycled through reactors.[67]

**3. R&D Requirements.** Among the preceding list of waste-disposal options, only the ultimate disposal in deep salt mines has been developed and fully assessed. R&D work is needed to explore the other alternatives and particularly (a) to provide a reliable near-term storage facility; (b) to explore Melt in situ technique and its central repository variation; (c) to study disposal in media other than salt; (d) to assess and improve chemical separation of key actinides with their recycling in reactors.

A total waste-disposal R&D budget several times the $5 million per year spent in the last few years has been suggested recently as appropriate to solve this problem.[68] With such a program the prognosis appears good.

### Low Btu Gas

**1. Present Status of the Technology.** Coal gasification to make low Btu gas (150 Btu/standard cubic feet) appears to be one of the cheapest methods of eliminating the sulfur problem arising from coal combustion for power generation, and so allowing the use of the plentiful supplies of "dirty" coal. Synthesis of low Btu gas is far simpler and cheaper than that of pipeline quality gas (1000 Btu/standard cubic feet), but because of its low heating value it cannot be transferred economically and has to be produced on the site of the power plant.

As 15—20 percent of the coal's heating value is lost in the process, low Btu gasification for electricity generation was economically unattractive before environmental considerations increased the cost of producing clean energy from coal-fired power plants (i.e., by stack gas scrubbing).

Combined-cycle systems, using both gas and steam turbines, could be associated conveniently with low Btu gas to produce electricity; in a combined cycle the exhaust gas of the gas turbine is channeled into a boiler to produce steam at 390°C for a steam-turbine-powered generator. This technique leads today to a total efficiency of some 39 percent—which is comparable to the best steam turbines—and is far higher than a conventional gas turbine system in which the exhaust gases escape at the relatively high temperature of 445°C.

Two approaches to low Btu gas use are currently under consideration. The first would utilize existing technology in operating a relatively low-pressure gasifier and a low-temperature gas cleanup system before passing the effluent directly into a boiler for combustion. Examples of the technology are the Lurgi process (the only one now commercially available) and the Wellman

Galusha system. Another example of a low-pressure, low-temperature system is the Applied Technology/Atgas process (currently in the stage of bench level experiments). This process circumvents the need for cleanup of the hot gas and allows direct use of the product gases in utility boilers.

A completely different approach is being pursued by Westinghouse, Combustion Engineering, Pittsburgh and Midway, and General Electric. This is to gasify the coal in a relatively high-pressure gasifier, perform a hot cleanup of the tar, dust and sulfur from the gas by a yet undeveloped process, and then pass the hot clean gases through an expansion-gas turbine and into a combined gas-turbine/steam-turbine cycle.

It should be noted that any of the high Btu gasification processes can be used to generate a low Btu gas by selective removal of process equipment (e.g., removal of the methanation process). Since the low Btu gasification unit will generally be part of an electricity generating plant, reliability of the gasification process is vital. Though the Wellman Galusha and Lurgi processes are proved and reliable, they have never been applied specifically to power-plant operations in the United States. The utility industry would therefore require demonstration of this technology on a commercial scale necessary before considering it as commercially available. One station for electrical power generation with a combined cycle system field with low Btu gas has just begun operating this year at Lunen, Germany.[69]

**2. Future Prospects.** Coal low Btu gasification provides a reliable way of producing clean power from high-sulphur coal. Present and future regulations on emissions and the abundance of high-sulfur coal in the United States would seem to suggest a large amount of interest in the future for this technique. Present estimates for the cost of low Btu gas manufactured in 250 million cubic feet per day (cfd) plants are about $1.05 per $10^6$ Btu (for the Lurgi Process, using coal at $35\cent/10^6$ Btu).[70] This is about $0.25 less than high Btu gas (SNG) per $10^6$ Btu.[71]

**3. Externalities.** Low Btu gas combined-cycle systems would allow the production of electricity with less environmental impact, the use of high-sulfur coal without excessive $SO_2$ release, and also cause less thermal pollution because of the higher efficiency of the system. Higher efficiency also means less primary resource use per unit of electricity produced. However, mining the large amounts of coal needed to produce low Btu gas will cause severe environmental problems. Deep mining leads to subsidence of land and pollution of streams caused by acid drainage from the mines and strip mining despoils the land unless extensive reclamation is carried out.

**4. R&D Requirements.** Currently Commonwealth Edison is assessing the feasibility of gasifying Illinois coal alone or in a combined-cycle using the

Lurgi technology at its Powerton station. Objectives of the Clean Power Fuel Demonstration Plant are to demonstrate that:

a. Various agglomerating and nonagglomerating coals can be successfully gasified.
b. Substantially all the particulates can be removed from the gas.
c. Desulfurization of the gas (remove about 90% of the sulfur) is possible.
d. Production of oxides of nitrogen upon combustion are reduced.
e. Low Btu gas can be reliably burned in present and future boilers.
f. The various systems will perform in concert reliably for the production of power.
g. Such a system can be substantially automated to minimize manpower requirements.
h. These systems operating in concert can be responsive to system load.
i. Gas quality can be reliably maintained.

Economic and design data for large conventional and combined cycle type plants will also be provided.[72]

The Applied Technology/Atgas process has a number of unresolved problems at present, including lance construction materials, controlling particulate emissions, and determination of refractory linings.

The higher pressure/combined-cycle processes all require:

a. Further development work on fluidization characteristics.
b. A high-temperature gas cleanup system that is not presently available commercially.
c. Higher gas turbine inlet temperatures to realize higher electrical conversion efficiencies. Gas turbines used today operate with inlet temperatures of from 1,600 to 1,800°F. An ultimate combined cycle thermal efficiency of 57.7 percent is projected by United Aircraft Research Laboratories, using 3,100°F turbine inlet temperature.[73]
d. New turbine blade materials in order to overcome the reliability problems of existing gas turbines.

The government, as part of the five-year R&D plan, proposes to:

a. Construct an entrained-bed gasifier type pilot plant (30 MWe to 50 MWe), which will include an advanced cycle plant. Its completion is expected by 1977.
b. Construct a fluidized bed gasifier (pressure type) pilot plant (30 MWe to 50 MWe) to start operating in 1978.
c. Operate a slurry feed system with high-temperature cleanup in a simple vessel in 1978.

d. Test three to five of the numerous new concepts of low Btu gasification at the pilot plant scale.

A total expenditure of $200 million over 1975–1979 is planned. Of this, items a and b immediately above will use about $130 million.[74]

## TECHNOLOGIES THAT CONTRIBUTE TO BETTER EFFICIENCY AND/OR A BETTER ENVIRONMENT WITH RESPECT TO ENERGY CONSUMPTION

### Conservation of Energy in Building Design and Operation

1. **Current State of the Technology.** According to a NBS study for the Task Force on Energy,[74] typical buildings consume approximately 40 percent more energy than would be required to maintain present levels of services and comfort, if best current standards had been used in design and construction and if careful selection and diligent maintenance were applied to heating and air-conditioning equipment. In 1971, a round-table on energy conservation, organized by editors of the *Architectural Record,* concluded that given the present state of the technology architects and engineers can reduce considerable energy losses in their design of buildings. Manufacturers could in a short time and at a modest extra cost produce equipment that uses appreciably less power (for example, the technology exists to manufacture more efficient air conditioners). "However, at present there does not exist an identifiable technological field concerned with energy conservation through effective utilization; existing techniques have not been integrated and applied and there is no disciplinary framework within which to pursue possible further development."[75]

2. **Future Prospects.** Since, in 1968, space heating, water heating, and air conditioning represented 14.3 percent of total energy consumption in the United States, a more effective utilization of energy in this area would have a positive impact on the energy consumption pattern.[76] The experience of early 1974 shows that simply by avoiding waste, considerable savings in energy consumption can be achieved without a change in lifestyle, or drastic limits on the use of energy, and without extensive research and development.[77]

Besides new legislation or economic incentives to implement current energy-saving techniques, improvements in the form of new techniques are needed in the short and medium range.

The National Academy of Engineering estimates that 1.5 million barrels per day of oil equivalent can be saved in residential and commercial heating, cooling and water-heating by means of improved insulation and equipment.[78]

**3. R&D Requirements.**  In 1972, the NBS gave the following list of R&D requirements for the next 10 years: (a) improve thermal design of buildings; (b) develop technology for upgrading thermal performance of existing buildings, such as inexpensive insulation and draft recycling systems; (c) develop methods for determining field performance of heating and air conditioning equipment; (d) develop methods for determining thermal performance of existing structures, including setting of standards for rating the efficiency of energy consumption of heating, air conditioning and other building equipment; (e) develop the application of solar energy for home heating and air conditioning and for water heating; and (f) carry out research to improve efficiency of heat pumps and absorption refrigeration equipment to use rejected heat from buildings or solar energy. The federal government plans to spend $50 million on R&D on energy conservation in buildings over 1975–1979 as part of a total R&D effort on energy conservation amounting to $180 million.[79]

### Energy Conservation in the Industrial Sector

**1. Present Status of the Technology.**  Industrial uses of energy presently account for about 41 percent of the nation's total energy consumption—mainly shared between primary metal industries, chemical and allied products and petroleum refining and related industries.

There are two basic ways to achieve a lower level of energy consumption in the industrial sector: (a) changes or new developments in process technology; and (b) thermal management techniques. The most important of these include waste heat recovery, recovery of combustable wastes to provide internal sources of energy, redesigning equipment to use fuel more efficiently, and maintaining steam systems properly to reduce losses.

With a few minor exceptions, the majority of industrial sectors have shown a decrease in energy consumption per unit of output during the last ten years, and this improvement in energy efficiency is the direct consequence of the fact that energy cost is becoming an increasing portion of production costs, as energy prices are rising.

In the steel industry, a major improvement was obtained ten years ago by introducing the Basic Oxygen Process, general use of which will cut steel energy consumption to two-thirds the previous amount or less, representing a saving of some 3 percent of U.S. energy consumption. In the aluminum industry, which is the highest user of energy per unit of output (100 to 200 million Btu/ton of aluminum as compared to only 25 million Btu/ton of steel), an important R&D effort has been made by Alcoa, which has recently conducted a new electrolytic smelting process that could reduce future energy use by some 30 percent. The chemical industry consumes some 20 percent of the total energy in industry. It appears to be a highly competitive industry in which reduction of energy consumption is strictly a question of economic trade-offs among various operating and capital costs.

**2. Future Prospects.** The industrial sector will remain the main energy-consuming sector for the next fifteen years, consuming some 40 percent of the total energy in 1985, and most of the energy savings can be expected from this area.

The following gives a sampling of some of the major energy-conserving processes that could be implemented during this period, and savings expected from them and from thermal management techniques:

| *Industry and Technologies* | *Estimated Savings in Energy Consumption* |
|---|---|
| I.   Steel | |
|    A.  Changes in furnace design, heat soaking pit design, and thermal management. | 20% of overall fuel requirements |
|    B.  Recycling using electric furnace. | 75% |
|    C.  Continuous casting. | NA |
| II.  Aluminium | |
|    A.  Alcoa smelting process. | 30% |
|    B.  Aluminum recycling. | 95% |
| III. Copper | |
|    A.  Smelting—redesigning smelters to use heat more efficiently, decreasing ore residence time in smelter. | 50% |
|    B.  Refining—decreasing residence time, recycling electrolytic solution, control of stalactites. | 5% |
|    C.  Recycling. | 89% |
| IV.  Chemicals | |
|    A.  Maintenance of steam systems. | As much as 50% of present steam consumption for a given system. |
|    B.  New caustic chlorine production process. | 20% |
|    C.  Processes which use vinyl acetate or vinyl chloride in place of energy-intensive acetylene. | NA |

| *(cont.)*<br>*Industry and Technologies* | *Estimated Savings in*<br>*Energy Consumption* |
|---|---|
| V.  Glass<br>    A.  Electric furnace for glass smelting. | 70–75% efficiency, opposed to 30% for fossil fuel-fired furnaces. |
| VI. Cement<br>    A.  New rotary cement kiln—<br>        fluidized bed, improved combustion system. | 30% |
|     B.  Preheater kiln. | 5%, but the system doubles the capacity of the main rotary kiln. |

Overall Savings on Consumption. Estimates of the total energy that could be saved run between 20 and 30 percent of present consumption. Charles Berg of the National Bureau of Standards says that with rising energy costs and the development of an effective market mechanism to facilitate the adoption of efficient equipment and practices industry's consumption of energy could be reduced by 30 percent. He adds that this could be done without reducing productivity using technology that is economically justifiable, and that it is either presently feasible or could be made so without excessive development efforts. The NAE estimates that improved efficiency in industry may save 2 million barrels/day in oil equivalent in 1985.[80]

3. Incentives for R&D. Two major incentives exist for the industrial sector to develop and implement energy-conservation practices—the increasing price and decreasing availability of energy supplies. These two factors are becoming more important now as energy prices have risen significantly and fuels have become more difficult to obtain, raising the percentage of total operating costs that companies spend for fuels. To some extent this may automatically increase the amount of R&D done on energy conservation. There are, however, a number of political and economic problems that affect the ability of companies to do such research.

First, regulatory barrier exists in the antitrust laws, affecting the smaller companies. These companies cannot afford to do the research individually, and are prevented from doing it collectively because of antitrust regulations.

Second, a common economic barrier is lack of capital. All of the industries concerned (primary metals, chemicals, pulp and paper, glass and cement, and food) are capital-intensive, and changes in process and equipment require major investments. Many companies cannot afford these investments, even though in many cases the technologies exist and are feasible. This is true because their profits are or have been low, and because they have spent millions on pollution control, which brings no return on investment in the traditional sense, though it allows them to stay in business.

As part of a general support for R&D on energy conservation totalling $180 million over 1975–1979, the federal government proposes to spend $55 million on R&D on end-use conservation of energy in industry.[81]

Appendix D

**Estimates of Government
and Private Funding for
Energy R & D**

**Table D–1.   Estimates of R & D Funding of the Private Sector 1972**
*(by industry group)*

|  | $ Millions |
|---|---|
| Oil | 660[a] |
| Oil Equipment | 50[b] |
| Natural Gas | 100[b] |
| Gas Equipment | 25[b] |
| Gas Transmission | 50[c] |
| Coal | 6[b] |
| Electric Utilities | 150[c] |
| Electric Utility/Equipment Suppliers | 350 |
|  | 1,391 |

a. American Petroleum Institute (API) estimate. This figure includes R & D on synthetic fuels, oil shale, tar sands, coal gasification and liquefaction, and expenditures by the petroleum industry on chemicals.

b. Oil Information Center, University of Oklahoma.

c. Federal Power Commission.

d. Informed Industry source. Includes expenditure on nuclear power.

**Table D–2.   Estimates of R & D Expenditure Undertaken by Electric Utilities, 1972**

|  | All Utilities | Top 20 Utilities | Share of Top 20 of Total |
|---|---|---|---|
| Revenue ($ millions) | 24,300 | 12,500 | 0.51 |
| R & D Expenditure ($ millions) | 142.5 | 101.6 | 0.72 |
| R & D Expenditure as Percent of Revenue | 0.59% | 0.81% |  |

Source: Compiled by our staff from data supplied by Federal Power Commission.

**Table D–3.  Estimates of R & D Expenditure Undertaken by Electric Utilities in 1970, 1971 and 1972, by Area** *(millions of dollars)*

|  | *1970* | *1971* | *1972* |
|---|---|---|---|
| Within Company |  |  |  |
| Power Plants |  |  |  |
| Fossil fuel steam (including environmental considerations) | 63.5 | 37.3 | 6.5 |
| Nuclear | 12.8 | 6.2 | 7.4 |
| Other | 1.6 | 3.3 | 1.4 |
| Transmission and Distribution | 8.4 | 4.9 | 4.6 |
| System Planning | 1.8 | 3.3 | 2.2 |
| Other | 5.5 | 6.1 | 3.4 |
| *Total* | 93.6 | 61.1 | 25.5 |
| Outside Company | 48.9 | 33.2 | 20.5 |
| *Grand Total* | 142.5 | 94.3 | 46.0 |

Source:  Compiled by our staff from data supplied by Federal Power Commission.

**Table D–4.  Estimates of R & D Expenditure Undertaken by Gas Transmission Companies whose Revenue Exceeded $100M, 1971**

|  | *All Companies* | *Top 10 Companies* | *Share of Top 10 of Total* |
|---|---|---|---|
| Aggregate Revenue ($ millions) | 7,196.3 | 4,884.4 | 0.68 |
| Aggregate R & D Expenditure ($ millions) | 14.9 | 10.11 | 0.68 |
| R & D Expenditure as Percent of Revenue | 0.21% | 0.21% |  |

Source:  Compiled by our staff from data supplied by Federal Power Commission.

**Figure D–1.** Federal Energy R & D Funding—FY 1973 *(millions of dollars)*

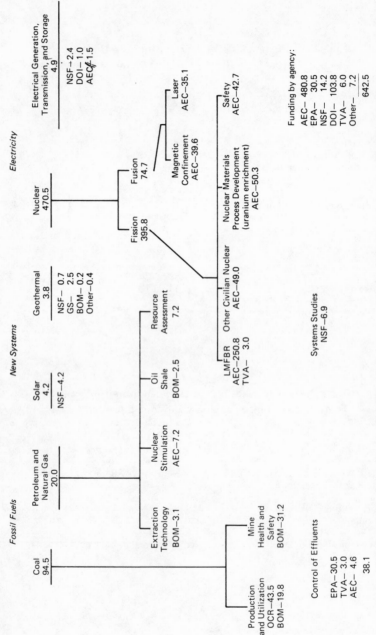

AEC—Atomic Energy Commission; EPA—Environmental Protection Agency; NSF—National Science Foundation; DOI—Department of the Interior; TVA—Tennessee Valley Authority; BOM—Bureau of Mines; OCR—Office of Coal Research.

Source: Compiled by our staff from published government data.

# Appendix E

# Reviewers' Comments

## COMMENTS, BY PHILIP SPORN, CONSULTANT

I find myself in difficulties with the very beginning of the report. Thus the first sentence in the final paragraph of the Preface, "Since October 1973, events have altered the world-wide energy situation," is a perceptive observation. However, the next sentence, "We have made *minor* adjustments in the report to reflect them," is not in consonance with that perception. The new circumstances require more than minor changes and, contrary to the philosophy expressed in the second sentence, *require changes in the basic approach.* The rapidly changing situation with respect to the supply and prices of energy not only makes some of the data in the report prepared in the summer of 1973 *appear to be dated, but they are in fact to badly dated* that their entire usefulness, it seems to me, is questionable; this will be developed in further comments.

### Chapter One
Page 5: The statement that our energy system is a market system may be so, but it fails to state that there is no longer a free market system because the market system has broken down: OPEC, by what under United States law would be held a criminal conspiracy, has demolished it.

Page 7: The statement that owing to the cheap and easy availability of energy in the past there has been little concern for using energy efficiently for all but the most intensive energy-using industries is true enough, but stops too quickly by failing to add that that condition must be brought to an end.

The analysis as to government involvement in the energy crisis is wholly incomplete. I have shown elsewhere that the current energy crisis is the result of multiple failures of public and private institutions (see: Sporn, "Multiple Failures of Public and Private Institutions," *Science,* April 1974).

Page 8: The statement that "the energy sector in the United States is mainly comparable to other industries that provide goods and services for consumption," is a most imperceptive observation. It definitely is not. It is even more definitely sui generis. It is so pervasive and so indispensable as a dynamic element entering into almost every activity of a modern society that its availability or nonavailability cannot be properly reasoned about or a research program set up for by assuming that it is just like any other industrial commodity.

Page 9: The observation that "comprehensive planning including the setting of public priorities *may turn out to be necessary,*" is much too cautious. They are critically necessary and planning with regard to availability of the total energy supply of the nation is badly needed right now.

The observation that the purpose of the report is to identify specific failures of the energy supply and demand system again is a nice piece of academic noncommitment, but does not go to the heart of the matter, which is very simple: Our energy use has been growing too rapidly from the standpoint of its availability from our own resources and from the standpoint of the world supply. We simply do not have the available energy, nor can we get it without violent upsets, to keep up that same rate of demand.

Page 9: Nor are we helped by a research policy statement that generalizes about setting up a program of resource commitments "for providing new technical capability through R&D for enlarging coal production or for expanding mass transit" and about comparisons that must be made "of their potential consequences . . within the private/public economy that constitutes the energy supply and use system." The fact of the matter is that an effective R&D program can only be carried out if it is set up to implement an adopted energy policy.

Page 10: The four conclusions reached may be academically interesting, but none has much worth from the standpoint of its contribution to the solution of the current energy crisis.

### Chapter Two

If I have so far expressed my unhappiness at the failure to recognize the energy crisis as being a great threat to our society and to the economy of our society, I am even unhappier, if that is possible, with the general tenor of Chapter Two.

Page 12: The social-economic philosophy expressed in, "When leasing land, however, according to our criteria, the government should act to maximize the net return on its holdings," may be a good standard, but I do not believe it is, and such a policy pursued by the government with the present energy crisis confronting the country could be deadly harmful to the people of the country.

Page 13:   Again the same overriding concern about profits is surprising in a document like this; this states that the criteria for investments in R&D by the Bureau of Reclamation, BPA, TVA, and the U.S. Army Corps of Engineers, "should be similar to that of private firms: that is, are the expenditures on R&D likely to produce opportunities for investments for which the benefits exceed the costs?" If adopted as it stands it will always be narrowly interpreted, and both R&D and society will suffer. In such an appraisal, will the negative social and economic costs of an additional 250,000 family heads thrown out of work be properly included? I doubt it.

Page 14:   A section shortly thereafter concerns itself with the development or the use of new techniques and with an understanding of the process of innovation. In an energy crisis any technology, whether an innovative one or an old one that is a hundred years old, if either of them can make a contribution to getting us out of the crisis, or to get us out more quickly, obviously it is a good technology to employ.

Pages 14 to 18:   A broad discussion of the justification of government in research follows. It is clear to me, however, that there is a complete misunderstanding of Project Independence and a willingness to leisurely evaluate self-sufficiency, even though self-sufficiency is not at all needed.

Pages 19 and 20:   There is also a long discussion of the government using different factors for discounting benefits of R&D versus private industry and using different time elements for discounting. This preoccupation with academic inconsequentialities leads, however, to what I would term the fallacy of the year.

Page 20:   This is indicated by two statements that follow. The first is, "There may then be some justification for government expenditures to improve the U.S. balance of trade. . . . If energy R&D is justified on such grounds, federal support for the improvement of hothouse technology to reduce our dependence on imports of bananas and coffee is likewise justified." Note the equivalency comparison between bananas and energy.

Then there is a second statement, "Energy is a commodity like any other; and if there is no divergence between private and social costs and benefits, this product should be utilized no more or no less efficiently than any other product. Indeed, adopting energy conservation as an explicit goal for federal support of R&D would result in resources being employed for finding ways of reducing energy use that could be more productively employed elsewhere." How about reducing energy use merely to reduce energy use when we so badly need to reduce our energy use?

I raise all these questions because it is obvious that the authors of this report simply have not brought their vision into proper focus. They do not recognize that our alarming adverse balance-of-trade figures not only are dollars running into many billions, which leave the United States and reduce our standard of living, but have also resulted as part of the same process in shutting down American industry and increasing our unemployment by hundreds of thousands.

"Energy is a commodity like any other," and if people who want work and find their jobs shut down cannot get work and their daily bread, surely Marie Antoinette gave the answer to that one some centuries ago: "Let them eat cake." I am literally dismayed at this lack of perceptiveness in social vision of the dreadful effect of the energy crisis.

Pages 22 and 23:    The report states that R&D itself is never an ultimate objective. True. But then it says, "R&D is only one—and not always the limiting—factor in the process of technological innovation." But surely technological innovation is not an end in itself, nor does it by itself justify R&D. But a deep national crisis such as we are in now is full justification for any research that will bring it to an end or bring it to an end more quickly.

My quarrel with this chapter, and I have a great quarrel with it, is summarized by my comments on the summary. The observation, "The government's basic role should be to assure that the energy supply system operates as efficiently as possible to deliver goods and services subject to various nonmarket social goals," is interesting but has nothing to do with our case.

Page 23:  The authors later state that the "role of government should be to moderate those consequences of the operation of the energy system that produce significant social costs." This again is an interesting academic conclusion; it is, however, irrelevant and has absolutely no place, in my judgment, in this report.

Finally there are given failures of the energy systems that we have today as justification for their claims for support by government. This is also perhaps of academic interest. But it has no applicability to our crisis and is not important.

Well, what is important? It is important to recognize that since the setting up of the Energy Policy Project of the Ford Foundation a major war was fought simultaneously with the military war that was fought between Israel and a group of Arab states—a nonshooting energy war between the Persian Gulf states and the noncommunist Western world and Japan, which the West lost. The consequences of that are barely beginning to be realized. Out of this have evolved the concepts of self-sufficiency as a United States policy aim in energy supply and the more pragmatic and indispensable Project Independence. If this latter is accepted, then *research and development acquire a totally different aim, objective, and time constant, all of them focussed on implementing Project Independence at the earliest possible date* and before the whole social-economic system of Western societies, again including Japan, collapses or their countries become a collective satrapy of a new OPEC—Persian empire.

The most important item for all parts of our energy society is the fact that last winter's long gasoline lines and rationing fears have become a distant memory for many motorists. People are trading in their smaller cars and are going back to the energy gulpers of pre-OPEC days, confident that the 1973–1974 energy crisis was a one-time thing. Oil imports are climbing and are expected to go higher. In the four weeks ending June 21, imports of crude oil and refined products averaged 6.7 million barrels a day against 6 million barrels twelve months earlier. At the same time "fuel prices, which many economists expected would drop, are still going up. Gasoline and other oil products in the United States are expected to rise in price as more domestically produced oil is freed from the $5.25 price limit." (*New York Times,* August 4, 1974.) Even if demand should drop, OPEC has shown that it does not intend to permit that to bring any price reductions.

Let us take a closer look at the primary energy situations.

The energy problem for the years ahead is very definitely not confined to this country. It is a worldwide problem. In the period 1968–1972, the total energy used by the noncommunist countries of the world increased at a rate of 5.6 percent per year and their oil use by 7.5 percent. We know today that continuation of use at this rate can only lead to disaster. In his usual perceptive style, Walter J. Levy ("World Oil Cooperation or International Chaos," *Foreign Affairs,* July 1974) has shown that if the recent growth in annual use of total energy by the noncommunist world were reduced about 20 percent to 4.6 percent, a reasonable scenario would yield an average oil import rate of growth between 1972 and 1980 of 5 percent and a Middle East import at an average annual growth of 6.4 percent to 29 million barrels per day in 1980 from 18 million in 1972. But even at present prices this rate could not be sustained by the oil importing countries on a current payments basis and, regardless of payments and the difficulties they would introduce, the oil probably would not be forthcoming.

To get a balanced situation with the oil consuming countries adopting a viable but definitely austerity condition and with the producing countries not to be under pressure to lower prices or increase production—both of which, and particularly the latter, are contrary to their long-term interest—Mr. Levy calls for a total energy growth in the 1972–1980 period of 3.3 percent. This yields figures for oil needed daily from the Middle East of 18 million, 19 million, and 18 million barrels for 1972, 1975, and 1980, respectively, and an average percentage growth in Middle East oil for the interval of 0.1 percent. Such an austerity policy could in time achieve some trade balance between the oil producing and consuming countries. It is, therefore, an excellent foundation on which to build the entire program of United States total energy supply and utilization for the balance of this century.

For a world energy growth figure of 3.3 percent, the United States figure should be somewhat lower, certainly not above 3 percent. Among the reasons for this moderate restraint on the part of the United States in the use of energy available to the world are: (1) the fact that with 6 percent of the world's population we have for decades utilized 35 percent of the world's total energy; (2) the fact that our per capita energy use is six times that of the rest of the world; (3) the fact that our social-economic development is highly advanced; and (4) the fact that the pollution caused by our enlarged energy utilization is far greater than in the rest of the world.

Thus building on this background and the cornerstone of a 3 percent total energy growth, a balanced energy policy can be developed.

I have prepared a table (E–1) showing a breakdown of the supply for a 3 percent growth in total energy and self-sufficiency in oil in the year 2000 and a comparison with actual performance in 1972. In the year 2000, nuclear and coal are shown in top positions with oil being maintained in a commanding position by virtue of increases from Alaskan, offshore production, and synthetic production. Gas is shown in a position not far from nuclear or domestic oil (but as a percentage far below its position in 1972) by virtue of imports amounting to 14 percent of the domestic supply. It is thus, clearly, a viable arrangement.

Since this calls for a doubling in total energy supply to or use by the United States in the year 2000 in the period elapsed between 1973 and the final date, that constitutes an increase in energy use from 75 quadrillion Btu to 150 quadrillion Btu per year, it is obvious that we cannot just find ways of implementing that policy and carry out the operation by fiat, governmental or economic. It will require a great deal of research and development, but the research and development will have as a specific aim and purpose to bring us into

**Table E–1.  Total Energy Supply of the United States in the Year 2000** *(Projected on the Basis of 3 Percent Annual Growth and Self-Supporting in Oil; Actual Supply in 1972)*

|  | 1972 Tons x $10^6$ | | 2000 Tons x $10^6$ | |
|---|---|---|---|---|
|  | BCE | % | BCE | % |
| Domestic Oil | 890 | 32.2% | 1,266 | 22.0% |
| Synthetic Oil | – | – | 345 | 6.0 |
| Domestic Gas | 860 | 31.0 | 1,040 | 18.0 |
| Imported Gas | 71 | 2.6 | 144 | 2.5 |
| Coal | 438 | 15.8 | 1,267 | 22.0 |
| Nuclear | 53 | 1.9 | 1,353 | 23.5 |
| Imported Oil | 387 | 13.9 | – | – |
| Other | 71 | 2.6 | 345 | 6.0 |
| Total | 2,770 | 100.0% | 5,760 | 100.0% |

These figures for the year 2000 are interesting. Nuclear and coal are shown in top position, with oil being maintained in a commanding position by virtue of coming increases from Alaska and expected increases from offshore drilling and from synthetic production. Gas is shown in a position not far from domestic oil and coal (but as a percentage far below its position in 1972) by virtue of imports amounting to 14 percent of the domestic supply.

a viable situation with regard to our total energy use, viable as far as our own resources—energy and economic—are concerned, and viable as to our relations with the rest of the world. Such an R&D program has not been prepared, and the program I have reviewed, if adopted, would certainly not bring it about. It therefore raises a question as to what to do with this report.

In his letter of August 28, Mr. Freeman says, "The revised draft is being sent to you to (1) review the final draft of the study and (2) to submit comments, if you wish, to be published in an appendix to each volume if, as seems likely, it is published." Mr. Freeman apparently has no doubts about the probability of the report being published. But I submit that this review of the final draft raises serious doubt as to whether it is in the interest of the authors and particularly of the Energy Policy Project of the Ford Foundation to publish this study in its present form.

September 9, 1974                                                        **Philip Sporn**


## SOME GENERAL CRITICISMS, BY JOEL PRIMACK, UNIVERSITY OF CALIFORNIA, SANTA CRUZ

### Important Problems Neglected

1. Perhaps the greatest difficulty in fitting R&D into government and industry is the fact that the characteristic time scales are so different: it takes nearly a decade to motivate and train a scientist or to bring a technological project to fruition; but governments and the economy fluctuate and change in much shorter periods. Any serious study of energy R&D must come to grips with this fundamental problem. The present report almost entirely ignores it, except for facile endorsements of the need for information and planning.

2. One of the most serious problems with large government technological programs is that, once they are initiated, bureaucratic and political forces conspire to insulate them from criticism. A solution is to make provisions for frequent outside review by competent scientists, engineers, and economists. They must have no personal stake in the continuation of the project, and they should report to officials (OMB, appropriate congressional committees) who also are in a position to consider the advice dispassionately. The nuclear reactor safety fiasco is a classic example of a program with inadequate outside review. The main reviewing body, the AEC's Advisory Committee on Reactor Safeguards, timidly suggested the need for a stepped up safety program in the late 1960s, but its appeals were ignored by the AEC. It was left to outsiders (chiefly Professor Kendall of MIT) to focus attention on the problem. The present report does not even mention the need for sustained, independent outside review.

### Shortcomings of Style,
### Organization, and Content

The style is bureaucratese, high-quality bureaucratese to be sure, but unleavened with so much as a single humorous remark. There is neither passion nor wit, and there is precious little new insight or information. It is hard to imagine that this report will find many readers except among government bureaucrats and other energy specialists—and I fear that these people will not be much enlightened by it. On the whole, I think it compares unfavorably in readability to the article by Eads (one of the authors) and Nelson on SST and breeder reactors [*Public Policy*, Spring 1971, as I recall].

It would be desirable for the report to make more use of the experience and information available from previous government and private ventures in large-scale technological innovation. For example, what lessons can be learned by contrasting the AEC–GE–Westinghouse development of LWR's with Gulf General Atomic's development of the HTGR? The report is full of sweeping generalizations unsupported by examples, let alone analysis.

As the report finally gets around to admitting at the conclusion of Chapter Four, it uses mainly rather conservative microeconomic ideas. It seems to me that the economic assumptions underlying the analysis should be presented early in the report, and in prose that noneconomists will understand.

**Joel Primack**


## COMMENTS BY S. FRED SINGER,
## UNIVERSITY OF VIRGINIA,
## CHARLOTTESVILLE, VIRGINIA

I strongly endorse the general and specific conclusions of the Report, especially the general philosophy of when and how government should support energy R&D, and how government should be organized to carry out this task.

My dissent therefore relates to items which may be considered peripheral to the main conclusions. Nevertheless these comments should be put on record in order to properly convey the tone of the discussions which led to the Report.

I.  First of all, there are some omissions:

1.  We should state explicitly the goals of an energy policy, namely (i) the importance of low-cost energy for consumer welfare; and (ii) the need to safeguard the U.S. against a cutoff of oil imports.

This statement has an important corollary: A heavy investment in R&D, say on oil from coal or on a breeder reactor, will inevitably produce a drive to put such technology into full-scale operation. (The fear of such inevitability provided the really believable opposition to the completion of the SST prototype program back in 1971). Yet this course may serve the consumer poorly by locking him into high-cost energy resources. The wiser course might be to *demonstrate* the technology only, while allowing the use of low-cost resources. The lowest-cost "insurance" against import interruptions might well be this demonstration, backing up an adequate program of oil stockpiles.

The Report should make it clear that we must be able to arrest the application of our newly developed technology, if this turns out to be in the public interest.

2. A time of perceived crisis may often be the poorest time for legislation and other decisions which have far-reaching implications. Thus the short-lived oil embargo (and events preceding it) triggered Project Independence, a $10 billion energy R&D proposal ($20 billion in the Congress), and two new federal agencies, FEA and ERDA—not to mention some 3000 legislative proposals, including the Emergency Petroleum Allocation Program and continued price ceilings on old oil.

The Report should propose that all legislation and similar proposals which tend to distort the market through taxes, subsidies and controls, or which constrain our flexibility of action, have a built-in time limit, a phaseout provision, or some other means of self-destruction.

II. Next, there are some matters of bias, emphasis and interpretation.

The Report (Chapter One) repeatedly gives the impression that the oil industry is monopolistic, adducing vertical integration and horizontal concentration as evidentiary. This is not sufficient; e.g., gas production by oil companies is a geological circumstance. Other economic tests give contrary evidence, such as the long-term drop in oil prices over the last 20 years, and the lower profitability of oil firms in comparison to other industries.

The Report further discusses only some examples of *indirect* leverage of governmental action on supply and demand. It neglects to mention the more important *direct* action of the federal and state governments which by and large distorted the market in favor of the consumer through the regulation of the price of natural gas, and in favor of the small independent oil producer who received favored treatment under market-demand prorationing, as well as the small independent refiner who benefited relatively more from the oil import quota program.

I therefore do not subscribe to the statement that "current energy supply problems are in large part an unintended by-product of governmental action in non-energy areas." The governmental responsibility for distorting energy markets is much more direct.

While concerned with supposed monopolistic practices by oil companies, the Report neglects to point out this possibility for manufacturers of electrical generating equipment, especially nuclear reactors and turbines.

I do not agree with the Report's conclusion (in Chapter Four) that reluctance of reactor manufacturers to bear the costs for LMFBR development is *prima facie* evidence that the current pace of development is too fast. The Report should face this issue squarely, especially in its discussion of R&D on nuclear breeders, by at least asking the following questions:

(i)   Is there underinvestment on private nuclear breeder R&D, because these firms wish to sell first many more light water reactors in order to break even on earlier development expenses?

(ii)   Or is there underinvestment by these firms, because they perceive the willingness of government to go ahead and make the necessary expenditures, with a good probability that these firms only will benefit from the government R&D?

(iii)   Can government arrange to do the necessary R&D in such a way as to increase competition in the area of nuclear reactors?

III.   Finally, the Report is strangely silent about the impact of U.S. energy R&D on other nations, and vice versa.

There is a great communality of interest among energy-consuming nations in developing energy sources, either based on coal or not based on fossil fuels. The U.S. simply cannot support *all* R&D options, nor should it. Licensing agreements are cheaper in the long run. It may be mistaken national pride which drives us into every kind of energy R&D. (And worse—into putting all the R&D into practice. This kind of thinking led us to adopt pressurized water reactors and has recently caused the British to adopt their home-grown steam-generating heavy water reactor (SGHWR) in preference to the PWR).

Yet we have many examples where independent development by other nations may yet benefit us: (i) the Canadian heavy-water reactor CANDU; (ii) the German Wankel engine and the Japanese stratified-charge engine.

Right now, many other nations, including the USSR, are putting a great effort into breeder reactor development. Japan has announced a major effort for solar power development based on photovoltaic cells.

Since the U.S. is blessed with huge amounts of coal, oil shale, uranium, as well as with oil which would yield to more advanced recovery methods, should we not concentrate more of our energy R&D effort there and make suitable agreements of cooperation and exchange with other technologically advanced nations?

It is my recollection that in our deliberations I touched on these questions and drew a positive response. I therefore wish to add these points to the Report.

**S. Fred Singer**

# Part I

# Notes

## CHAPTER ONE

1. Stanford Research Institute, *Patterns of Energy Consumption in the United States [for] Office of Science and Technology,* (Washington D.C.: U.S. Government Printing Office 1972).
2. James M. Utterback, "Innovation in Industry and the Diffusion of Technology," *Science* 183 (Feb. 15, 1974); Erik A. Haeffner, "The Innovation Process," *Technology Review* 75 (March/April 1973).

## CHAPTER TWO

1. J. de V. Graff, *Theoretical Welfare Economics* (Cambridge: Cambridge University Press, 1957), particularly Chapter X: "Marginal Cost and the Just Price."
2. A. C. Pigou, *The Economics of Welfare* (4th ed.). (London: Macmillan & Co. Ltd. 1952). R. Coase, "The Problem of Social Cost," (October 1960), in Breit and Hochman eds., *Readings in Microeconomics* (New York: Holt Rinehart and Winston, 1968).
3. R. A. Musgrave, *The Theory of Public Finance* (New York: McGraw-Hill, 1958), Chapter I.
4. F. M. Bator, "The Anatomy of Market Failure," *Quarterly Journal of Economics* 72 (1958): 351–379.
5. Haeffner, "Innovation Process," op. cit.; Panel on Invention and Innovation, U.S. Department of Commerce *Technological Innovation: Its Environment and Management.* (Washington D.C.: U.S. Government Printing Office, January 1967).
6. T. Scitovsky, "Two Concepts of External Economies," in K. and T. Scitovsky, eds.), *Readings in Welfare Economics* (Homewood, Ill.: Richard D. Irwin, 1969).
7. Council of Economic Advisors, *Annual Report 1972,* p. 126.

8.  T. Scitovsky, *Welfare and Competition* 5th ed., 1973 (Homewood, Ill.: R. D. Irwin 1971).
9.  This has been extensively discussed in welfare economics literature under the topic of public utility pricing.
10. Musgrave, *Theory of Public Finance,* op. cit.
11. K. J. Arrow, "Economic Welfare and the Allocation of Resources for Invention," *Essays in the Theory of Risk Bearing* (Chicago: Markham Publishing Co., 1971).
12. Nearly everyone would rather receive an additional dollar today than a year from now or some other time in the future. Among other reasons, this time-preference for money arises because a dollar available today can be invested and used to earn more money.
13. C. P. Kindleberger, *International Economics,* 5th ed. (Homewood, Ill.: Richard D. Irwin, 1973).

## CHAPTER THREE

1.  Edward B. Roberts, *The Dynamics of R&D* (New York: Harper & Row, 1964).
2.  Lord Rothschild, "The Organization and Management of Government R&D," in *A Framework for Government R&D* (London: Her Majesty's Stationary Office, 1971).
3.  R. R. Nelson and G. Eads, "Governmental Support of Advanced Civilian Technology: Power Reactors and the Supersonic Transport," *Public Policy* 19 (Summer 1971): 405–427.
4.  *Economic Analysis and the Efficiency of Government,* Part 4, *Supersonic Transport Development,* Hearings before the Subcommittee on Economy in Government of the Joint Economic Committee, Washington, D.C., 1970.
5.  R. Witherspoon et al., *Governmental Approaches to Air-Pollution Control* (Washington, D.C.: Institute of Public Administration 1971), and works mentioned therein.
6.  Center for Policy Alternatives, Massachusetts Institute of Technology, *National Support for Science and Technology: A Description of Foreign Experiences,* Vol. 1 (March 1974).
7.  See Appendix B.
8.  Paul W. MacAvoy, *The Economic Effects of Regulation,* (Cambridge, Mass.: MIT Press, 1965).
9.  Panel on Invention and Innovation, U.S. Dept. of Commerce *Technological Innovation: Its Environment and Management.* (Washington D.C.: U.S. Government Printing Office, January 1967).
10. Denis Douillet, "L'Aide au Developpement: Un Premier Bilan," *Le Progres Scientifique* (January–February 1974).

## CHAPTER FOUR

1.  National Academy of Engineering, *Toward U.S. Energy Self-Sufficiency: An Engineering Evaluation* (April 1974).

2. I. C. Bupp and J. C. Derian, "Breeder Reactors in the U.S.: A New Economic Analysis," *Technology Review* (July/August 1974).
3. See Appendix C and references quoted there.
4. Harvey Brooks, "Science and the Future of Economic Growth," *Journal of the Electrochemical Society,* Vol. 121, No. 2, February 1974.
5. D. Braybroke and C. Lindblom, *A Strategy of Decision* (New York: The Free Press, 1970).

## APPENDIX C

1. Extraction of Energy Fuels Panel for the Committee on Energy R&D and Goals, Federal Council for Science and Technology, June 1972.
2. U.S. Energy Outlook—NPC, December 1972.
3. National Academy of Engineering (NAE), *U.S. Energy Prospects, An Engineering Viewpoint* (Washington, D.C., 1974).
4. *Oil and Gas Journal,* August 26, 1970, pp. 42–43.
5. "Interior Leases Colorado's Oil Shale Research Facilities to Denver Firm," U.S. Department of the Interior News Release, May 26, 1972.
6. NAE, *U.S. Energy Prospects,* op. cit.
7. Ibid.
8. Ibid.
9. Extraction of Energy Fuels Panel.
10. Informed industry source.
11. NAE, *U.S. Energy Prospects,* op. cit.
12. Ibid.
13. Dixy Lee Ray, *The Nations Energy Future: A Report to the President,* December 1, 1973.
14. "Energy Research and Development." Report of the Task Force on Energy of the Subcommittee on Science Research and Development of the Committee of Science, Research and Development: U.S. House of Representatives, December 1972.
15. Dixy Lee Ray, *Nation's Energy Future,* op. cit.
16. U.S. Senate, Hearings before the Subcommittee on Minerals, Materials, and Fuels, November 18, 1971.
17. H. Perry, *Energy R&D—Problems and Prospects: Prepared for the Committee on Interior and Insular Affairs, U.S. Senate,* 1973.
18. NAE, *U.S. Energy Prospects,* op. cit.
19. H. Perry, *Energy R&D,* op. cit.
20. U.S. Senate, Hearings before the Subcommittee on Minerals, Materials and Fuels, op. cit.
21. H. Perry, *Energy R&D,* op. cit.
22. Dixy Lee Ray, *Nation's Energy Future,* op. cit.
23. Office of Coal Research, U.S. Department of Interior, *1973 Annual Report.*
24. NAE, *U.S. Energy Prospects,* op. cit.
25. H. Perry, *Energy R&D,* op. cit.
26. NAE, *U.S. Energy Prospects,* op. cit.
27. MIT Energy Laboratory Policy Study Group, *Project Independence: An Economic Evaluation* (Cambridge, March 15, 1974).
28. NAE, *U.S. Energy Prospects,* op. cit.

29. Dixy Lee Ray, *Nation's Energy Future,* op. cit.
30. Dixy Lee Ray, *Nation's Energy Future,* op. cit.
31. H. Perry, *Energy R&D,* op. cit.
32. Dixy Lee Ray, *Nation's Energy Future,* op. cit.
33. A. D. Little, *Competition in Nuclear Power Supply Industry,* (Cambridge, 1968).
34. Milton Shaw's statement before the JCAE, March 1973.
35. Dixy Lee Ray, *Nation's Energy Future,* op. cit.
36. Dixy Lee Ray, *Nation's Energy Future,* op. cit.
37. D. J. Rose: Nuclear Eclectic Power *Science* Vol. 184, No. 4134, 19 April 1974, pp. 351–359.
38. Committee on Energy Research and Development Goals, Federal Council of Science and Technology, *Assessment of Geothermal Energy Resources* (Washington, September 28, 1972).
39. Briefing before the Task Force on Energy of the Subcommittee on Science Research and Development, October 1971.
40. H. Perry, *Energy R&D,* op. cit.
41. Geoffery R. Robson, "Geothermal Electricity Production," *Science,* April 19, 1974.
42. Committee on Energy R&D Goals, *Geothermal Energy Resources,* op. cit.
43. Dixy Lee Ray *Nation's Energy Future,* op. cit.
44. OST, Solar Energy Panel, *Solar Energy Utilization: A Plan for Action* (July 14, 1972).
45. Briefings before the Task Force on Energy, op. cit.
46. Dixy Lee Ray, *Nation's Energy Future,* op. cit.
47. *Task Force on Energy Report,* op. cit.
48. Ibid.
49. Dixy Lee Ray, *Nation's Energy Future,* op. cit.
50. OST Synthetic Fuels Panel, *Hydrogen and Other Non-Fossil Synthetic Fuels,* July 1972.
51. Ibid.
52. Ibid.
53. Briefings before the Task Force on Energy, op. cit.
54. Hearings before Subcommittee on Science, Research and Development of the Committee on Science and Astronautics, May 1972.
55. Ibid.
56. *Task Force on Energy Report,* op. cit.
57. Briefings before the Task Force on Energy, op. cit.
58. Hearings before the Subcommittee on Science, Research and Development, op. cit.
59. *Task Force on Energy Report,* op. cit.
60. Dixy Lee Ray, *Nation's Energy Future,* op. cit.
61. "Managing Radioactive Wastes," *Physics Today* (August 1973), pp. 36–41.
62. Ibid.
63. Ibid.
64. *Task Force on Energy Report,* op. cit.
65. Ibid.

66. A. S. Kubo and D. J. Rose, "Disposal of Nuclear Wastes," *Science* 182 (December 1974): 1205. A. S. Kubo, "Ph.D. Thesis, Nuclear Engineering Department, MIT, 1973.
67. *Task Force on Energy Report,* op. cit.
68. Kubo and Rose, "Disposal of Nuclear Wastes," op. cit., p. 1205.
69. *Science,* January 5, 1973, p. 54.
70. H. M. Siegel, and T. Kalina, "Technology and Cost of Coal Gasification," *ASME Paper,* No. 72–WA/Fa–2 (July 1972).
71. MIT Energy Laboratory Policy Study Group, *Project Independence,* op. cit.
72. J. Agosta et al, "Status of Low Btu Gas as a Strategy for Power Station Emission Control," Commonwealth Edison Company, Chicago, Illinois, Paper presented at 65th AGM of AlChE, November 1972.
73. Ibid.
74. Dixy Lee Ray, *Nation's Energy Future,* op. cit.
74. *Task Force on Energy Report,* op. cit.
75. C. A. Berg, "Energy Conservation through Effective Utilization," *Science,* July 13, 1973.
76. Stanford Research Institute, "Patterns of Energy Consumption in the U.S.," *OST,* January 1972.
77. MIT Energy Lab Policy Study Group, *Project Independence,* op. cit.
78. NAE *U.S. Energy Prospects,* op. cit.
79. Dixy Lee Ray, *Nation's Energy Future,* op. cit.
80. NAE, *U.S. Energy Prospects,* op. cit.
81. Dixy Lee Ray, *Nation's Energy Future,* op. cit.

## Part II

## Energy Research and Development in Industrialized Countries Other Than the United States

*Michel Grenon*

# Chapter Five

# Summary and Conclusions

This study has been an attempt to appraise energy research and development in major industrialized countries outside the United States, before the energy crisis erupted in late 1973. Its aim was to discover which options each country has investigated, the budgetary support given, the relative contribution of private and public organizations, and the governmental mechanisms used.

## GENERAL ATTITUDE TOWARD ENERGY SUPPLY AND ENERGY R&D IN INDUSTRIALIZED COUNTRIES

Before environmental problems and oil supply availability brought new factors into play, it was generally considered in Western Europe's industrialized countries (and apparently in Japan as well) that there were two poles for any energy policy: (1) self-sufficiency, or (2) low cost of supply. There is no question that, facing their coal "crisis" (end of the 1950s in Europe), industrialized countries chose the low costs, with imported oil. They tried to allay any fears they had about dependency by dealing with more than one producing country. Recent history has shown this solution to be an illusion, shattered when the various producers united together under the same banner.

While it was still an illusion, however, imposed low prices of Middle-East oil became a "reference." As a result, noncompetitive coal mines were systematically closed, in spite of the fact that, in Europe, coal reserves are evaluated at 350–400 billion tons (which may be equivalent to total oil reserves *in the world*).

Nuclear energy, developed first for military and political reasons, was considered in the mid–1950s (after the first Geneva Conference on Peaceful Applications of Atomic Energy) to be a possible universal (and miracle) solution. But after the first enthusiasm, it became clear that this solution would not be so easy. This initial enthusiasm and subsequent discouragement is reflected in the history of Euratom. After the Suez crisis of 1956, the Three Wise Men of Euratom proposed an "ambitious" nuclear program, which soon appeared "unrealistic" and was eventually abandoned.

Almost twenty years later, this program is finally being accomplished, but under different conditions. By the mid–1960s, with the United States making a massive start on its commercial LWR program, nuclear power again promised to become more or less competitive. On this assumption, Europe could plan to stabilize in the medium term (possibly around 1985) its import of oil, although at rather high levels, by stepping up nuclear power development.

Then came some warnings that access to the cheap oil reserves would not last forever (after the Teheran agreement, February 1971). The result generally was a gentle acceleration of nuclear programs, with the competitive situation of nuclear electricity gradually gaining ground; however, no serious program was aiming toward other applications, such as nuclear process heat. The relative position of electricity on the energy market was the main winner of this new situation.

With the oil crisis, nuclear development programs were still further accelerated. In France and Italy, for instance, for power production; in Germany, nuclear process heat received a growing interest.

Notwithstanding various and diversified suggestions, there were no serious attempts to utilize other possibilities. In both Europe and in Japan, all kinds of resources or new energy techniques have been investigated, at one time or the other—from wind to geothermal energy, from thermal gradient of the oceans to solar energy conversion. All were ruled out as commercial alternatives, often on the basis of outdated economic and technical studies. In any case, the energy alternative inevitably was demonstrated to be much more expensive than past oil, or future nuclear.

Although it may be that Europeans are simply reluctant to change their minds, it must also be recognized that Europe's resources are *not* comparable to those of the United States (coal, oil, shales, geothermal . . . and sunny deserts!). But still, there did seem to be a stubborn resistance to looking at energy possibilities other than nuclear, a point to which we will return. This was less true of Japan, which had initiated a broad assessment of various possibilities. Now, after the events of late 1973, other countries have started assessment programs on new energy resources.

Could this research on new energy resources be performed on an international, or at least on a European basis? Perhaps, but it would need more conviction on the part of all concerned. Surprisingly, only two energy R&D programs are efficiently coordinated in the European Community: research on coal (fuel from the past), and research on thermonuclear fusion (energy for a far future).

As for conservation of energy, no such program turned up, nor was the subject mentioned, except in a Swedish personal communication received during this inquiry. As the reference cost of energy was low-cost Middle-East oil, it can be said that the "reference level" of energy consumption was that of North America, about three times that consumed by the industrialized countries. Although not conservation-minded in those precrisis times, some organizations took proud note of the low gasoline consumption and high performances of the European and Japanese automobiles. But the best proof that conservation could have been studied earlier is that it is intensively studied now.

The social value of scientific and technical research in general has been questioned in Europe, as it has been recently in the United States, not so much in the scientific community itself, but more generally by politicians, and sometimes by the general public. An interesting document[a] has been published by OECD, on the aims and objectives of R&D. Concern over its social impact has surfaced in the United Kingdom, France, Germany and elsewhere. Some R&D budgets have been stabilized, or even decreased in relative value (in France, but not in Germany and Japan, starting in fact from a lower value), but all countries have been looking for a more efficient and more socially-oriented utilization.

There may be no direct connection, but at the same time, many among the biggest nuclear research centers have "diversified" some of their activities into nonnuclear and *nonenergy* sectors. This may appear somewhat paradoxical at a time when nuclear energy has been exclusively chosen as the energy solution of the future, and when it is clear that all its problems are not completely solved, not to speak of the potential interest of other energy alternatives. But now there is a tendency to correct this situation, and many nuclear centers have expressed interest in new energy resources R&D.

Finally, regarding pollution, although the problem is generally less severe in Europe than in the United States and in Japan, this had a much greater impact on R&D than the "supposed" energy crisis, until late 1973. In all countries, energy R&D includes a sizable effort on pollution problems and pollution abatement. Stack gas cleaning and scrubbing, fuel desulfurization, new refining processes and new products, thermal discharges, siting problems, and so on are intensively studied, and possible solutions are tested.

## COAL RESEARCH AND DEVELOPMENT

The largest—though declining—coal production is in the United Kingdom; in the other coal countries (Germany, France, Belgium, Netherlands, Japan), coal production has actually shrunk, and the coal industry has generally faced tremendous financial and social problems.

Most of the R&D has been in the "retreat" spirit, except in the United Kingdom where it is sound, but largely market-oriented (development of coal uses).

a. "Science, Growth and Society: A New Perspective," OECD, 1971.

There are few, if any, studies on desulfurization, because European coals are low in sulfur. (In Europe, the sulfur problem is mainly related to oil and heavy fuel oil, especially from the Middle East, which is the main supplier, with an average sulfur content of around 3 percent). The cost of coal is so high, and the utilization of natural gas sufficiently low in most countries (until the discoveries in the Netherlands and in the North Sea), that there has been no economic incentive to study coal gasification. There are two exceptions: in Germany, researchers are investigating nuclear coal gasification, and in the United Kingdom, gasification research (developed successfully through many years of reliance on coal gas) now is being continued primarily for export to the United States. (The British, with their new supplies of natural gas from the North Sea, no longer need gasification for their own use.)

Coal mine safety, a problem as old as mining itself, is a continuing concern in the industrialized countries, with a continuing search for safer mining equipment and techniques.

Research and development has also focused on production and on utilization of coal. Production has progressively been concentrated in high-performance mines (others being closed), and research is aimed at increasing it; studies are made on fast-working tools, long wall equipment, drilling of galleries, rock mechanics, methane release and climate (mines going deeper and deeper, automation, and so on).

Utilization research has concentrated primarily on power production (declining) and on steel manufacture. For production of coke for use in steel-making, some interesting studies have been made of methods to extend the range of coking coals. In the United Kingdom, where 50 percent of the coal is used for power production, researchers in both the coal and power industries are studying combustion, fluidized bed combustion (jointly with the Office of Coal Research of the United States) and related processes. In the United Kingdom, where domestic uses of coal are still important (and coal authorities are not prepared to lose them), studies continue on various smokeless coals or coal mixtures.

Excepting thermonuclear fusion, still in the pure research phase, coal is the only sector of energy where R&D is coordinated among the various European countries. The United Kingdom, Germany, France, and Belgium each has its individual research laboratories (which date back to before the European Communities) and individual programs (mainly for specific problems and for studying new commercial coal products). However, the most important studies related to production—safety and coking—are coordinated and sponsored by the Communities in Brussels. Between 1957 and 1972 (before the Community expanded from six to nine members, with the United Kingdom, Denmark and Ireland), the share of Communities expenditures in coal R&D totalled 43 million UC;[b] from 1970 to 1972, the Communities' share was roughly 3.5 million UC,

b.   UC: European Unit of Count.

and represented about 10 to 15 percent of total coal R&D of the six member countries.

## OIL RESEARCH AND DEVELOPMENT

Oil is buried deeply in the ground, and the secrets of its R&D are also well hidden. Unless the well runs dry. . . .

Oil business in industrialized countries is shared between international oil companies (mostly the seven major ones: Exxon, Gulf, Mobil, Standard Oil of California, Texaco, of the United States; Royal Dutch Shell of United Kingdom and the Netherlands; and British Petroleum of the United Kingdom; plus a few independents, such as Continental, Occidental, Phillips, etc.), a few national oil companies (with very different experience and ability, high for the oldest ones, less for the most recent ones), and numerous independent refiners (mostly in Germany and Japan).

The five U.S. Majors have various large research organizations in industrialized countries, but almost exclusively devoted to product development, refining processes improvements, petroleum chemistry, and other processes; that is, the R&D is mostly market-oriented. This contribution is important, and there is fruitful exchange between the U.S.-based and the foreign-based research organizations and laboratories; but to our knowledge, most and possibly all of the research related to exploration and production (in which we were mainly interested in this inquiry) is performed in the U.S. organizations of these companies.

The European-based Majors, namely Royal Dutch Shell and British Petroleum, own and operate very large research organizations and laboratories, about which they are not too eager to talk. Royal Dutch Shell has a reputation for high-quality work, but it is kept as confidential as possible. Many research projects are process- or product-oriented. As far as exploration and production are concerned (and this is usually the part of R&D kept most secret by all the oil companies in the world), there is a difference between the two companies: BP has traditionally owned some of the richest oil fields in the world, and produced more than it could refine, while Royal Dutch Shell has been traditionally short of rich fields (except in Venezuela), with the need to buy crude to adjust to its refining capacity, and with consequently greater incentive to improve exploration and production.

Perhaps the reason it is so difficult to discover information about some sectors of the R&D performed by international oil companies is that actually they have not been performing that much. . . . It is possible that until late 1973 there was little profit incentive to pursue R&D, as long as oil production costs (mainly in new areas like the Middle East) were so low.

Among the European oil companies, it seems that the highest volume of integrated R&D is performed in France, through the joint collaboration between French oil companies and the rather unique IFP (French Petroleum Institute); of particular importance is an intensive off-shore research and development program.

Practically everywhere, many studies are now devoted to environmental protection, such as crude or fuel oil desulfurization, pollution abatement in automobile engines, and so on.

## GAS RESEARCH AND DEVELOPMENT

Conversion from town gas (produced initially from coal, and then from oil) to natural gas is quite recent in most industrialized countries outside the United States; it is not yet accomplished in Japan, which is awaiting LNG import increases in the coming years. In Europe, it was started by the post-World War II gas field discoveries in Italy and France, was boosted by the discovery of the very large gas field of Groningen in the Netherlands in 1959–1960, and followed, for the United Kingdom, by important discoveries in the North Sea. But natural gas is not expected for the time being to supply more than 10 percent, or 15 percent at best, of the total energy mix in most industrialized countries. This percentage will be considerably less for Japan, and consistently higher for the Netherlands, of course, where it may reach 30 to 40 percent.

Usually, exploration for and production of natural gas are the responsibility of oil companies. Transport and distribution are accomplished by gas utilities, some of them covering the whole national territory and publicly owned. Most R&D is oriented toward the quality of the service, and the promotion of new utilizations. In the United Kingdom, for instance, more than 50 percent of R&D funds (totalling between £5 and 6 million per year)[c] of the British gas utility is devoted to development and improvement of gas uses and to new applications.

Some studies are being conducted on gas production from oil or naphtha, and on farther-away processes such as nuclear coal gasification and nuclear hydrogen production. Important studies have been done (mainly in France) on natural gas liquefaction and LNG transportation.

## ELECTRICITY RESEARCH AND DEVELOPMENT

The electricity sector is both the most traditional and the most future-oriented (because of nuclear energy) in the industrialized countries we have studied. No doubt electricity will benefit the most from the changing oil situation. If the countries had continued to rely on a declining and expensive coal resource, or on "fluctuating" oil imports, the future of electricity development in these countries perhaps might have been somewhat compromised; with nuclear energy

c.  $12 to $14 million in U.S. dollars.

prospects, it is bright, and even generally encouraged by many governments, which consider it the main—if not the only—route to an improved energy self-sufficiency. However, "Projects Independance" are still a distant prospect.

In all countries studied, we have found quiet, sound programs of R&D covering practically all sectors, from production to transmission, from distribution to utilization. Due to the fact that thermal production through fossil fuels will still dominate electrical energy for many years, most of the studies in the sector have been reoriented towards environmental protection, such as gas stack treatment, fuel desulfurization, fluidized bed combustion, chimneys studies for dispersions of pollutants, thermal discharges, etc. Nuclear power production is mostly studied by national nuclear authorities and by industry.

The biggest shift in R&D programs perhaps is found in the development of new electricity uses: electrical heating (mainly for households, and progressively for special industrial or agricultural applications), and the electric car, for which there is a growing interest for urban uses.

Magnetohydrodynamic generation was much in favor during the last decade. Many R&D programs on MHD have been discontinued; others are continuing (mainly in Germany and in Japan). In general, little effort has been devoted to other methods to improve the conversion efficiency, either by topping cycles (potassium vapor) or low-temperature cycles (freon, isopropane); again, this is probably a result of the low cost of fuel oil.

The same comment applies to fuel cells as to MHD. There was a peak of enthusiasm and support for these programs. There is much less now. It is not clear how the oil crisis may change these situations.

## NUCLEAR ENERGY RESEARCH
## AND DEVELOPMENT

The major energy R&D programs fall under this category. Taken altogether, the nuclear programs of the industrialized countries (if only civilian applications are considered) largely exceed the United States program. Two of the largest programs, the German and the Japanese, have no military application at all.

In the beginning, the industrialized countries considered almost all possible types of burners, and the main type that was partially developed by the United Kingdom and France was the natural uranium-graphite-gas-cooled reactor. Now, like the United States, most have finally chosen Light Water Reactors (LWR), generally starting with American licenses, and aiming for subsequent independent national developments. The United Kingdom has made another choice with the Advanced Gas Cooled Reactor (slightly enriched), but is it definite?

For second choice, although many people would name the High Temperature Reactor (HTR), it is not clear which type is really second, the HTR or the Liquid Metal Fast Breeder Reactor (LMFBR). If estimates were based only on achievements, we would say the LMFBR is ahead, with two prototypes in operation, the French Phoenix and the British PFR (to say nothing of BN−350 in the USSR), as compared to only one prototype HTR under construction (the Pebble Bed type, in Germany, due to operate in 1976). But of course there remains uncertainty, and the HTR benefits from the commercial success of this reactor on the U.S. market through General Atomic. At any rate, the total effort (however dispersed it is among various nations) on LMFBR exceeds by far the total effort on HTR.

There are some interesting programs on nuclear process heat, mainly in Germany (coal gasification, methane reforming, long-distance heat transportation through chemical energy) and in Japan (nuclear steel-making). Some recent announcements point to increased efforts in this direction, as well as to obtaining nuclear hydrogen though thermochemical water-splitting. This can also increase the interest in the HTR.

Unfortunately, most of the industrialized countries are as short of uranium as they are of oil. France, with about 60,000 tons, is the exception. The others will have to look intensively for foreign sources of uranium.

Two separate large programs have developed uranium enrichment techniques: gaseous diffusion and gas ultracentrifuge. Other possibilities are being studied. It is clear that in the next decade, industrialized nations in Europe, and Japan, will reach some degree of "enrichment self-sufficiency," this degree probably improving with time.

The high quality of the R&D in nuclear energy in the industrialized countries cannot be denied. Unfortunately (this is a personal opinion), it could have been still higher with faster results if duplication-multiplication could have been avoided. Within the six-member European Community there was a tentative attempt toward unification of the R&D program with Euratom, but it collapsed in such dramatic failure that "Euratom new style" has almost nothing more to do with nuclear energy, except for thermonuclear fusion, which will be discussed later.

Unity has been replaced by multiplicity, and a common program by a variety of multinational enterprises. The associates for centrifuge enrichment, for instance, are quite different from those associated for LMFBR, etc. To the layman, the make-up of these associations seems to rely more on game theory than on energy policy. As a result, there are more than twice as many reactor manufacturers in Europe (and still more if Japan and Canada are included) than in the United States (five only), for a program of construction which is less than half the present U.S. program.

## NONCONVENTIONAL ENERGIES
## RESEARCH AND DEVELOPMENT

It seems impossible to mention any nonconventional source of energy—even the most exotic ones like energy of the ocean waves—and not find at least a small group (and very often more than one) working with enthusiasm for these new prospects. But, as far as we have been able to judge, these researches have not received any strong financial or political support, at least prior to the 1973 oil crisis. The only exception seems to be thermonuclear fusion, appropriately supported and even (a noteworthy exception) efficiently supported and coordinated by a Euratom common program.

Introduction of a new energy technology needs a "tunnelling effect," usually through government funds or incentives to overcome the "potential barrier" of economic disadvantage. Most of the industrialized countries have generously provided these funds for implementation of nuclear fission and, to a lesser extent, for nuclear fusion. They have appeared not to wish to sponsor a competitor to their cherished child, nuclear energy, certainly not competitors (such as solar energy) about which they have publicly expressed their doubts.

## CONCLUSIONS AND RECOMMENDATIONS

The present study, though incomplete, indicates clearly that most of the industrialized countries, in spite of short supplies of cheap domestic energy, have not relied much on the potential of research and development programs, other than nuclear development, to ease their energy situation. Most of these countries, if not all, have relied massively on oil imports, on the assumption that such a situation would last at least until their nuclear energy could take a growing share of the burden. Apparently, since the late 1973 oil crisis, some countries have started a thorough assessment of new energy resources (especially Japan); it is difficult to say, for others, if it is more than lip-service for the time being.

As a conclusion, our opinion is that the United States has wasted its abundant energy resources by using them too freely and carelessly; we think that other industrialized countries (and this is especially true for domestic coal resources) have wasted their scarce energy resources by deciding *not* to utilize them (a closed mine is often a lost mine), and by not capitalizing on their vast human resources to find energy solutions. Instead, they settled for an inadequate R&D effort incapable of meeting a severe energy situation, one which they had fatalistically to accept. This does not mean that nothing has been done, but it is our conviction that much more could have been accomplished.

In his April 1973 Energy Message, former President Nixon mentioned the possibilities of broad international cooperation for energy R&D. During the recent oil crisis, Secretary of State Henry Kissinger invited other nations to coordinate energy R&D. Highly desirable as these goals might be, our past experience suggests the need for caution in this field. Unfortunately, most international organizations are very difficult to create (the more so the bigger they are), and need a long lead time before becoming operative. If such an objective were to be pursued, the best approach would probably be to assign long-term projects to such an international organization.

Nevertheless, intermediate steps on this road could bring faster results. There is in most of the industrial countries a very high potential of energy R&D teams, whose efficiency could be boosted by clear and well-defined, limited objectives. Joint ventures (as Conoco-British Gas, Exxon-Alsthom, etc.) seem objectively to be a good solution. This suggestion for "ad hoc" joint developments is not contradictory with the reservations we expressed about some of the multinational associations in nuclear Europe: these associations were not made to fit into a larger political framework with long-term goals, but were pragmatically aiming only toward better short-term efficiency.

Finally, we think that it would be highly beneficial for all concerned if an international conference on energy R&D could be organized in the not too distant future. We remember how much all industrialized countries benefited from the first Atomic Conference in Geneva in 1955. Such an international conference on energy R&D would benefit the whole energy community as well.

## LIMITS OF THIS STUDY

Conducted over a period of nine months, this study involved canvassing several countries on a variety of factors in their energy R&D. None of these countries publishes a catalog of energy R&D programs, and most of the energy research is scattered in various separate organizations. Even in the countries with a fair amount of R&D centralization, energy per se was generally not a "Head Chapter" for listing of the R&D activities.

The canvass of countries and organizations for this information did not yield uniform results. Most of those contacted (with a few exceptions) supplied generously the information they had. Even so, the information was not uniformly useful, some data requiring more contacts and discussions than the study allowed. Some organizations replied that they had no available information on the subject for the time being; finally, a few organizations may inadvertently have been passed over.

It should be noted that most of the information and *opinions* were gathered before the energy crisis became more acute in America, and progressively so in Europe. Collected now, some of these opinions could well be different.

In the course of this study, we discovered that various countries (Sweden, Japan, etc.) and organizations were surveying energy R&D activities.

The Research Committee from the OECD is said to be preparing an international document inventorying energy R&D, though not for publication, and it is understood that the Joint Group for Energy and Science of this same organization has been preparing a study of coal technology. Under the leadership of Mr. Johnson, from the U.S. Bureau of Mines, this synthetic study focuses on various new technologies in the coal sector, to assess the status of development, needed amounts of coal, environmental factors, and so on, the main purpose being to assess the influence of such coal technologies on future coal demands.

The European Communities have also started a broad inquiry on energy R&D programs in the member countries. Questionnaires have been prepared and sent to national organizations with a listing of all possible activities, and a computer program has been prepared for treatment of data sheets. The time span of this study is uncertain, perhaps a year or more.

Much profitable work remains to be done in the area that this study covers, especially by covering a greater number of countries and organizations, by describing in fuller detail the specific R&D programs of interest, and by trying to assess the fall-out (and possible modifications) due to the actual energy crisis.

## PRESENTING THE MATERIAL

We considered two possible methods of assembling the information, both of which would be useful in any subsequent, broader study. The first one was a mere listing of research organizations and research facilities, such as the complete ones established by the International Union of Électricity Producers (UNIPEDE) for experimental facilities in electrical research. This would have required more time and staff work than was allowed. The second method, which was the one chosen, though less complete, is more descriptive, and thus likely to be better suited to a general understanding of the energy R&D situation in industrialized countries. In this approach, we summarize briefly the energy situation in each country, describe the general organization for R&D, and review the R&D currently being pursued.

The summaries of each country's energy situation serve to put R&D in perspective. It is clear that a country without any domestic coal resources has little reason to perform coal R&D; but the picture is different with a country with declining coal resources. In most countries in Europe, for example, the coal industry has met enormous technical and financial difficulties. A country faced with these problems can decide either to launch a massive R&D program to salvage its valuable coal, or to resign itself to minimum activity. Such a choice depends on the structure of the energy industry, and on governmental energy policies; on both, we have made a few comments when it seemed appropriate.

In summarizing the general organization for R&D, we have not tried to define R&D, on which many experts do not agree, nor to take it in its broadest aspect. Tentatively, we have tried to emphasize the respective responsibilities taken by governments and industry in the various countries. We have relied somewhat on the very interesting studies of OECD on research policies, although some of them are unfortunately out of date, and more oriented toward basic research.

The review of main energy research and development concentrates on fuel sectors, on electricity and, when available, on nonconventional energy resources and techniques.

As for any international study, we faced the problem of units,

**Table 5–1. Production and Consumption of Energy, 1971** *(in million tce)*

| Countries (Population in 10^6) | Production | | | | | Consumption | | | | |
|---|---|---|---|---|---|---|---|---|---|---|
| | Solid fuels | Liquid fuels | Natural gas | Primary electricity | Total | Solid fuels | Liquid fuels | Natural gas | Primary electricity | Total |
| Canada (21.8) | 16.0 | 94.0 | 94.0 | 21.0 | 225.0 | 24.0 | 96.0 | 61.0 | 20.0 | 201.0 |
| France (51.2) | 33.8 | 2.5 | 9.6 | 7.3 | 53.2 | 48.1 | 132.2 | 15.5 | 7.3 | 203.1 |
| F. R. Germany (59.2) | 148.5 | 9.6 | 18.7 | 2.5 | 179.3 | 141.0 | 169.4 | 26.5 | 2.5 | 339.4 |
| Japan (104.7) | 33.0 | 1.0 | 4.0 | 11.0 | 49.0 | 80.0 | 245.0 | 6.0 | 11.0 | 342.0 |
| Sweden (8.1) | – | – | – | 6.5 | 6.5 | 1.5 | 37.5 | – | 6.5 | 45.5 |
| U.K. (55.6) | 150.4 | – | 24.8 | 3.8 | 179.0 | 147.8 | 131.7 | 26.0 | 3.8 | 309.3 |
| U.S.A. (207) | 505.0 | 637.0 | 848.0 | 39.0 | 2,029.0 | 452.0 | 970.0 | 867.0 | 39.0 | 2,328.0 |

Source: Based on UNO statistics. Some of these figures may differ somewhat from figures given by the specific countries in the reports.

physical and monetary. We have generally used the metric system, and more specifically, for energy-mix tables, the TCE or ton of coal equivalent, as it is used in United Nations statistical publications (unless figures were given otherwise), with accompanying rough U.S. conversions, and we kept financial information in the national money in which it was provided, to avoid the problem of fluctuating changes (giving the approximate dollar value as of beginning 1974).

# Chapter Six

# Canada

Canada has the good fortune to be endowed with substantial supplies of all five main sources of energy: coal, oil and gas, hydropower and uranium. But with its climate, and with the transportation demand imposed by the vast land-area, the demand for energy is also substantial (second only to the United States). Nature has frequently placed major Canadian energy resources in rather inconvenient places in relation to where energy is needed and used.

Canada's biggest problem is to decide how much of its reserves (considerable, but not inexhaustible) it will be willing to trade in the coming decades, or to keep for future generations, taking into account the growing population (expected to increase from 22 million in 1971 to 35 million in 2000). In the year 2000, energy consumption could be four times the present value.

Research and development, which appeared hardly necessary compared to many other needs, is proceeding on a low level, and is loosely coordinated. The R&D is under strong influence of universities, where some basic research is outstanding, and of world high standards. The importance of foreign companies has not favored domestic industrial R&D.

## THE ENERGY SITUATION

Primary energy consumption in Canada has tripled during the past twenty-five years. Oil and gas now meet almost two-thirds of the total energy consumption, compared with less than one-quarter twenty-five years ago, while coal's share has declined from one-half to one-tenth. The other major energy source is hydro-electricity, which has been meeting about one-fourth of total energy needs since the late 1950s. Nuclear energy has yet to make a significant impact on the national energy scene.

It can be seen from Table 6–1 that Canada has progressively changed

Table 6–1.   Energy Production and Energy Consumption in Canada *(in million metric tons of coal equivalent)*

|  | 1950 | | 1960 | | 1970 | |
| --- | --- | --- | --- | --- | --- | --- |
|  | *Production* | *Consumption* | *Production* | *Consumption* | *Production* | *Consumption* |
| Solid fuels | 16 | 37 | 9 | 20 | 13 | 24 |
| Liquid fuels | 5 | 21 | 33 | 53 | 88 | 92 |
| Natural gas | 3 | 3 | 20 | 16 | 86 | 57 |
| Primary electricity (hydro and nuclear) | 29 | 31 | 13 | 12 | 20 | 19 |
| *Total energy* | 53 | 92 | 75 | 101 | 207 | 192 |

Source:   United Nations statistics.

from a net importer to a net exporter position. However, in spite of all its fuels (apart from uranium), and due to geographic factors, Canada is simultaneously an energy importer (to some provinces, generally the eastern ones) and an energy exporter (from other provinces, generally middle or western ones). To change this historical situation, as illustrated by the "Ottawa Valley Line," which brings Canadian oil from the West to the East, raises many political and economical problems. Nevertheless, we would expect this to be one of the main trends of future Canadian energy policies.

**Coal Industry.** In 1972, the coal industry produced 20.6 million tons of coal, exported 9.4 million tons of coal and 260,000 tons of coke, and imported 19.3 million tons of these products. Exports have risen markedly since 1969 and imports have increased by 50 percent since 1962.

Much of the Canadian coal industry is in the hands of private investment. Foreign investors control 73 percent of coal mining now being conducted in Canada. The concentration of the industry into the hands of the large corporations is a result of the large financial and technical challenges that must be met.

Canada has extensive coal reserves estimated at about 120 billion tons, of which about 113 billion tons are in British Columbia, Alberta and Saskatchewan. These are geological estimates of reserves in place, but even on the basis of economic mineability criteria, Canada has sufficient mineable coal for the foreseeable future; but much more information must be obtained as to its quality and mineability for purposes of determining future export policy and best use within Canada.

**Oil Industry.** In 1972 the oil industry produced 1.7 million barrels of crude oil daily, exported 1.1 million barrels of crude and products, and imported 900,000 barrels daily of crude and products. The producing rate has more than doubled in a decade. Export controls were placed on oil in March of 1973.

The petroleum industry (oil and gas)—exploration, production, refining and distribution—is dominated by foreign-controlled firms, which account for over 91 percent of the assets and over 95 percent of the sales of the industry. About four-fifths of the nonresident-controlled assets are held by U.S. interests. Most territory that is expected to yield new oil and gas reserves is already under permit to firms doing exploration. Canadian controlled firms hold the rights to only about 15 percent of federal and provincial permits and leases.[a] For a while now, talks have been continuing on the founding of a "national petroleum

a. In fact, the desire of Canadians for rapid development, which was often beyond the immediate capacity of Canadian firms, and which foreign firms were ready and eager to undertake, has made for high levels of foreign control in this sector.

company," NPC. Its proponents foresee NPC taking part in the exploration for Arctic oil and exploitation of tar sands, to begin with.

In the case of oil (and this is also true for gas), there is a fair amount of uncertainty about how large the resource base actually is, as shown in Table 6–2.

Most of the potential resources are expected to be found in Canada's as yet largely unexplored frontier areas. Supply-demand studies have indicated that Canada has sufficient total oil-resources potential to meet domestic demand well beyond the year 2000.

It is worth mentioning that the recent rapid production increase has led to a decline in the ratio of the proven reserves to the annual production from 24.5 to 15 in the period 1966–1972.

**Gas Industry.** In 1972, the natural gas industry produced 2,500 billion cubic feet (2.8 times more than in 1962), and exported 1,000 billion cubic feet (3 times more than in 1962).

Proven natural gas reserves yet to be produced total 53 trillion cubic feet. Estimates of gas potential, based on 1972 and 1973 assessments by the Geological Survey of Canada, range from 834 to 711 trillion cubic feet. As in the case of oil, the potential resource base appears large, but new reserves must be developed for the domestic market before there can be any further growths in exports. Annual reserve additions will have to increase substantially from the 1970 increase of 2,800 billion cubic feet if they are to support a pipeline for the transport of Arctic reserves.

**Electricity Generation.** The gross generation of electrical energy in 1972 was 238 billion kWh. Over the years, exports and imports have been more or less balanced, but in 1972 exports totaled 10,372 million kWh, about four times as much as imports. The net exports represent 3.3 percent of total Canadian generation. New high-voltage direct-current technology and large nuclear units will lead to increasing interconnections between provincial power systems.

**Table 6–2.   Canada's Oil Resources** *(billions of bbl)*

|  | In Place | Recoverable |
|---|---|---|
| Proven oil reserves (conventional) | 44.5 | 16.0 |
| Potential oil (conventional) |  | 83–118 |
| Alberta oil sands |  |  |
| Open-pit mineable |  | 65.0 |
| "In situ" recovery |  | 236.0 |
| Alberta heavy oil | 75.0 | 30.0 |
|  | 119.5 | 430–465 |

Source: "An Energy Policy for Canada–Phase I," Minister of Mines, Ottawa, 1973.

At best, hydroelectric energy production might double to about 310 billion kWh by 1990, compared to 157 in 1970. Table 6–3 compares the various sources of electricity generation in 1970, and the forecasts up to the year 2000. It is clear that the growth of hydroelectricity will be moderated from now on through competition from nuclear power.

About 75 percent of Canada's electrical energy is presently produced by domestic hydroelectric sources; more than one-half of the remainder is generated from imported fuels. The imported fuels are used in Ontario and in the Maritime Provinces; all other regions are self-sufficient on the basis of Canadian energy sources.

**Nuclear and Uranium Industry.** A distinction must be made between the two aspects involved here, namely: nuclear reactors, and the uranium market.

*Nuclear Reactors.* The present Canadian nuclear power program is based upon the CANDU natural uranium heavy water reactor concept. This is the culmination of over twenty years of research and development by Atomic Energy of Canada Limited (AECL), the government agency formed in 1952 to continue the work begun at Chalk River by the National Research Council. Created in 1958, the AECL Power Projects group designed the first full-scale power station at Douglas Point. Later, in conjunction with Ontario Hydro, the group built the 4 X 500 MWe Pickering (a notable success) and the 4 X 750 MWe Bruce Generating Stations. It also, in conjunction with Hydro Quebec, built the 250 MWe Gentilly-I nuclear power station (based on an alternative to the CANDU reactor, where the coolant is steam).[b]

As of mid-1973, there were about 2,000 MWe of nuclear power capacity operational in Canada, and 4,100 MWe under construction or committed. It is estimated that by 1985 there will be about 15,000 MWe of nuclear power capacity installed in Canada. By 1990 this is expected to grow to over 30,000 MWe, and by the year 2000 to about 100,000 MWe.

*Uranium.* The uranium industry reached its peak production in 1959, and then entered upon a dramatic decline due to the loss of the U.S. and U.K. markets. Federal government action, in establishing two successive uranium stockpiling programs, prevented a complete collapse of the industry. An era of large commercial uranium sales began in 1966, and one-quarter of presently known low-cost reserves are now under contract.

The uranium industry is under mixed public and private ownership, with over 20 percent of the assets under foreign control. Consideration is being

b. Canadian type reactors have been adopted by India, Pakistan, Argentina, Thailand and, recently, by Rumania. AECL or Canadian General Electric (in Pakistan) have contributed actively to these developments.

**Table 6–3. Sources of Electricity Generation, 1970–2000**

| Source | 1970 Billion kWh | % | 1980 Billion kWh | % | 1990 Billion kWh | % | 2000 Billion kWh | % |
|---|---|---|---|---|---|---|---|---|
| Hydro | 157 | 76.5% | 235 | 59% | 310 | 44% | 344 | 30% |
| Thermal Total | 47 | 23.5 | 161 | 41 | 388 | 56 | 788 | 70 |
| Coal | 34 | 17.0 | 76 | 19 | 127 | 18 | 151 | 13 |
| Oil | 7 | 3.5 | 29 | 7 | 72 | 10 | 118 | 10 |
| Natural Gas | 5 | 2.5 | 11 | 3 | 9 | 1 | 17 | 2 |
| Nuclear | 1 | 0.5 | 45 | 11 | 180 | 26 | 502 | 44 |
| Total | 204 | 100% | 396 | 100% | 698 | 100% | 1,132 | 100% |

given to the question of reducing this percentage, and even, in some circles, to the possibility of placing an embargo on uranium exports. This subject will probably be an important point for future energy policy issues.

Known uranium resources are estimated to be 400,000 tons of $U_3O_8$ available at prices up to $15 per pound. Canada's cumulative domestic needs up to the year 2000 could total 100,000 tons, while committed exports amount to some 60,000 tons (mid-1973). In addition there is estimated to be a further 500,000 tons of $U_3O_8$ available at $15 per pound or less.

## GENERAL ORGANIZATION FOR RESEARCH AND DEVELOPMENT[c]

The three main governmental organizations dealing with R&D are the Scientific Secretariat (itself a part of the Privy Council Office), dealing with day-to-day problems, the Science Council of Canada (its government and university members report to the Prime Minister), and the National Research Council (NRC), founded in 1917. The Economic Council is also interested in scientific policy.

Inspired by the British model for planning, coordination and execution of science activities, as well as for university training (the British model was the Department of Industrial and Scientific Research, set up in 1915), the NRC has developed a number of laboratories of its own. Twenty-one NRC laboratories were established during World War II, and within a few months the number of staff had increased from a few dozen to almost 2,000.

At the beginning of the 1950s, federal government funding of R&D in industry was less than $3 million per annum. This grew to about $50 million a year in 1957–1958, after which it dropped sharply and did not again reach $50 million a year until 1965–1966. Large technical projects had been funded at the frontiers of the most advanced fields: avionics, supersonic aircraft, large jet engines, nuclear power reactors, and computers. These programs involved hundreds of millions of dollars.

The three sectors that are performing research are the government (federal and provincial), the universities, and industry. There is no doubt that industry has the least favorable position, notwithstanding official declarations for more than fifty years which have stressed the importance of scientific developments for promoting industrial capability. One of the most frequently mentioned reasons for such a situation is that a good part of the industrial

c. It was particularly difficult to obtain up-to-date information for this section. There are complete, valuable studies, like the 1969 OECD "Science Policy in Canada," which information dates back to 1967, or the *Report of the Senate Special Committee on Science Policy,* published in 1970, but these are somewhat old. Various up-to-date inquiries are now being made, but are not yet available for publication.

companies are subsidiaries of foreign corporations (mainly U.S. and British), and these mother companies perform most of their research in their home country.

In 1967 the Industrial Research and Development Incentives Act (IRDIA), administered by the Department of Industry, was initiated. This is a grant-based general incentive program intended to stimulate industrial R&D. This grant amounts to 25 percent of eligible capital investment in R&D facilities and 25 percent of the increase in current R&D expenditures over the average of the previous five years.

In 1969 the NRC began a program of negotiated development grants to universities, aiming at the formation of "centers of excellence," with an industrial or regional development objective.

It is generally thought that, due to the impressive number of programs involving different agencies, the lack of coordination is particularly acute. A big weakness of the overall system seems to be its inability to promote national industries: even in the nuclear energy sector, where achievements and success with the CANDU reactor are outstanding, there is no national industrial company. The Senate Committee has stated that renewed attempts by successive governments to promote technological innovation by industry have all failed; what progress has been made in this respect results almost exclusively from the initiative of industry itself.

To sum up:[d]

1. Canada devotes about 60 percent of its R&D budget to scientific research, and only about 39 percent to technological development (these proportions are reversed in the United States, United Kingdom or Sweden).
2. Canada relies heavily on the academic sector as a performer of research (more than do other advanced countries), and the government directly finances close to half of that effort, producing a growing supply of well-trained scientists.
3. The government performs a large share of R&D (larger than in any other advanced country). Together, the academic and governmental sectors perform more than 60 percent of R&D activities.
4. The Canadian government finances only a low proportion of extramural R&D acticities and, moreover, a substantial share of this support is allocated to the academic sector.
5. While Canadian universities are concentrating on their various missions ("as they see them"), provincial research organizations, at the other end of the R&D spectrum, emphasize the use of knowledge and the introduction of new technology in industry. But not all provincial agencies have the same degree of affiliation with their provincial governments, and some provinces have no research agency at all. Generally, provincial groups complain that

d. These are some of the main conclusions of the Senate Committee.

the federal government has ignored them and does not make good use of their particular capabilities.

For 1969–1970, it was estimated that 69 percent of the total government expenditure on scientific activities was spent in government laboratories, 13 percent was assigned to industry, and 18 percent to universities and other nonprofit-making organizations.

For the 1973–1974 budget of $19,663 million (as compared to a 1973 GNP of $118,678 million, at market prices), 3.7 percent were devoted to scientific research, which amounts to $722 million. Of this, it was estimated that about 15 percent, or $100 million, were devoted to energy research and development, a major part thereof going to nuclear research.

## ENERGY RESEARCH AND DEVELOPMENT

According to the White Book on Energy Policy,[e] R&D expenditures in the mineral industry in general in Canada have been lower than in many other countries. The high degree of foreign control was thought to be a probable contributing factor. The Canadian Statistics data for 1970 show that "oil and gas wells and petroleum products" firms together spent $18.1 million on current research and development. Of the $18.1 million, the petroleum products group reported having spent $16 million, and "oil and gas wells" firms, only $2.1 million. The latter group consists principally of the junior firms of the petroleum industry: the large-scale integrated firms, which are virtually all foreign controlled, are grouped in the "petroleum products industry," which in 1967 spent $15.9 million and in 1969 spent $19.8 million on current research and development. The integrated firms of the petroleum industry had, in 1970, sales of close to $4 billion, so that their current R&D spending of $16 million was about 0.4 percent of sales. Moreover, there is no ready measure available of the nature of the R&D work done in Canada. The expenditures shown could relate to activities varying from the simple gathering of data to the actual experimentation, assessment and product innovation work.

As far as fossil fuels are concerned, most of the R&D is performed under sponsorship or in the laboratories of the Ministry of Energy, Mines and Resources, which includes the Geological Survey of Canada, founded in 1842. One of the problems of resource evaluation is the challenge of vastness: in 1960, it was estimated that "not more than 15 to 20 percent of Canada was now geologically mapped in adequate detail." For oil and gas research, valuable research is performed in Alberta, by various public and private institutions.[f]

e. "An energy policy for Canada, Phase I" issued under the authority of the Minister of Energy, Mines, and Resources, Ottawa, 1973.
f. Due to difficulties in obtaining up-to-date data, information as gathered here is somewhat incomplete.

### Coal Research and Development

The energy branch of the Ministry of Energy, Mines and Resources (MEMR) is responsible for establishing guiding principles for the coal industry and defining adequate programs for coordinated and long-term utilization of Canadian coal. The energy branch has founded the Ministerial Advisory Committee on coal, for coordinating expertise and facilities of the federal government, as well as maintaining relations with industry, and with the Coal Association of Canada.

The energy branch is administering various grants for coal research to universities or other research organizations. In 1971, for instance, grants amounted to $100,000, three-quarters going to four research centers in Canada.

The mine branch operates the Metals Reduction and Energy Centre, in which, for instance, the metallurgical fuel engineering group performs studies on coal treatment and carbonization. These studies have been particularly helpful in developing an export market for western coals (6.6 million tons to Japan in 1971, expected to grow to over 20 million tons in 1980, to Japan and possibly Europe). The Canadian Carbonisation Research Association has joined in this effort.

### Oil and Gas Research and Development

Oil and gas production is mainly concentrated in Alberta, and oil and gas exploration is more and more oriented toward the frontier provinces, northwestern territories and Arctic islands; moreover, oil sands are of growing interest.

Regarding exploration in the frontier provinces, the energy branch of MEMR founded in 1968 a working group for studying problems of oil exploration, and of pipeline construction, maritime transportation and environmental problems.

The Institute of Sedimentary and Petroleum Geology at Calgary, Alberta is performing studies for the Canadian Geological Survey of the MEMR. These studies are divided among seven main sections: Arctic Islands (aiming to evaluate their economic potential), Structural Geology, Paleozoic Stratigraphy, Mesozoic Stratigraphy, Western Paleontology, Petroleum Geology and Special Projects. Technical staff totals about eighty people. The institute is also very active in geological mapping, and has scheduled completion of a broad reconnaissance coverage of the unmapped parts of mainland territory by 1976; also important are basin analysis studies, such as the Sverdrup Basin in the Arctic.[g]

Regarding production, there are two main research organizations in Alberta, the Petroleum Recovery Research Institute and the Research Council of Alberta. Some research is also performed in universities, partly in the regular university budgets, and partly under programs sponsored by industry. The

g. Due to recent renewal of interest in coal, the institute plans to initiate studies on coal potential, such as drilling programs.

Energy Resources Conservation Board acts as an advisory capacity in the development of programs for other organizations.

The Petroleum Recovery Research Institute (PRRI) was established December 2, 1966, to carry out fundamental research related to the enhancement of the recovery of oil and gas from underground reservoirs. Industry participation in PRRI is on a voluntary membership basis, with companies agreeing to maintain their membership for five consecutive years. As of 1973, some thirty-five companies were contributing about $108,000/year, the government of Alberta matching this contribution to a yearly maximum of $100,000 (from 1967 to 1973. total revenues have been $1,369,000). PRRI has been working on an average of five research projects annually, the principal projects to date being:

1. Relative permeability measurement using reservoir fluids (completed).
2. Polymer solution flood (completed).
3. Reservoir statistical analysis (completed).
4. Interfacial phenomena in porous media.
5. Retrograde condensation and revaporization.
6. Hot water floods.
7. Diffusion and dispersion in miscible flooding.
8. Oil well coning.

Alberta Research is performing various energy-related work, including: resource surveys (coal and oil sands deposits); mining and extraction (in-situ extraction techniques for oil sands bitumen); processing and utilization (from tailing treatments from oil sand processing to conventional and in-situ coal gasification); environmental studies; transportation and transmission (coal-oil slurries, LNG), etc. Approximate expenditures for 1973 are $660,000, and the biggest research project being the development of in-situ extraction techniques for oil sands bitumen ($150,000).[h]

### Electricity and Nuclear Energy
### Research and Development

Hydro potential remains high in Canada, and hydro electricity production (150 billion kWh in 1970) could be doubled in the coming decades. Interest is continuing (with reassessment of past studies) for the tide plant at Fundy. Many rivers offer high potential, and are actively studied: upper Yukon, Columbia, Nelson, and others. Exploitation of these resources raises a severe transportation problem, which is being studied (direct-current transmission, studies of very high voltage performed in Hydro-Quebec Laboratories, etc.)

h. Early in 1974, Energy Minister Donald MacDonald announced a $40 million program (with much more to come) on frontier oil and oil sands, and the proposed founding of a National Oil Company.

But by far the biggest energy program in Canada is the nuclear energy research and development program, performed by Atomic Energy of Canada Limited (established in 1952). The two main AECL laboratories are at Chalk River (biggest R&D center of Canada) where, just at the end of World War II, Canada built the first nuclear reactor outside the United States, and at Whiteshell (Manitoba). The Chalk River establishment employs about 2,500 people, and has numerous research facilities such as NRU, critical facilities, van de Graaf, and so on. Whiteshell was founded in 1963 and employs about 700 people; the main research tool has been the WR−1 reactor, heavy water moderated and organic cooled.

As is well known, Canada has concentrated its efforts from the very beginning on heavy water reactors, and has achieved a noteworthy success with the Pickering power plants. All components and processes have been developed by AECL, including the important pressure tubes (initially of Zircaloy, and later from cold-worked zirconium−2.5 percent niobium), development of heavy water production processes (such as amine–hydrogen exchange), organic or boiling water cooling (Gentilly-I plant), studies on recyling of plutonium and on carbide fuels, etc. Interesting studies have also been performed on neutron breeding of fertile materials with accelerators. Yearly budgets of AECL total about $100 million.

Due to its very high uranium potential (more than 700,000 tons of uranium, proven and probable reserves, at less than $15/lb $U_3O_8$),[i] Canada has shown interest in uranium enrichment (in Quebec Province, combined with huge hydroelectric resources), although little research has been done on enrichment technology (which will probably be brought by possible foreign partners, such as France for instance). The weakest point of this nuclear energy research and development program seems the lack of success in involving industry in the program.

### Thermonuclear Fusion

The Institut National de la Recherche Scientifique, of the Université du Quebec, is doing research on thermonuclear fusion. This R&D includes four research programs: two on scientific feasibility, one on plasma applications and one on fusion reactor technology.

Program I.   Interaction between matter and laser beams ($CO_2$). Laser has been developed, and used to study plasma heating and solid targets; two lasers of different frequency have also been used.

Program II.   Plasma containment. Theoretical studies on plasma equilibrium in electrical and magnetic containment, and KEMP devices development (cinetic, electrical and magnetic containment).

i. In 1944 a crown company was established for uranium: Eldorado Mining and Refining. However, most of the market is dominated by Denison Mines and Rio Algom.

Program III.   Plasma applications. Interactions between plasmas and aerosols, plasmas dusts, and shock-waves.

Program IV.   Fusion reactor technology. Materials behavior under intense neutron and ion bombardment (10 to 20 keV ions and 14 MeV neutrons), and breeding studies.

## REFERENCES

### Energy Situation
"An Energy Policy for Canada, Phase I."—Minister of Energy, Mines and Resources, Ottawa, 1973.

### Research and Development
National Research Council of Canada Reports.
OECD. *National Policies for Science: Canada.* 1969.
"A Science Policy for Canada." Senate Special Committee on Science Policy. Ottawa, 1970.
*Science Dimension* (six issues per year). Periodic publication of the National Research Council of Canada.

### Energy Research and Development
Alberta Research (E. J. Wiggins, Director). Personnal Communication.
Atomic Energy of Canada Ltd. Annual Reports.
Canadian Geological Survey. Annual Reports.
Energy Resources Conservation Board (G. A. Warne). Personnal Communication.
Fourth Atomic Geneva Conference. Canadian Papers.
Institute of Sedimentary and Petroleum Geology. Descriptive Brochures.
Merril Lynch, Toronto. "Canadian Uranium—An Industry Review."
Ministry of Energy, Mines and Resources Annual Reports.
———— . Mines Branch. Metals Reduction and Energy Centre. Divisional Reports.
Petroleum Recovery Research Institute. *History and Accomplishments of the Petroleum Recovery Research Institute* (November 22, 1973).
———— . *Report of the Interim Board of Directors.*
Université du Quebec. Institut National de la Recherche Scientifique. Brochure, 1972–1973.
———— . *INRS–Energie. 3^eme Rapport Annuel* (1 September, 1972–31 Mai, 1973).

# Chapter Seven

# Federal Republic of Germany

Because of its powerful industries and the high standard of living of the people, Germany is the biggest energy user in Western Europe. Many German companies (such as Volkswagenwerke, Siemens, Daimler-Benz, Badische Anilin und Soda Fabrik BASF, Bayer, and Krupp) rank high in the *Fortune* directory of the largest industrial companies outside the United States in the sectors of iron and steel, automobiles, electro-technical and electronic equipment, and chemistry.

Historically, there has been no large German energy company comparable to the oil companies in America, the United Kingdom, France or Italy.[a] The free-enterprise system has resulted in a spread of small or medium-size energy companies (with multiple and complex interconnections), which was not favorable for long-term energy research and development. Moreover, the political Federal system, with the states having high autonomy in matters such as education and research, was similarly unsuited to foster long term "big" science.

In recent years, through financing large projects (especially nuclear energy development), the federal government has increased considerably its role in research and development, and, in the early 1970s, even began a progressive reorganization of all research activities in Germany, reinforcing coordination and centralization. It is too soon to draw any conclusions about its success. In late 1973, the federal government put together its first national energy policy, which was badly needed.[b]

## The Energy Situation

In 1950 the energy structure in Germany was very similar to that of the United Kingdom, essentially based on coal. Since then, however, Germany

a. In late 1973, the government announced it would promote and participate in a new major oil company, to be formed through a series of mergers.
b. "Energy Policy Program for the Federal Republic of Germany" (September 1973),

*157*

has forged ahead in economic and industrial development, and the share of coal in the energy mix has steadily decreased. Coal contributed less than one-third of the energy mix in 1972, while oil, now the major fuel, accounted for more than 55 percent of the total energy consumption. Almost 95 percent of the oil is imported. Natural gas is expanding; and nuclear energy is expected to become more and more important, as can be seen from Table 7–1 on past energy consumption and recent forecasts.

In the Federal Republic of Germany, it is in principle left to the initiative of private undertakings to obtain the supply of energy; this applies to all forms of energy as well as to the various levels of energy production and distribution. None of the different branches of the energy industry is national-ized or subject to extensive government control. The forms of management of all undertakings of this sector are based on the principles of private industry, even those in which the state or other public authorities hold a part interest. "Public utility undertakings," i.e., the electricity and the gas industry, are independent as to their decisions in technological and economic fields, but their investment projects are subject to control as to whether they are likely to serve the purpose of supplying the public with reliable and cheap energy.

The Federal Ministry of Economics is the competent authority at the federal level for energy matters, while at the state level, the Ministry of Economics of the particular state is responsible for the energy sector. Coopera-tion between the administration and the energy industry is not institutionalized, but proceeds through informal contacts. Institutions representing the industry have also assumed duties, some of which are of a public character (such as statistics in coal mining and supervision of self-restraint in fuel-oil sales).

**Coal and Lignite.** As can be seen from Table 3–1, solid fuel produc-tion has steadily decreased since the end of the European coal crisis of the

**Table 7–1.  Energy Consumption and Forecasts, 1955–1985**
*(million metric tons of coal equivalent)*

|                    | 1955  | 1960  | 1972  | 1975[a] | 1980[a] | 1985[a] |
|--------------------|-------|-------|-------|---------|---------|---------|
| Coal and lignite   | 158.6 | 157.6 | 114.7 | 107     | 97      | 88      |
| Oil                | 15.5  | 44.4  | 196.4 | 230     | 275     | 330     |
| Natural gas        | 0.4   | 0.8   | 30.6  | 48      | 82      | 92      |
| Nuclear energy     | –     | –     | 3.1   | 12      | 45      | 90      |
| Others             | 8.8   | 8.8   | 9.6   | 9       | 11      | 10      |
| *Total consumption* | 183.3 | 211.6 | 354.4 | 406     | 510     | 610     |

a. Forecasts, from FRG, Ministry of Economics, "Energy Policy Program of the Federal Republic of Germany (September 1973).

published by the Federal Minister of Economics. In this document, energy R&D is mentioned (generally reinforcing existing programs, such as nuclear process heat), but no figure is given for the energy R&D budget increases.

1950s, and continues to decrease. In fact, one must distinguish between hard coal and Braunkohle or lignite. The production of lignite, widely used in power plants, is slowly increasing. About 115 million metric tons (about 35 million metric tons of coal equivalent) was produced in 1972; it will probably level off at around 35–37 million tce/year. Bituminous coal production fell from nearly 140 million metric tons at the end of the 1950s to 84 million metric tons in 1972, and is expected to continue to decrease to 50 million metric tons in 1985.

Coal and lignite reserves are still important, and there are people arguing for keeping a higher domestic coal production, but the recent energy policy proposals from the federal government apparently do not plan to change the present trends, (only to consolidate present production levels), and coal continues to be considered a noneconomical fuel. The two main uses of solid fuels are steel manufacturing and power production.

Before 1969, the coal and lignite industry was divided among about 100 different companies, many belonging more or less to the steel or to the power industry. In 1969, many coal companies in the Ruhr district were merged together in a new private company, Ruhrkohle AG, receiving financial support from the federal government. Unexpectedly, the financial losses of this new big concern continued to increase, and amounted to about DM 1 billion ($400 million) in the first three years. These difficulties were due in part to steady increases in costs, and to the obligation to sell coking coal at low prices to the previous owners of the coal companies. Finally, all the measures taken (reorganization of the industry, taxes on fuel oil, subsidies to coal users such as power plants), as well as improvements in production efficiency (from 1652 kg per day per worker in 1956 to 3830 kg in 1971), have not been able to alter the coal situation, or to change the trends.

The poor financial situation of too many coal companies could have been considered as unfavorable to coal research and development as a whole. Nevertheless, corporate research has been well developed, and was also supported by the European Coal and Steel Community.

**Oil.** There is a small amount of domestic oil production in Germany (mainly in the North), which came to 8 million metric tons (160,000 b/d) of oil in 1968, and has been slowly decreasing at a few percent per year since 1969. Exploration is proceeding in the German sector of the North Sea, but without any success so far. Oil reserves are about 75 million metric tons (525 million barrels).

Oil is imported mainly from the Middle East and Africa. Libya was the main source of imported oil through the 1960s, but its role has been decreasing in favor of the Middle East. About 75 percent of Germany's oil supply is commercialized by foreign companies (mainly U.S. and British or Dutch-British), and there has been no important national oil company either in research and production or in refining. The German producing or refining companies were either subsidiaries (or closely related) to previous coal companies (Gelsenberg), or to electricity producers, or to chemical companies (such as Veba, for refining).

In 1969 a new consortium, Deminex ("However late, nevertheless appropriate . . . "), was formed with the aim of finding new sources of oil supplies in foreign territories. Shareholders of Deminex are Veba-Chemie, Gelsenberg (formerly a coal company, actually shareholder of Ruhrkohle, involved in Libya, and now diversifying to nuclear fuel cycle), Union Rheinische Braunkohle Kraftstoff, Wintershall (subsidiary of BASF), Deutsche Schachtbau (a drilling equipment and exploration company), Saarbergwerke, and Preussag. Deminex was to receive DM 575 million ($230 million) from the federal government during the first six-year period (1969–1975), but its success has been somewhat limited. For the time being, it is only an exploration consortium. This survey found no indication that Deminex is performing any research and development program on its own.

Due to environmental difficulties during recent years, construction of refineries has been delayed, and the refining capacity is insufficient. This means that, in addition to crude oil imports, Germany must also import oil products (most of them from the Netherlands, France, and Belgium). Germany's new energy plan of 1973 proposed that the government join in a merger of the main independent German refiners, under Veba leadership, in a national refining undertaking. Deminex and this new refining consortium, with the government as a major shareholder, could become the two poles of a stronger integrated national oil company.

**Natural Gas.** There is significant natural gas production in the Federal Republic of Germany (about 17 billion $Nm^3$ [630 billion $ft^3$] in 1972),[c] covering about two-thirds of the requirements. In 1972, gas reserves were estimated to about 350 billion $Nm^3$ (12,950 billion $ft^3$). It is forecast, as is shown in Table 3–1, that gas consumption will multiply by a factor 3 between 1972 and 1985, with most of the increase to come from imports—from the Netherlands, the Soviet Union, the Norwegian Sector of the North Sea, and Algeria, according to already signed contracts. Other contracts are being negotiated with other producing countries, situated farther from Germany, such as the Persian Gulf.

Exploration and production of widely spread small gas fields are performed by about fifteen companies. The most important, Wintershall (German ownership, subsidiary of BASF), produces about one-third of domestic natural gas; foreign companies (mainly Exxon and Shell) control more than 50 percent of domestic gas production. Transportation and distribution are performed by other companies (about fifteen also), acting locally; share owners

c. $Nm^3$ or normal $m^3$ refers to cubic meters at "normal" conditions: 15°C (59°F) and one atmosphere.

are big industrial manufacturing companies (and gas users), national or foreign oil companies, as well as states and urban communities. There is no vertical integration in the gas industry.

The federal government, according to its new energy policy, now guarantees the bonds for development and import contracts, and plans to subsidize a seismic program aiming to look for possible deep, or very deep gas fields in the national territory.

**Electricity.** Total electricity production in 1972 was roughly 280 billion kWh, two-thirds produced by public plants, and one-third by industrial plants (in Germany, industry is producing a major part of its own power requirements). In 1973, the total installed capacity was slightly over 60,000 MWe, about one-third owned by industrial corporations. It is forecast by the Federal Minister of Economy that total installed capacity will reach 140,000 MWe in 1985, which means that about 90,000 MWe will have to be built in the next 12 years (due to the shut-down of old power plants). About half will be nuclear plants. In 1972 about 7 percent was hydroelectricity, and the remaining thermal power, the main fuels being coal and lignite. The federal government will try to keep a level of about 30 million metric tons of coal for power production between 1973 and 1980, through subsidies, and wants to limit use of fuel oil and natural gas to a minimum value.

There are more than 700 entities for the production and distribution of electricity, of very different sizes. The biggest one, Rheinisch-Westphaliche Elektrizitats Gesellschaft (RWE), produces more than one-third of the total electricity. The 600 or so public utilities are grouped in the Vereinigung Deutscher Elektrizitatswerke (VDEW), and the companies producing electricity for their own needs and for public distribution are grouped in the Verband Industrielle Kraftwirtschaft (VIK). About two-thirds of the electricity companies mix private and public shares. Most of the undertakings cooperate together and exchange power, but each one generally has a local or regional monopoly. As a result of the high number of companies, many power plants were undersized relative to economical optimum; some companies (such as RWE) have a strong financial position, and diversified interests in other industrial sectors (coal, oil, uranium, etc.). Costs and rates have been relatively low, as well as investments compared to annual turnover (nuclear energy can change this situation).

As in the United States until the recent creation of EPRI, a major part of electricity research and development was in fact performed by equipment manufacturers, such as Siemens, AEG-Telefunken (which have now merged their electrotechnical capabilities in Kraftwerk Union, KWU), Brown-Bovery-Company Mannheim (BBC), etc.

**Nuclear Energy.** Nuclear energy developments had to wait until after the first Geneva Conference in 1955; that is to say, German research laboratories and nuclear industry started about ten years later than many other developed countries, such as the United Kingdom and France, to say nothing of the United States. From the very beginning, unlike its British and French neighbors, German industry took the lead, strongly supported by the Federal and the state governments, in this process avoiding some of the ambiguities that have weighed so heavily on the British and French nuclear programs with their big centralized and monolithic nuclear authorities. It must be recognized that nuclear developments in Germany have been impressive. Many reactor types were studied at the beginning, even such exotic ones as zirconium hydride moderated and sodium-cooled plant, KNK in Karlsruhe. Efforts very soon concentracted, however, on light water reactors, initially using American licenses: Westinghouse Pressurized Water Reactor (PWR) for Siemens, and General Electric Boiling Water Reactor (BWR) for AEG; by improvements, these two German companies have more or less freed themselves from their American licences; the two companies in 1969 merged their nuclear activities in KWU, and compete eagerly with American companies on the international market (power plants already sold to Argentina, the Netherlands, and Austria).

Starting with experimental and prototype nuclear power plants (the first 16 MWe BWR Kahl plant began operation in 1961), continuing with demonstration nuclear power stations (250 MWe BWR Gundremmingen station in operation in 1966, and 345 MWe PWR Obrigheim station in operation in 1968), KWU's two companies built their first commercial plants for operation in 1971–1972 (670 MWe BWR at Wurgassen, and 662 MWe PWR Stade). All this was accomplished in a period of ten years. Nuclear plants were generating 2,300 MWe by the end of 1972. Nuclear plants under construction (including 1,200–1,300 MWe plants like Biblis), will supply another 7,500 MWe, and planned units will supply 10–12,000 MWe. These developments would raise nuclear capacity to around 20–22,000 MWe by 1980. All the reactors are manufactured by KWU, except one by BBR-Babcock Brown Bovery Reaktor GmbH, Mannheim, subsidiary of U.S. B&W, German B&W and BBC.

German industry is also active in the various aspects of the nuclear fuel cycle, from uranium prospecting (sponsored by the government) to fuel elements manufacture, enrichment, radioactive transport, and reprocessing. These activities involve companies acting independently, cooperatively (reactor manufacturers, chemical companies, utilities, coal and/or oil companies), or through international associations. There are joint projects with the Netherlands and the United Kingdom for enrichment, and with France and the United Kingdom for reprocessing and radioactive transportation.

There is some environmentalist opposition. Safety measures and administrative procedures have been increased accordingly, but it seems that so far environmentalists have not been able to stop or seriously delay reactor construction.

### General Organization for Research and Development

Research in the Federal Republic of Germany has generally been performed in universities, in various laboratories sponsored by the German Association for Research, in the laboratories of the Max Planck Gesellschaft, and in various industrial laboratories, virtually without any kind of central co-ordination or planning. The states were financing most of the basic research. Recently, and more or less spurred by the development of big nuclear research, the federal government has sponsored large research centers and federal laboratories, and increased considerably its share of financial support. In the place of what was sometimes called "the imitation phase" (of American, British or French research), the federal government and the recently appointed new Ministry for Research and Technology plan to substitute a new and dynamic research policy, through systematic planning, public dialog (periodic hearings on main programs), and the participation of the scientists themselves in the decision-making process. In contrast to the situation in many Western countries, where public research budgets have been leveling off (or even relatively decreasing, as in France in recent years), the funds for research and development in Germany have been steadily increasing.

### The Government and Scientific Research

One important factor in the reorganization of research by the federal government is the definition of Major Fields, with the basic purpose of orienting research toward social goals and social developments (similar to OECD research policy objectives as defined in October 1971 by the Ministers for Science and Technology of the member countries). The government is also reorganizing the university and the education system along this same idea of Major Fields; as noted above, a good part of basic research is performed in university laboratories, financed 50 percent by the Lander and 50 percent by the government. In 1971 the federal government devoted DM 1685 million ($675 million) to general scientific development (exclusive of applied or specific projects), of which DM 1031 million ($410 million) went into the universities.

Independent research is also performed in the unique organization—Max Planck Gesellschaft—which has developed so spectacularly during the last twenty years. Today, the Max Planck Gesellschaft comprises some fifty-two institutes and lesser research units, employs some 8,000 people, of whom some 2,000 are graduates,[d] and operates on an annual budget of some DM 500 million ($200 million). Apart from some special income for space science and nuclear activities, a now relatively diminished contribution from industry and the foundations (such as Fritz Thyssen, Volkswagen, and Alfred Krupp), and a very

---

d. Engineers and M.S. degrees, and most often Ph.D. degrees.

small profit of its own, the annual budget of the MPG has, until recently, been raised in deliberately equal proportions from the federal and regional governments; however, the huge Institut fur Plasma Physik of Garching, near Munich, has been funded with only 10 percent from the Bavarian authorities. The share of the government may well also increase for other institutes.

Although some institutes have especially close ties with industry (for example, the one for iron and steel), there is no contract research as such. The institutes vary considerably in size, from the relatively large ones of physics (Munich) to very small units. The very large Institut fur Plasma Physik in Garching dwarfs all others with its scientific establishment of over 200.

The founding of such a large unit is quite atypical of the Max Planck Gesellschaft and does not seem to represent a significant change of policy. Among the various MPG institutes, the Institut fur Plasma Physik is the main one concerned with energy problems; to a lesser extent, hydro and gasdynamics is studied at the Max Planck Institut fur Stromungsforschung in Gottingen; two institutes, previously dealing with coal research (Max Planck Institut fur Kohlenforschung), are no longer concerned with coal and energy: one is dealing with metallic-organic compounds, and the second with radiation chemistry.

Basic research is also sponsored by the German Association for Research (about DM 220 million [$88 million] a year), financed equally by the federal government and by the states, plus about 10 percent by foundations. Now this Association is also more or less following the division in normal and major (or priority) fields.

These major fields are enhanced by governmental technical programs. The overall budget for these technical programs (as defined by pluri-annual plans) was DM 2300 million ($840 million) in 1971. The main technical programs are: (1) atomic programs (see below); (2) space program (1969–1973); (3) information and communication program (No. II, 1971–1975); (4) oceanography research (1969–1973); (5) technology improvement program; and (6) environment research projects.

**Industrial Research.** In recent years the rate of increase of industrial funding for research and development has been about the same as the rate of increase of government-sponsored research. Industry is financing about half of research and development in Germany. In 1969, industry spent DM 7.4 billion ($3 billion), of which DM 6.4 billion ($2.5 billion) was their own money, compared to DM 4.8 billion ($1.9 billion) in 1967.[e]

Main efforts are more and more concentrated in three sectors: chemical industry (including refining and petroleum chemistry), steel, and mechanical equipment (including the automobile). Then come electrical equip-

e.  These comparisons are made with 1974 dollar value for the DM, which is overvalued by about 40 percent compared to mid-1960s.

ment, precision mechanics, and opticals. The three first sectors were using about 81 percent of total expenses in 1965 and 86 percent in 1969; chemistry in 1969 received 31.7 percent of companies own funding, electronics and electrotechnique, 26.5 percent; and automobile, 17.2 percent.

From the DM 520 million ($210 million) granted by the federal government in 1970 to industrial companies for R&D, 48 percent was for steel, equipment and automobile industries; 17.2 percent for electro-technical, precision and optical industries; 13.1 percent for chemistry; and 6.4 percent for energy and water supplies.

An organization somewhat similar to the Max Planck Gesellschaft was created in 1949: The Fraunhofer Gesellschaft for applied research, which comprises some twenty institutes and seven research groups. The Fraunhofer institutes perform contract research for industry and for the public sector in addition to their own research projects. Part of the budget is financed by the federal government.

Interprofessional research represents only about 4 percent of the total industrial research and development, with DM 300 million ($120 million). The main sector (more than 50 percent) is for the mining industry, where interprofessional research is somewhat traditional. Outside the mining sector, only small or medium companies use this kind of joint research, and it can be said that industrial R&D is mainly performed by the biggest companies. Nevertheless, there is a growing tendency for cooperation, even sometimes between competing companies (such as electrical equipment and aeronautics).

## ENERGY RESEARCH AND DEVELOPMENT

One may gather from the above that it was extremely difficult to assemble valuable information on energy research and development, because of the great number of professional and industrial organizations linking numerous and independent companies. Nevertheless, an important set of documents has been collected on energy economics and energy-sector statistics.

Before dealing with the various fuels research and development, it should be noted that there is in the Federal Republic of Germany an organization that is somewhat similar to the U.S. Geological Survey combined with the U.S. Bureau of Mines. It is the Bundesanstalt für Bodenforschung (Hannover), which is supplemented also by geological services in the various states, and which works in an especially close association with the Niedersachsiches Landesamt für Bodenforschung. The Bundesanstalt für Bodenforschung performs geological studies, with a high priority on improving prospecting techniques (including geochemical methods), and develops mining technology such as drilling, hydromechanical extraction, washing, roof support, front mining, as well as air and water control methods.

## Coal Research and Development

Initially, research and development for coal was mainly oriented toward coal utilization, and was performed by individual mining companies; safety was also a major subject for research. The introduction of mechanization has largely increased the needs for R&D, and changed the classical type of R&D into a new and modern type. In 1952, all the coal mining companies created a common research organization—the Steinkohlenbergbauverein—divided in two closely associated main organizations—the Bergauforschung GmbH and the Bergwerksverband Kray laboratories—with more than 1,000 people, about half of the academic level. The yearly budget is about DM 115 million ($46 million), 80 percent financed by mines, and 20 percent by the federal government, the state governments and the European Communities; it is expected that the federal government's share will increase in the coming year.

The lignite industry has an independent research organization that is attached to the Deutsche Braunkohle Industrie Verein, in Koln. There are also some companies studying coal production and power production, but it is somewhat difficult to determine whether the research they are doing on combined coal gasification and gas turbine should be classified as coal utilization research or as power production research and development.

The three main items of research from the Steinkohlenbergbauverein/Bergbauforschung/Bergwerksverband are: (1) safety and basic research; (2) mining technology; and (3) coal utilization and coal products development. A few comments and examples will be given.

**Safety and Basic Research.** Safety research includes medical studies on silicosis, and development of rescue procedures in case of accident. Methane research has been done on the extent of gas release by neighboring layers, improvement of gas concentration measurement, release of gas by coal storages in the mine, and development of measuring equipment (ventor, and Unor-$CH_4$ recorders).

Important studies are being done on ventilation of mines, with laboratory mock-ups, to improve the climate in the mines, decrease the risk of accidents with teledetecting systems, measuring temperatures, and to assess heat-flow patterns and cooling requirements.

Geological and geophysical basic research is being performed for a better understanding of rock mechanisms. Television equipment has been developed for observation in bore-holes a few hundred meters deep. Many studies are devoted to ground-pressure measurements and correlations, so as to be able to improve planning of coal extraction; mock-ups are also used for hard rocks or for less hard ones, and for rectangular cross-sections of coal mine walls or working faces. Four kinds of experiments are successfully performed: (1) systematic measurements in the mine (and neighboring grounds); (2) model studies; (3) checking on prototype equipment at the surface; and (4) final testing of new mining equipment.

**Mining Technology and Mining Machines.** This sector has made an all-out effort to increase productivity, studying everything from rock mechanics to long-wall developments and transport of material and people. Mechanization has made impressive progress in recent years, since the decision that the only way German mining could survive was by concentrating high levels of coal extraction in a small number of mines with few working faces. One objective is to reach a yield of 3,000 metric tons of coal per day per working face. Mechanization, automatization, and remote control are being progressively integrated in the various mining steps. Developments are continued on coal-cutters, with varying angles related to the slope of the seams, with advancing roof support. New ploughing machines are tested in experimental facilities (6,400 m$^2$ and long-wall mock-up of 100 m) where varying rock compositions are reproduced (by chalk, concrete, etc.), surface tests allowing careful measurements before proceeding to final tests in the mine itself. High-speed boring machines are also being developed for very deep mining, and hydraulic fluids are also studied for remote-control equipments.

**Coal Utilization.** Considerable effort has been devoted to coking, to try to produce metallurgical coke from coals generally not used for this purpose; included is research to produce coke from lignite (Deutscher Braunkohlenindustrie Verein, Koln). There is also, as in the United Kingdom, active research to promote coal products or by-products in various industrial sectors, such as electrometallurgical electrodes, building materials, Rhodanide, polyurethane, and so on.

In the sector of energy, there are studies on combustion process versus particle sizes of various coals, and on fluidized bed combustion, in cooperation with the Steag company (absorption of sulphur oxides of the flu gases by a special coke, low-temperature carbonization product formed to a cylindrical shape, and transformation to sulfuric acid). Long-term studies include the following:

Coal gasification. Due to the high cost of coal, and the expected low cost of nuclear process heat, some projects are being developed, in cooperation with Aachen Technical University and the Julich nuclear research center, to use the heat of a high-temperature pebble bed reactor OTTO (Once Through Then Out) for coal or lignite gasification.

Low BTU gas (from coal and steam reaction). A conceptual design of a commercial plant uses a 3,000 MWth (heat production capacity) reactor to process about 2.6 million metric tons of coal per year and also produce electricity. Such a project would need outlet temperatures of 1,100°C (reaction temperature 900°C), which are not yet proven. If supported, such a project could become a major energy project for Germany, and possibly for Europe.[f]

f. Some conceptual studies are also performed on possible methanol production from coal.

MHD. Calculations have shown that an open-cycle MHD topping cycle above a conventional steam cycle could raise efficiency to 49–52.5 percent. For many years, Bergbauforschung has carried out studies on MHD (using, preferentially, coal, but possibly using oil or gas), aiming to build a demonstration plant VEGAS–II of 30 MWth, and beginning with a small demonstration plant VEGAS–I of 2 MWth. The experimental program covers electrode materials, seed injection and recuperation, and so on. Although progress has been made (and a cooperative effort agreed upon between Germany and the United States), no time-schedule has been settled for VEGAS–II, and no decision has been taken on the construction of VEGAS–I. Work is continuing on a research basis (Argas experiments developed with Julich nuclear research center).

**Land Reclamation.**  One achievement worth mentioning in connection with lignite production in the Koln district is the outstanding land reclamation program carried out by the industry. The Rheinische Braunkohlenwerke A.G. has a special department with a worldwide reputation for land reclamation and land planning and management. It has developed a high technology for simultaneous mining and reclamation. The system uses giant bucket wheel excavators that separate valuable topsoil (loess) from worthless or toxic materials. A sophisticated network of pipelines and rail transport carries the extracted materials, either lignite, loess, or spoil, away from the area. The loess goes by hydraulic pipes to small waiting fields or "polders," where Dutch reclamation techniques are used to restore the land to full agricultural productivity. This technology, used in the context of careful regional planning, has permitted the lignite industry to cut large swaths through the country side, even at times transplanting whole villages, and to later recreate a liveable and productive landscape.[g] Two processes are used, a wet process and a dry process. Such reclaimed lands compete with the most fertile lands around Koln. Studies began early in the 1950s and the first big operation (Schirhof) begun in 1963, was terminated in 1971 (8.30 km² –2,075 acres). Other areas have been converted into water-recreation areas.

### Oil and Gas Research and Development
As noted earlier, there has been no large German domestic oil company comparable (even without mentioning the major U.S. companies) to the British BP, the Dutch-British Shell, the French CFP and Elf/ERAP or the Italian ENI, either/or for oil and gas research, or for refining. Moreover, there is no centralized research organization, comparable for instance, to the French Petroleum Institute.

The most important oil research organization in Germany seems to

g.  "Surface mining and land reclamation in Germany" E.A. Nephew – ORNL–NSF–EP–16 (May 1972).

be the Deutsche Gesellschaft für Mineralolwissenschaft und Kohlechemie E.V. or DGMK, in Hamburg. This is a technical association for coordinating and sponsoring research, and for publication of research and development results, either through meetings and congresses, or through publication of monthly technical review: "Erdohl und Kohle-Erdgas-Petrochemie, vereinigt mit Brennstoff-Chemie." The overall budget of DGMK for 1972 was DM 1,141,000 ($450,000) (expenses) of which DM 788,000 ($315,000) was for research budget.

The main research and development sectors dealt with by DGMK range from oil and gas exploration techniques (in connection with geology, geophysics, geochemical and field engineering), drilling technology and production process, refining and petroleum chemistry, transport and distribution equipment, (for crude, oil products and natural gas), to environmental studies, improvement of products quality, regulation, and standards.

### Electricity Research and Development

There are two main organizations for research and development for electricity: the Forschungsgemeinschaft für Hochspannung-und Hochstromtechnik e.v. (FGH), for electricity production, transport and distribution, resulting from the merging of two former research organizations: the #400-kv-Forshungsgemeinschaft e.v., and the Studiengesellschaft für Hochspannungsanlagen e.v., financed by utilities for distribution and by electrical industry.

Moreover, big power companies (such as RWE or STEAG) or big electrotechnical manufacturing companies, such as KWU (power equipment common subsidiary of Siemens and AEG-Telefunken) or BBC have their own research programs carried out in their own research facilities.

**Forschungsgemeinschaft für Hochspannung-und Hochstromtechnik e.v. (FGH).** Main laboratories of FGH are in Mannheim-Rheinau and in Dossenwald (Mannheim), and include open-air high-voltage equipment for D.C. or A.C. power. All the problems related to the use of higher D.C. or A.C. voltages in interconnected networks are studied, in close connection with electrotechnical equipment manufacturers (operational difficulties, statistics of accidents, analysis of operation, and so forth): tests of switching devices (such as switchgears, transformers, and busbars), tests on dynamic and thermal effects of high-current arcs, investigation of over-voltage phenomena, load-flow and short-circuit currents (by steady-state network analyser and digital computation), and so on. In its new energy policy, the federal Minister for Economy also has stressed the importance of high-capacity underground transmission systems.

Before merging, the two organizations employed about eighty people.

**Elektrowarme Institut Essen e.v.** Main studies are related to household and industrial applications of electrical heating, covering all aspects of the problem, including temperature measurement and control, development of materials, furnaces, heat pump, and checking procedures. HF and infrared heating applications are tested, together with cooling for conducting materials, and high temperature heat storage.

Some examples of the R&D activities of private companies follow.

**RWE. (Rheinisch-Westfalisches Elektrizitatswerk AG).** As mentioned above, RWE is by far the most important electricity producer in the Federal Republic of Germany—in 1971 production was 31.8 billion kWh, turnover DM 4.57 billion ($1.8 billion), investment DM 1.76 billion ($0.7 billion), R&D cost DM 3.5 million ($1.4 million). Research is mainly concentrated in the field of electrical heating and energy uses and conservation in industry, household, commerce and agriculture. The biggest research project has been that of developing nuclear reactors, especially the fast breeder, with about DM 80–85 million ($32–34 million) going into the Kalkar SNR prototype.

**Steag.** Another example of private R&D comes from the Steag company. In 1972, Steag was operating twenty-five powerplants with a total capacity of 3,500 MW. Ruhrkohle AG is the biggest shareholder, and RWE the third. Steag's Kellerman station at Lunen is used for a broad development program on desulfurization and combined gas/system turbine generating plant with bituminous-coal high-pressure gasification. Three different pilot plants are being tested for reducing $SO_2$ emissions ( (1) Bischoff process by lime scrubbing; (2) Bergbau-Forschungs process with dry $SO_2$ absorption on coke; and (3) Lurgi $H_2S$ scrubbing with "Claus-Gas" generation).

**Siemens.** One of the biggest electrotechnical and electronics companies in the world, Siemens spends yearly more than DM 1 billion ($4 million)—about 7 percent of worldwide sales volume—on research and development. Unfortunately, it was not possible to earmark the share devoted to energy problems among a very broad R&D program. This program (mainly in the Erlangen research center [staff over 2,300] and in the Erlangen and Munich laboratories) deals with components, data systems, telecommunications, power engineering, electrical installations, medical equipment, fuel cells (prototype of 5 kW for power emergency supply source), superconductivity (prototype of a superconducting stellarator magnet for MPG Institut für Plasma Physik in Garching), plastics, plasma physics, together with reactor engineering, automation engineering and system engineering.

Finally, in its basic document on reorganization of research and development in Germany, the federal government has mentioned in the Technology Improvement Program, its aim to develop electrochemical and catalytic energy conversion, as well as other energy production and transport technologies. There is a program on batteries and on fuel cells, partially oriented toward future electric-car propulsion (prototype vehicles are foreseen for 1974–1975). Other projects are aimed at developing superconducting cables for high-power transmission.

### Nuclear Energy Research
### and Development

The commercial and technical success of the German nuclear industry, however great its reputation for quality, would not have been possible without a massive effort of public funding, from the states and from the federal government. The federal government has progressively assumed the major role in nuclear energy research and development, through its four successive Nuclear Programs. During the past seventeen years, more than DM 11 billion ($4.4 billion) have been spent by the federal government and the state governments, and the Fourth German Nuclear Program (1973–1976) envisaged government expenditures of approximately DM 6.5 billion ($2.6 billion),[h] covering reactor development, the entire fuel cycle, safety and radiation protection, isotope and radiation technology, as well as fundamental research.

Part of research and development is performed by industry on government funds. But most of the research is performed in the big nuclear research centers, which will consume about DM 3 billion ($1.2 billion) within the next four years. Initially, these centers were funded equally by the state and federal governments; now, the share of the federal government is 90 percent. However, all the centers are registered as companies (GmbH), and industries own 49 percent of the shares. Due to their importance in the nuclear energy R&D picture, the nuclear research centers are briefly presented in Table 7–2, with their main projects, employees, budgets, and so forth; as can be seen from the table, these nuclear research centers are generally divided in rather independent institutes. A project, under supervision of a project leader, makes use of several institutes.

Recently (before the oil crisis), the federal government decided that although the nuclear research centers should still be mainly devoted to nuclear energy research, they must also perform nonnuclear (and nonenergy) research and development of general interest. It was reported that already 20 to 40 percent of the staff works in the nonnuclear fields, in close collaboration with industry.

We will briefly review some of the major programs for reactor development and for the fuel cycle, leaving aside fundamental research (the importance of which can be measured by the fact that DM 2.2 billion [$880 million] are planned during the Fourth Nuclear Program, more than half this

h. Apparently under inflation pressure, the government decided early in 1973 on a small decrease of budget for research and development, which will unfortunately affect the Nuclear Research Centers and oblige them to make slight staff reductions.

Table 7-2.   Details of the German Nuclear Research Establishments

| Name (founding date) | Main Projects | Number of Institutes | Employees | | Annual Budget 1971 (1972) million DM | Reactors |
|---|---|---|---|---|---|---|
| | | | Total | Scientific | | |
| GFK–Karlsruhe (Gesellschaft für Kernforschung mbH) (19-July-1956) | Fast breeders Safeguards Transuranium-elements Reprocessing Data processing Nozzle enrichment | 14 | 3,400 | 1,000 | 183·9 (201·7) $74M 80M | FR´-2 MZFR KNK |
| KFA–Jülich (Kernforschungsanlage GmbH) (11-December-1956) | HTGR's Gas turbines Nuclear process heat Fusion Life sciences | 14 | 3,600 | 700 | 199·0 (209·3) $80M 84M | FRJ-1 (Merlin) FRJ-2 (Dido) AVR |
| GKSS–Geesthacht (Gesellschaft für Kernenergieverwertung in Schiffbau und Schiffahrt mbH) (18-April-1956) | Nuclear ship Propulsion Desalination Marine techniques | 3 | 544 | 135 | 33·3 (40·4) $13M 16M | FRG-1 FRG-2 FDR (Otto Hahn) |

| | | | | | | |
|---|---|---|---|---|---|---|
| GSF–Neuherberg (Gesellschaft für Strahlen und Um-weltforschung mbH) (1-July-1964) | Radiation effects Environmental effects Radioactive waste Disposal | 9 | 900 | 300 | 50·9 $20M | TRIGA Mk III |
| HMI–Berlin (Hahn-Meitner-Institut für Kern-forschung GmbH) (1956) | Nuclear chemistry Radiation chemistry Low energy phys. Solid-state phys. | 4 | 460 | 130 | 30 $12M | BER–1 (closed down) BER–2 |

amount being for high-energy physics), isotopes and ionizing radiation or radiation protection research. In the reactor development sector, high priority is given to the advanced reactor lines: the high-temperature reactor (HTR) and the sodium-cooled fast breeder reactor (LMFBR); light water reactors (LWR) are expected to receive only additional funding for some technological improvements or safety studies. There is also an R&D program on nuclear ship propulsion, under which one ship, the *Otto Hahn* has been completed. Also under way are various studies and projects (in association with Japan) on nuclear container ships, from 80,000 hp up to, eventually, 240,000 hp. These projects are receiving a new push as a result of recent oil price increases. For LWR power reactors, KWU is studying the use of water reactors not only in a baseload regime but also in a load-following regime (new control concepts).

**High-Temperature Reactors (HTR).**    A first 15 MWe prototype HTR was successfully built at Julich by Arbeitsgemeinschaft Versuchreactor AVR, and started operation in 1967, achieving excellent performance; in February 1974, outlet temperature of this reactor was raised to $950°C$ ($1,750°F$). The enriched uranium-graphite fuel is of the pebble-bed type. A second plant using the same basic principles is being built at Schmehausen in the Ruhr district; the THTR–300 (Thorium High Temperature Reactor of 300 MWe) is expected to be in operation by 1976.

Although this type of reactor has very attractive features, its promoters (the BBC–Brown Bovery Company Mannheim) have apparently been impressed by the commercial success of Gulf-General Atomic with HTGR-prismatic fuels. A commercial company has been formed, HRB (Hochtemperatur-Reaktorbau GmbH, 55 percent BBC and 45 percent GGA), to promote Gulf reactors in Germany. Nevertheless, research and development is continuing on HTR (and pebble bed) reactors, with two projects of special interest:

(1) the HHT project, or direct-cycle HTR with helium turbine; studies aim to establish complete specifications for the construction of a 300 MWe prototype power plant (participants in this study include Julich Research Center, BBC, HRB, fuel manufacturer Nukem and a utility).

(2) The application of HTR to process heat. The first step proposed involves the OTTO type of reactor (Once Through, Then Out, without recirculation of the fuel balls), with an outlet temperature of $850–900°C$ ($1,560–1,650°F$). Various nuclear process heat applications have been studied: steelmaking, hydrogen production through methane reforming (experimental loop EVA in Julich), and of growing importance now, coal gasification (mentioned above, in coal research), hydrogen production through thermal-chemical water-splitting (in cooperation with Aachen University), and long-distance heat transport through chemical energy (methane splitting, Adam and Eva concept). Although these projects have not been sufficiently funded till now, this has

apparently changed recently; the Julich group under Professor Schulten is presumably one of the most valuable working on nuclear process heat.[i]

**Fast Sodium Cooled Breeder Reactors.** With the AVR and the THTR described above, Germany can be considered ahead in high-temperature reactors in Europe; compared to the United Kingdom and France, on the other hand, German fast reactor developments can be considered rather slow. Sodium experience has been gained with experimental loops (Karlsruhe and Bensberg/ Interatom) and with a sodium thermal reactor KNK (which will receive next year a fast core and become KNK–II). A first prototype, of 300 MWe, the SNR (Schnell Natrium Reaktor) has started construction recently at Kalkar, in close association with Belgium and the Netherlands (Germany 70 percent, Belgium and the Netherlands 15 percent each, the shares applying to construction costs as well as to supporting research and development performed by national organizations). Differing from the British PFR in Dounreay and the French Phenix in Marcoule, the SNR–1 is of the loop type.

Loop type of construction has also been chosen for the next step. Considered by some experts to be somewhat ambitious! is the SNR–2, of 2,000 MWe, on which construction is foreseen to begin in 1979, about one year after the expected operation of SNR–1. A second major difference with the other European fast reactor projects has been a recent decision to use "big" fuel pins, say of 7.5 mm diameter (against 6 mm) for SNR–2, and possibly for the second loading of SNR–1; such a solution requires more plutonium, but would allow more conservative specific power rating for the core.

Not including SNR–2, but including SNR–1, the total cost of the fast reactor program in Germany has been estimated at more than DM 2,000 million ($800 million), including basic research in the nuclear research centers, mainly Karlsruhe. The main industrial partner is Interatom.

**Nuclear Fuel Cycles.** All phases are studied. The main emphasis is on enrichment, and, on a much smaller scale but worth mentioning, on waste treatment and storage.

Some studies have been performed on gaseous diffusion, and a German group of companies has participated during a few months in the international study group, Eurodif, under French leadership, on the French gaseous diffusion process.

The main efforts for enrichment are concentrated on ultracentrifugation, which studies began in fact in the mid–thirties, and have been strongly

i. Eight German industrial firms founded the working group "Nuclear Process Heat" in February 1974, and presented a development program that will cost about 1.45 billion DM ($600 million). This covers the construction of a demonstration power plant for coal gasification with a high-temperature reactor of 750 MWth, the operation of which is considered for 1982.

supported for about ten years; over DM 600 million ($240 million) have been allocated up to 1976. Since the Almelo Treatise (March 1970), German developments have been integrated with those of the United Kingdom and the Netherlands, in two joint organizations: Urenco Ltd. at Marlow, U.K. for plant operations, and Centec (Gesellschaft für Centrifugentechnik mbH, Bensberg, FRG), responsible for development and construction of centrifuge enrichment plants to be purchased and operated by Urenco. At the end of 1973, the two organizations merged in a common organization, Urenco–Centec. Uranit (Nukem, GmbH, Gelsenberg AG, and Farbwerke Hoechst) is the German partner in this organization; centrifuges are fabricated by MAN (with Dornier and Erno), and architecture-engineering is the responsibility of Interatom, which has carried out extensive R&D work in plant technology.

Under a contract from the federal government, Uranit has built the first German prototype plant in Almelo; in 1974, the complete plant will have a capacity of 25mt SWU/y.[j] Continuous progress is reported on centrifuge performances, separating capacity and availability, and centrifuge fabrication (from 15 to an expected 30 units per day). Plants for the first trilateral joint plant of 250 t SWU/y have been recently upgraded to 2,000/3,000 in 1980, and 10,000 in 1985.

No less impressive, although on a smaller scale, are the developments of the nozzle process developed by Professor Becker in Karlsrube, very attractive since there are no moving parts other than the pumps or valves, and no critical diffusion barrier. According to some experts, the nozzle process is the next competitor to centrifugation. About DM 24 million ($9.6 million) have been spent on this work since 1957, and the present rate of public funding is now about DM 7 million ($2.8 million) yearly, part of the financing being supplemented by Steag (Essen) which expects to contribute a total of DM 20 million ($8 million) by 1975. Construction of a few prototype stages—with an initial capacity of about 25 t SWU/y, aiming toward 600–800 t SWU/y at the end of the 1970s—will probably commence in 1974, by an association of Gesellschaft für Kernforschung (Gfk) of Karlsruhe with Steag.

Finally, as regards nuclear waste disposal, there are various studies on conditioning of radioactive wastes (Karlsruhe) by solidification. Experimental storage of low-activity wastes was started in 1967 in an abandoned salt mine at Asse; initial test storage of high-level radioactive waste is planned for 1974, based on a broad R&D program aimed at demonstrating the suitability of the mine for ultimate disposal of highly active wastes (in the form of glass blocks placed in boreholes within the mine workings).

**Thermonuclear Fusion.** R&D on thermonuclear fusion is closely coordinated in the joint Euratom fusion research program; as a consequence, the

---

j.  SWU, Separative Working Unit, is a measure to define the work which has to be accomplished for enriching uranium isotopes. It is expressed in kilograms or metric tons of uranium.

German program is incomplete, but nevertheless looks for internal coherence. Studies and experiments are concentrated in two main places: the Institut für Plasma-physik der Kernforschungsanlage (KFA) Julich, and the Max-Planck-Institut für Plasmaphysik (IPP) Garching, near Munich; some universities, and the Nuclear Research Center of Karlsruhe, are contributing some fundamental theoretical studies. The configuration: Stellarators (of the Wendelstein type), Pulsator (of the Tokomak type, 70 cm [27.5] minor radius, 28 kilogauss toroidal magnetic field strength), toroidal theta-pinch machines, Julietta (linear theta pinch), ISAR (screw pinch), etc. Plasmas studies are performed with powerful lasers, and thermonuclear reactor concepts are in the preliminary design stage.

## REFERENCES

### General Organization for Research and Development

Deutsche Forschungsgemeinschaft. Aufgaben und Finanzierung, 1972 bis 1974. Wiesbaden 1972.

Die Aufgaben der energiewirtschaftlichen Forschung heute und in der Zukunft. von H. Schaeffer (Brennstoffe, Warme, Kraft 21, 1969).

Die Max Planck Gesellschaft und ihre Institute. "Portrat eirer Forschungorganisation." (Brochure.)

Jahrbuch der Max Planck Gesellschaft, 1971–1972.

Max Planck Gesellschaft: A Model for "Small Science"? *Nature* 237, No. 5352 (May 26, 1972).

Rapport de recherche (IV) du Gouverment de la Republique Federale d'Allemagne, 1972. (Bundesberich Forschung IV.)

Umweltforschung, Aufgaben und Aktivitaten der DFG 1950 bis 1971. Bonn, 1971.

Zur Tatigkeit der M.P.G. zur Forderung der Wisenschaften. (Information Bildung, Wissenschaft, Dec. 16, 1972).

### Coal Research and Development

Bergbau-Forschung (Steinkohlenbergbauverein). (Brochure.)

Blickpunkt Braunkohle (Rheinische Braunkohlenwerke Aktiengesellschaft, Koln). (Brochure.)

Die Stellung der Braunkohle im Rahmen der Energiewirtschaft.

Energieprognose fue die Bundesrepublik Deutschland unter Berucksichtigung des Ensatzes von Kernwarme zur Vergasung fossiler Rohstoffe. (Julich, KFA, 745–RG).

Private discussions with scientist from Bergbau-Forschung.

Steinkohle 1971/1972 (Gesamtverband des Deutschen Steinkohlenbergbaus).

Steinkohlenbergbauverein. Jahresbericht 1971. Jahresbericht 1972.

### Oil and Gas Research and Development

Deutschen Gesellschaft fur Mineralolwissenschaft und Kohlechemie e.v. DGMK. Jahresbericht 1972.

Gelsenberg. Annual Reports.

### Electricity Research and Development

BBC-Mannheim. Geschaftsberich 1972 (private communication).
Elektrowarme Institut (list of publications).
Rheinish. Westphalisches Elektricitatswerk A.G. (private communication).
Studiengesellschaft fur Hochspannungsanlagen e.v. (list of publications).
Vereinigung Deutscher Elektrizitatswerke VDEW. Arbeitsbericht 1972.
Vereinigung Industrielle Kraftwirtschaft e.v. Tatigkeitbericht.
VGB Technische Vereinigung der Grosskraftwerkbetreiber e.v. Tatigkeitsbericht
    1972/1973.

### Nuclear Energy Research and Development

*Atomwirtschaft* (main German nuclear periodical).
Deutsche Reaktortagung, 1973, Karlsruhe.
IV Bundesrepublik Deutschland Atom-programm.
Survey of the Federal Republic of Germany (Nuclear Engineering International,
    February 1973), pp. 93 to 123.

### Thermonuclear Fusion

Etat de la recherche sur la fusion thermonucleaire controlee en Allemagne
    Federale. A. Schluter. Geneve IV. A/Conf. 49/A/377.
Max Planck Institut fur Plasmaphysik, Garching (various publications).

### Energy Situation

Brennstoffe, Warme, Kraft (technical review).
Daten zur Entwicklung der Energiewirtschaft in der Bundesrepublik Deutsch-
    land. Ausgabe 1972.
Die Erdöl-und Erdgasexploration in der Bundesrepublik Deutschland im Jahre
    1972 (Erdöl und Kohle-Erdgas-Petrochemie vereinigt mit Brenn-
    stoff-Chemie 26−381−388, 1973).
Energiewirtschaft und Umweltbeeinflussung in der Bundesrepublik Deutschland
    (Forschungsstelle fur Energiewirtschaft. München, Sept. 1972).
Forschungsstelle fur Energiewirtschaft (München). (Many publications on energy
    problems.)
Gegenwartige und kunftige Probleme der Energieversorgung. (Studie 7. Heraus-
    gegeben von der Esso A.G. Hamburg. Jahresbericht 1973.)
*Jahrbuch fur Bergbau, Energie, Mineralol und Chemie.* (Unfortunately, this
    Jahrbuch, however complete it is, does not contain budget figures,
    especially for research organizations and technical associations.)
Mineralöl und Energiepolitik (MWV Mineralölwirtschaftverband e.v., Hamburg).
Mineralölwirtschaftsverband e.v. (Hamburg). Arbeitsgemeinschaft Erdölgewin-
    nung und-Verarbeitung. Jahresbericht 1971.
Steinkohle Energiemarkt Wirtschaftpolitik (Gesamtverband des deutschen Stein-
    kohlenbergbaus).

# Chapter Eight

# France

France is generally said "to be late by one war." Perhaps this is another way of saying that France is often somewhat out of step. Curiously, in fact, many options taken by the French are correct, but they are taken and developed *too early*; often, when their time comes, the nation (or its representatives) has lost confidence in its own power. And then the counter-measures are taken too late.

In the sector of energy, France is one of the few countries that has tried to have an energy policy, dating back half a century to the "petroleum law" of 1928. The potential impact of events on such a policy have too often been underestimated. Many of the principles were right, and continue to be so. But the results are sometimes far below expectations: France is probably, after Japan, the second most heavily dependent nation on energy imports.

Because of administrative centralization (which principle dates back many centuries), and because the main energy sectors have been nationalized since the end of World War II, a very large amount of energy research and development has been performed in France, based on a strong and historical research tradition, and on a well-known creative inventiveness. Unfortunately, as time has passed, most of the research programs have tended to become somewhat academic, and disconnected from the fundamental needs of the nation; and research facilities initially planned for energy research have increasingly been used commercially in other fields. Cleverly "domesticated," the research and development potential could certainly be one of the highest among industrialized countries.

### The Energy Situation

Self-sufficiency in energy consumption was, in 1972, less than 30 percent. This situation was somewhat hidden by the fact that oil imports were made through French companies controlling their own oil production abroad.

*179*

There are few hopes of changing such a situation in the coming years. Most hopes rely on nuclear energy development, but however hard it will be pushed, the trend of an increased energy dependency can hardly be reversed before about 1985. Table 8-1 shows (in million tons coal equivalent) the structure of energy consumption in France, and the forecasts up to 1985.

The coal industry, gas manufacture and distribution, and electricity production and distribution have been nationalized since the end of World War II (apart from a few exceptions, such as electricity production for some specific industrial uses). If we add to this that the state has a share of 35 percent of the semipublic oil company, and owns totally the second largest oil company in the country, it is clear that the government rules the energy sector almost completely, through the Ministry for Industrial and Scientific Development. The energy program is coordinated by a Secretary for Energy,[a] assisted by Technical Departments (for Mines, for Motor Fuels, and for Gas and Electricity), by various advisory committees, such as the one for the production of nuclear electricity (commission pour la production d'electricite d'origine nucleaire [PEON]).

France's economic (and now, also social) development is guided by Plans that are called "indicative," and not mandatory, as they are in socialist countries. The Plan (France is now in the Sixth Plan, 1971–1975) is prepared through close cooperation between the public authorities and business circles, involving technical preparation by the High Commission for the Plan and various specialized commissions, and a process of consultation. With regard to energy, there is an energy commission (plus subcommissions for oil, coal, gas, and electricity), which is practically responsible for the whole energy policy. Finally, the Plan is voted on by the Parliament after final (political) adjustments.

Table 8-1. Energy Consumption by Fuels (in million tce)

|                    | 1960  | 1965  | 1970  | 1972  | 1975    | 1980    | 1985    |
|--------------------|-------|-------|-------|-------|---------|---------|---------|
| Solid fuels        | 70.2  | 68.5  | 57.2  | 46.9  | 37–42   | 27–32   | 22–29   |
| Oil products       | 40.3  | 74.6  | 131.1 | 159.5 | 180–205 | 235–280 | 270–345 |
| Gaz                | 4.5   | 7.9   | 14.6  | 20.3  | 23–27   | 30–41   | 37–55   |
| Hydro and nuclear  | 13.5  | 16.1  | 20.4  | 18.8  | 24.5    | 39      | 60–90   |
| Total              | 128.5 | 167.1 | 223.3 | 245.5 | 275–290 | 345–375 | 425–470 |

Source: Derived from "Commisariat au Plan," Report on Sixth Plan.

a. Beginning of 1974, due to the energy crisis, the Secretary for Energy was replaced by a General Delegate to Energy, with extended power and responsibilities. A general program for energy R&D was being planned, but not yet available at time of reviewing this survey. Only a few actions (solar house prototype, oil shale assessment) have been launched.

Since 1969, there has been a Ministry for Environment, which works in close association with the Ministry for Industrial and Scientific Development.

**Coal.** Coal was the main fuel before, and for a decade after World War II. In the late 1950s production reached an absolute maximum of over 60 million tons per year. However, it became evident at this time that for technical reasons (rather thin and generally irregular coal seams in the major beds in the northeast of France) it would become more and more difficult to continue to increase production. Then came the European coal crisis,[b] and it was in fact decided to decrease production, a decision that led to dramatic social events and consequences. Production was decreased first to 53 million metric tons in 1965, then to 39 million metric tons in 1970, 25 million metric tons in 1975, and possibly only 15 million metric tons in 1980. Meanwhile, it has been necessary to import 14–18 million metric tons of coal every year for metallurgical purposes.

Coal use in industry and in households is continuously shrinking. The two main uses of significance are steel manufacture and electricity production, either at the coal mine mouth by coal producers, or by the French nationalized utility EDF; many EDF power plants have been adapted to burn either coal or fuel oil.[c]

Nationalized mines are managed by Coalfield Authorities (Houvilleres de Bassin) with a central supervisory body—Charbonnages de France, or CdF— which is a public industrial and commercial undertaking endowed with legal personality and is financially independent. The number of employees has been drastically reduced, from 217,000 in 1960 to 119,000 in 1970, a heavy social burden requiring the creation of new industries in the most affected regions. The "recession plan" (unfortunately, not only expansion and development must be planned, but regression also . . . ) could not avoid a deficit that reached about 1.5 billion francs ($300 million) yearly, which the Government had to cover.

b. At the end of the 1950s, after a short period of recession in Europe, and due to important wage increases, the price of European coal began to grow vigorously: one ton of coal in Paris coming from the east of France was much more expensive than one ton of coal coming from the Appalachians and crossing the Atlantic. Moreover, oil was discovered in growing amounts in the Middle East, by international oil companies and U.S. independents. When President Eisenhower imposed oil import quotas in the U.S., most of this oil, now available, and very cheap, found its way to Europe. Mining and coal authorities, under the pressures of governments and of industry, claiming the need for cheap energy, began to "retreat," close mines, and decrease production. This was the "coal crisis." Another solution would have been to tax imported oil and to subsidize domestic coal, but it was not thought feasible. The coal crisis had many political, social and psychological impacts in the most hard-hit countries: France, Belgium, the Netherlands, and even Germany.

c. It is clear that this gives the feasibility to the fuel user to choose the cheaper fuel, between coal and oil, available on the market. But this introduces uncertainties in the planning of the fuel supplier.

Even if coal could make a strong comeback in Europe, France would benefit from it (if ever) much later than the United Kingdom and Germany, because of the physical structure of the coal fields, which are hard to mine and very difficult to mechanize. From the purely industrial point of view, let us mention that Charbonnages de France is diversifying in various other sectors, such as chemistry and petroleum-chemistry.

Oil. There is a small and decreasing domestic production of oil in the southwest of France (by a subsidiary of Exxon), around 2 million metric tons (40,000 bpd) per year, a few very small fields in the Parisian Basin, and some hopes off shore (West of Brittany, possibly in the Mediterranean Sea where the depths are, unfortunately, very great—3,000 to 6,000 feet).

France is, perhaps, with Japan, one of the countries that has profited the most from the 10 to 15-year period of low-cost world oil. They both suffer now from their dramatic dependence on imports. As can be seen from Table 8–1, oil satisfied 65 percent of France's energy mix in 1972; between 1970 and 1985, oil is planned to cover about 70 percent of energy requirements. In 1960, oil from North Africa and the Middle East was about 25 percent of the total energy mix; in 1975, this will reach about 60 percent. Terminal facilities are planned accordingly, such as the first 500,000 TDW tanker terminal being built near LeHavre.

Laws that were instituted 50 years ago, and more or less permanently confirmed since that time, were aimed toward a national organization of petroleum development: French-controlled companies must handle worldwide capacity of production about equal to French needs; at least two-thirds of oil consumption must be transported under the French flag; national refining must always exceed domestic consumption (leading to a positive export balance); all petroleum activities are closely controlled by state authorities (even the opening of a service station), who also impose very strict price controls. In the framework of controlled refining and distributing permits, the domestic market of oil products is about equally divided between French national companies and subsidiaries of foreign oil companies (mainly Exxon, Shell, BP and Mobil).

There are two national oil companies. The first one is Total/ Compagnie Française des Petroles (35 percent owned by the state), which was created in the 1920s to handle the French share of the Turkish Petroleum Company; with a 1972 production of about 60 million metric tons of crude (1.2 million barrels per day), Total/CFP ranks high in world international oil companies; due to its interests in the Middle East and many other continents, it is sometimes called the eighth "International Major." The second company, Elf/ERAP (100 percent state-owned) was founded from various state organizations dealing with oil research, exploration or production (mainly in the Sahara). Like Total/CFP, but with a smaller capacity of 15 to 20 million metric tons a year (400,000 bpd), it is now a fully integrated company.

Research and development activities by the oil companies are prominent, as well as those performed by the French Petroleum Institute, the national research organization for all petroleum sectors.

**Gas.** France began its conversion to natural gas in the 1950s, with the discovery of the Lacq field (southwest), first only of local importance, and then of national importance after the construction of gas-lines to Paris and the East of France. Lacq is producing now about 7–9 billion $Nm^3$/yr (260–330 billion $ft^3$/yr), and will probably continue to do so during the next decade (decrease of reserves being somewhat counterbalanced by a few surrounding discoveries). France is also importing gas from the Netherlands (Groninguen field) and from Algeria (4.5 billion $Nm^3$/yr) (160 billion $ft^3$/yr), and has played a leading role in the technology of natural gas liquefaction and liquefied natural gas maritime transportation. Contracts have also been negotiated with the Soviet Union for imports of Siberian gas.

In fact, possibly because of the long distances from the possible foreign suppliers to the main domestic market, France has been somewhat less aggressive in negotiating supply contracts than other countries, such as Germany. As a result, it is foreseen that gas consumption will probably cover about 9–10 percent of the energy mix in 1975–1980s, instead of 14–15 percent for other European countries, and the growth rate is in fact between 1.5 and 4 times less than for these other countries.

Gas production is associated with oil companies (Elf/ERAP group for Lacq). Gas manufacture (or imports) and gas distribution were nationalized in 1946; the national enterprise is Gaz de France. Gross income in 1970 was about 2.5 billion francs ($500 million). Unfortunately, because of price control (plus the heavy charges induced by shifting from town gas to natural gas), the long-term debt is very heavy, 5.5 billion F ($1.1 billion) (with acculated deficit of 1 billion F ($200 million), and can increase to more than 8 billion F ($1.6 billion) by the end of the present (sixth) Plan. The number of employees is stable, around 29,000.

**Electricity.** After a steady growth at 7.5 percent per year up to 1965, electricity consumption in France slowed down considerably to 6.5 percent per year between 1965 and 1972, the slowest rate of increase in Europe. This may be due to the lack of an active commercial policy (as compared, for instance, to the commercial policy of oil companies), and to a relative decrease of high-tension sales because of a higher tariff than in neighboring countries.

Total electricity consumption in 1972 was 146 billion kWh, which corresponds to a value of 2,888 kWh per capita. The share of electricity in the energy mix was a low 22 percent in 1970–1972; in 1972, production was 49 billion kWh from hydroelectricity, and 114 billion kWh from thermal plants (about 14 billion of which was from nuclear power plants). More than 50 percent of thermal electricity comes from burning fuel oil, and less than 30 percent from coal.

Created in 1946 as a domestic monopoly for electricity transportation and distribution, and by far the most important power producer in France, Electricite de France (EDF) had a turnover of about 14–16,000 million francs ($2.8–3.2 billion) and employs about 100,000 people; as an electricity enterprise, it is second only to the British CEGB.

To ease the pressure of oil imports in the future, the government, in close coordination with EDF, has decided to increase the rate of growth of electricity (at a minimum 8 percent per year during the Sixth Plan) *and* to promote the shift from fuel oil and coal to nuclear uranium. To be able to promote its industrial and commercial activities and fulfill these new prospects, EDF has signed with the government a development agreement, with social and economical objectives and "a posteriori" governmental controls. EDF has developed an active commercial policy to promote new uses of electricity in France, such as for electrical heating, and this policy relies on actively supporting research and development programs on electricity applications.

From the industrial point of view, there is a large concern of international dimension, the Group CGE (Compagnie Generale d'Electricite, whose total turn-over was 11 billion Francs [$2.2 billion] in 1972). Its main activities are in electrotechnical equipment (the well-known Alsthom company), civil works, electronics, communication, electrochemistry, household appliances, etc. Alsthom manufactures steam and gas turbines (GE-licenses). CGE group performs a great deal of R&D.

**Nuclear Energy**. As noted above, nuclear energy is considered the best hope for France to recover a better energy self-sufficiency. From the very beginning in 1946, with the creation of the Commissariat a l'Energie Atomique directly under the Prime Minister, with control being exercised by the Ministry for Industrial and Scientific Development, developments in this field have been original, and tentatively independent of other countries.

The first French power reactors were natural uranium-graphite, and gas cooled. Unlike the British, who built a series of the same kind of reactor, the French built their plants one by one, with continuous technical improvements from one to the other, from EDF–I (60 MWe) to Bugey I (540 MWe with annular fuel). Perhaps as an illustration of French "timing" discussed in the introduction, it is unfortunate that France did not continue reactors already built and operating well, for it is questionable if their cost would have skyrocketed as much as LWR's. However, that belongs to history. France did make a late shift to LWR in 1969, with five plants now under construction (PWR type), by a company licensed by Westinghouse (which is also a shareowner). In 1974, the nuclear development program was vigorously accelerated. Sixteen reactors have been ordered, most of them PWR, plus one BWR; and one 1,200

MWe LMFBR. There have been very promising achievements in the LMFBR development, with Rapsodie-Fortissimo, the steam generator facility, and the 250 MWe Phenix prototype plant.

France also has a strong position in the nuclear fuel cycle: in uranium production (in France and abroad) French interests control about 10 percent of world reserves and world capacity; in enrichment, there is a military gaseous diffusion plant, and the decision was made late 1973 to build, jointly with European associates, a civilian plant of 9–12 million tons SWU/yr; there are also fuel reprocessing facilities in The Hague.

Most of the research and development has been performed by the French CEA. This is both a strong point and a weak one. Notwithstanding its broad industrial and commercial activities, CEA cannot be compared to large industrial concerns like those in Germany or the United States, and a real equilibrium has not yet been found between a very powerful CEA, a unique customer EDF, and a somewhat "shy" French nuclear industry.

### General Organization for Research and Development

There is a fair amount of research and development performed in France; in 1972 the total budget for R&D was somewhat higher than 17 billion F ($3.4 billion) with about 210,000 people employed in R&D activities. Research is highly centralized (even from the geographical point of view, with roughly 61 percent of researchers in the Paris area!). The main research organizations come under the administration of various ministries but are coordinated by a central interministerial administration, the Delegation Generale a la Recherche Scientifique et Technique (DGRST) (General Delegation for Scientific and Technical Research), reporting to the Ministere du Developpement Industriel et Scientifique (MDIS) (Ministry for Industrial and Scientific Development, mentioned above).

From 1958 to 1968, responding to General de Gaulle's wish for modernization, there was a considerable, steady increase in public budgets for R&D in absolute as well as in relative values, aiming to reach 2.5 percent of GNP in 1975 (starting from a low 1.2 percent of GNP in 1960). Since 1968, budgets have increased only slowly, and in 1973 the ratio was back to around 1.7 percent GNP. As in the United Kingdom and United States, research suffered from budget restriction policies. But, in addition, there has also been a national questioning of the aims of research, as in many other developed countries, and a tentative effort is presently being made for a better, and more socially oriented, research policy.

**Research and the Government.** It is no surprise, in a highly central-ized state such as France, that the government deals with practically every aspect of research and development. For the last ten or more years, the government has financed about 69 percent of total R&D, the share of industry averaging 31 percent and expected to rise to 35 percent. Government action can be looked at from three different points of view: the five-year plans, yearly programs, and research organizations.

As in many other sectors of activity, R&D is periodically submitted in France to the process of "flexible" (nonmandatory) planning, with a special Commission for Research, initiated by DGRST with advice of the "12 Wise People Committee" (Advisory Committee for Scientific and Technical Research). The result of this work and the work of numerous subcommittee ("brainstorming" committees on fundamental aspects of R&D activities and R&D policy, sectorial committees such as the one for energy, etc.) is a proposal to the government and the Parliament for a financial frame or envelope (the "Enveloppe-Recherche") for the five years covered by the Plan. Once accepted, yearly budgets will be set according to this general frame: in the last five years, it must be mentioned, the yearly budgets have been systematically less than the minimum included in the frame.

The aim of such a process is continuous improvement, to correct oversights and reassess past judgments. But there is a grave defect in that a differentiation is made, for past financial reasons, between operating budgets (which are not included in the Plan process) and investment budgets (which are included). The division made between the two is sometimes more than arbitrary. Moreover, some R&D activities are not "programed" in the Plan, and still complicate the picture. Such factors diminish somewhat the usefulness of the Plan, which nevertheless is of value.

Compared to the Fifth Plan, where funds were mainly assigned to research organizations, the lion's share going to so-called "big programs" (mainly space and nuclear research), the Sixth Plan (1971–1975) reflects a questioning and reorientation of national R&D effort. Funds have been allocated according to program objectives, and emphasis has been directed toward industrial development. Development as a whole, which was generally getting less than 48 percent of the funds, will progressively receive more now, up to 52–53 percent. Priority among the various industrial sectors has been given to competitive ones, mainly electronics, chemistry, metallurgy, and mechanics; "big programs" have been more or less stabilized.[d] The total five-year public budget for programed research and development (investment budget only, excluding operations) has been fixed at between a minimum 19.5 billion ($3.9 billion) and a maximum 21.4 F billion ($4.3 billion) (1970–Francs). About 10 percent is for research aimed at social-economical improvement (such as habitat, transportation, relations between man and his environment, etc.); one-third for fundamental research; and the remaining 56 percent for research aimed at industrial development.

d.  It is nevertheless a little bit surprising that the nuclear energy budget, in an energy-hungry country, has received the same treatment as space research.

Practically all the basic research is performed in national laboratories and national organizations, the most important being the Centre National de la Recherche Scientifique CNRS, covering practically (but not exclusively) all fields, from basic natural sciences to human sciences or nuclear research. CNRS comes under the Ministry for Education, and is closely associated with the universities.

Most of the technical organizations and laboratories (some of which are prominent in their field) come under the Ministry of Industrial and Scientific Development, and perform research which, in fact, could as well be performed in industrial laboratories. This is generally agreed now, and the DGRST has developed a broad system for promoting industrial research and development, even sharing on an equal basis with industry innovation and development activities, through an original and efficient system; about 2 billion francs ($400 million) have been earmarked to such "industrial aid" in the Sixth Plan.

Finally, in 1972, the *total* effort in France for research and development was evaluated at about 17 billion francs ($3.4 billion) (investment and operation): two-thirds were public funding, half of this about corresponding to the "Enveloppe-Recherche." Roughly 2.6 billion francs ($520 million) was for fundamental research (university, CNRS, etc.); 2.5 billion francs ($500 million) for military research; 1.9 billion francs ($380 million) for nuclear research (civil applications); 1.5 billion francs ($300 million) for aeronautics and space research; 2.3 billion francs ($450 million) for social, economic, medical and agricultural research; the remaining 6.2 billion francs ($1.24 billion) was industrial research directly funded by industry. To be sure, part of the research sponsored by the government (such as nuclear energy) is also related to industrial applications.

**Industrial Research.** As noted above, development, or applied research, is less important in France than in many other industrial countries. First, there was generally more interest in pure research than in industrial applied research; and second, the structure and general organization of French industry (with a large number of somewhat small companies compared to other industrialized countries) was rarely favorable to an intensive R&D effort. Exceptions worth mentioning are the electronics industry (with a research effort strongly supported by the government, such as through "Plan Calcul"), and the chemical and metallurgical industries, where successive mergers since the end of the World War II have finally resulted in large, competitive concerns, which perform high-quality research. Through the Sixth Plan, and especially the DGRST special industrial-aid program, the government has decided to reinforce the R&D capability of chemical and metallurgical industries.

Although it is also planned to support mechanical industry R&D, this sector is an example of too many small companies, and it is generally agreed that some pressures will have to be exerted on structures . . . and minds. . . .

The changes and improvements in industrial R&D have been noteworthy in the last ten years.

## ENERGY RESEARCH AND DEVELOPMENT

From the foregoing description of the French energy situation, it is clear that France is certainly one of the countries in the world (with Japan) where energy research and development is most needed. Moreover, the centralized organization, and the fact that the energy industry is nationalized or government-controlled, are favorable factors for a highly coordinated energy research and development. However, these positive aspects are somewhat counterbalanced by what could be called a fatalistic approach to the energy situation by the politicians, the best example of which is that when the research program for the Sixth Plan was discussed in Parliament, it was the energy sector that suffered the most severe cutbacks. (This decision was a result of a wrong assessment that cheap oil prices would continue for a long time.)

Some achievements have been outstanding, such as deep off-shore oil research, or the Liquid Metal Fast Breeder Reactor program. Nevertheless, it is our opinion that much more could have been done in many other sectors.

Studying energy research and development through the Sixth Plan would unfortunately be misleading, because only part of energy R&D is programed in the Plan, mainly nuclear energy (but as a whole, military and civilian, investment and operation). Some of the research in coal, gas, and electricity, although in the public sector, is included in industrial research, as well as most of oil research and development (part of it financed by special taxes).

### Coal Research and Development

Virtually all the coal research and development is performed by Charbonnages de France (CdF), which owns an important research organization, the CERCHAR (Centre d'Etudes et de Recherches des Charbonnages de France). CERCHAR has one main laboratory at Verneuil-en-Halatte (more than 600 employees, including about 140 from the academic level). It also has one experimental station in Marienau (Moselle) especially devoted to applied coke research, and owned equally by IRSID (Steel Research Institute), employing about 80 people. Founded in 1947, CERCHAR'S evolution can be summarized by three successive phases, closely related to the coal situation in France. From 1947 to 1960, most of the research was devoted to safety in mines and production techniques. From 1960 to 1969, the main effort was devoted to improvement of mine production efficiency (related to best producing fields for concentrating coal extraction) and development of related industries due to a partial conversion of CdF (in chemistry for instance), together with continued safety studies. Since 1969, a strong effort has gone into trying to keep active the few remaining centralized mines, and to use valuable research experience through diversification in noncoal industries (such as general mining and environment). Although the share of coal research is decreasing with the decrease of national coal production, the budget is slowly continuing to increase due to noncoal industrial activities, the commercial part of which is handled by a specialized department: CERCHAR–INDUSTRIE.

In 1972, the total budget of CERCHAR was 54.4 million F ($11 million) from which about 32 percent went for coal production and safety research, 13 percent for coal utilization, 24 percent for chemical research and 31 percent for noncoal industrial research.

### Coal Production and Safety in Mines R&D

Studies are performed on explosives and flammable dusts, aimed toward a better understanding of the dangerous conditions in mines and toward formulating rules for the safest and most efficient means of extraction with explosives. Experiments are performed on electrical detonators and shotfiring accessories, and for improving ways to deal with dust-explosions (water-dams, etc.).

Ventilation is studied by calculation and simulators; temperature effects have been explored in relation to greater depths and increasing size and power of working equipment. Numerous studies continue to be devoted to methane from occurrence to release (general laws, measuring devices, prevention, and studies of instantaneous outbursts of methane or of mixtures of $CO_2$ and $CH_4$). As for mine fires, there has been a complete analytical study of all fires that have occurred in the last decade (about 100 cases).

Noxious dust (in thin, medium or thick inclined seams, together with process of removal) and pneumoconioses are traditionally studied, from both the point of view of technical preventive measures and of basic biological and medical research (well-known research on aluminum compounds preventive effects and on the role of quartz dust).

Continuous progress has been achieved in respect to rock mechanics, and on the influence of certain mining factors on behavior of roadways and faces. Resulting from a more than fifteen-year effort, this study is aimed at the prevention of deformations and degradations of mine works and at designing control and corrective measures for abnormal behavior, so as to optimize production conditions, mainly for inclined seams.

Numerous mining machines are being studied, such as machines for driving roads in coal, machine-gripping hands, remote-control of winding machines, test bed investigation of shearer drums, coal-cutters, ploughing, supported by technical research on various equipment (such as hydraulic transmissions, control of plough faces, and valves for hydraulic props).

Regarding studies of hydraulic stowing, it is worth mentioning hydraulic stowing in strongly inclined seams and investigation of the behavior of tubings in steep seams.

Finally, improvements have been made in the protection of electrical networks, in flameproof equipment, of communication means in face and roadway with calling facility, the "phasophone," speech communication for trapped miners, and remote-control systems for surface industries.

Part of these activities, as for the Bergbauforschung in Germany and the INIEX (Institut National des Industries Extractives, Liege) in Belgium, are coordinated and partially financed by the European Communities.

**Processing and Utilization of Coal.** Research activities in this field are related to studies of coal and coke structure and of process products (and properties of flammability), coal cleaning, sundry activities such as transformation of washery shale into building materials, economic exploitation of ash and industrial applications of plastic materials.

Most important is coking research (mainly performed in Marienau experimental station): tests on coal and coke (oxydation after storage), thrust on the coke-oven walls (development of laboratory ovens), coke quality (for Usinor factory in Dunkerque and Solmer future plant in Fos), studies and industrial testing.

**Pollution and Explosions Problems.** The general experience accumulated by CERCHAR has well prepared it to look efficiently at industrial problems, among which are pollution and explosion risks.

Air pollution and air cleaning (scrubbing, catalytic, oxydation, absorption) are studied, together with pollutant formation, mainly nitrogen oxides. Interesting studies are also performed on burning of solid refuse, and on noise pollution (mine work and thermal plants).

Explosions studies have been extended to various industrial conditions (gases, vapors, flammable dusts), both for determining the possible causes and for prevention or for safety measures against the effects of occurring explosions.

**Table 8–2.  Petroleum R & D During the Sixth Plan, 1971–1975**
*(millions of 1970 dollars)*

| | | |
|---|---|---|
| *Processing and product uses* | | 188 |
| Refining | 90 | |
| Product uses | 88 | |
| | | |
| *Exploration and production* | | 145 |
| Drilling and production | 57 | |
| Geophysics | 20 | |
| Geology | 22 | |
| Offshore program | 46 | |
| *Total (not including petroleum chemistry)* | | 333 |

### Oil Research and Development

Although only a very small part of oil research and development belongs to the programmed R&D of the Sixth Plan "Enveloppe-Recherche," basic general information on the oil R&D programs can nevertheless be gathered from the work performed by the Subcommission for Oil, a chapter of its final report being devoted (on a purely indicative basis) to oil R&D. The total effort of petroleum research and development has been estimated (see Table 8–2) for the Sixth Plan at about 1,835 million F (1970), excluding research in the petroleum chemistry sector. The biggest part, about 1,045 million F, was foreseen for processing and product uses: refining (490 MF), and product uses (480 MF); exploration and production were supposed to use about 800 million F, divided in drilling and production (310 MF), geophysics (110 MF), geology (120 MF), offshore program (250 MF). The number of people employed comes to around 3,400, more than 80 percent working in refinery process developments and utilization of petroleum products. For the last few years, great emphasis has been given to environmental problems, leading to new refining processes or new less-polluting products. All the above-mentioned figures were nonmandatory, and it was mentioned that final programs will depend on the evolution of the economic and international situation. Recent international developments will probably influence this program, but it was not possible to know how much, or which way, at the time of writing or at the time of reviewing (because plan modifications were still being studied).

Based on past experience (for instance, on the Fifth Plan, 1966–1970, during which about 1.1 billion Francs [$220 million] were spent, practically in equal shares between refining product uses and exploration/ production), the programs are about equally shared by the Institut Français du Petrole (IFP) (French Petroleum Institute) and the French oil industry. Founded in 1944, the IFP is a renowned research organization, performing research and development in all sectors of the oil industry. IFP employs about 1,600 people (30 percent of the academic level). It is considered that roughly 75 percent of the IFP R&D program is closely coordinated with oil companies. IFP is financed by a special tax on oil products (for instance, 0.18 F per hectoliter [0.14¢/gal] of gasoline). The total budget for 1972 was about 200 million ($40 million) Francs, 20 percent of which came from external contracts or research programs. Moreover, IFP participates in nine or ten subsidiaries, especially founded (with or without industrial partners, depending on the objectives) for exploiting some of the IFP licenses or processes, generally on an international basis. Some similar institutes have been initiated on a smaller scale in a few countries (India, Egypt, Indonesia) with the help of IFP, but to our knowledge, such a strong and efficient petroleum R&D organization with industrial extension is unique in Europe.

The other part of oil R&D in France is performed by the oil industry itself, primarily by the two main national oil companies, Compagnie Française des Petroles and Elf/ERAP. There are also the research laboratories of foreign subsidiaries, almost entirely devoted to process and product improvement, such as the Mont-Saint-Aignan laboratories of Exxon/Esso France, the Grand-Couronne laboratories of Shell, and the Lavera laboratories of British-Petroleum (world known for their work on oil proteins). These various laboratories exchange and receive knowledge and experience from their mother companies in mutually fruitful relationships.

Other industries, such as off-shore drilling or platform manufacturers, or companies like the Compagnie Française de Geophysique, also contribute to and participate in petroleum research programs (mainly in the off-shore development program), as well as with some university laboratories (Ecole des Mines, Nancy, Strasbourg). The Compagnie Française des Petroles' main laboratories are in Gonfreville, and cover all the activities, from reservoir research to refining processes and to fuel cell research. Due to historical reasons, arising out of mergers of various organizations, research activities of the Elf/ERAP group are spread in various laboratories (such as Boussens for production and Chambourcy for geophysics, Solaize for refining); they also cover all the sectors of the oil industry, and are often closely associated in common programs with IFP.

As it would take too long to review all the research programs for oil in France, we will give a few noteworthy examples of the main achievements in the field of exploration/production, the offshore development program, and energy-related applications.

**Exploration/Production.** Geological studies are performed on the formation and migration of oil, by laboratory experiments, on-site studies, and theoretical work aimed at a better understanding of fundamental phenomena. Procedures for analyzing nonsoluble organic material (kerogen) associated with rocks have been developed, and the phenomenon of migration of oil has been studied (detailed studies for Parisian basin and East-Sahara). A mathematical model to simulate the formation of oil has been worked out. Structural geology is used for a better understanding of oil traps and for forecasting characteristics of oil reservoirs and fracturation. An analytical study of many sedimentary basins and oil fields is aimed at estimating possibilities of discovery of future oil fields. Photogeology and teledetection systems are being developed.

In geophysics, a large effort has been devoted to computerization of analysis and results, and to the possible uses of holography. For drilling studies there is an active association between the various oil companies and IFP.[e] There are also optimization studies for turboratory with flexodrilling, or with normal piping systems; promising results have been obtained, based on improved measurements at the level of the drilling tool. IFP is also continuously developing flexodrilling (some experiments are performed in USSR in association with Russian technicians).

e.  Association de Recherche sur les Techniques d'Exploitation du Petrole A.R.T.E.P.

Production itself is studied by improving knowledge of oil fields and oil production process, in the frame of the above-mentioned ARTEP association between oil companies and IFP: characteristics of reservoirs and of various fluids, wetting behavior of oil and water in reservoirs, flow in fractured reservoirs, models for reservoir behavior, methods for reservoir stimulation (chemical or hydraulic fracture), and secondary/tertiary recovery by fluid injection (polymers, froth, or microemulsions), or by thermal process.

**Offshore Development Program.** As early as 1963, the French government, more precisely the Directorate for Motor Fuels in the Ministry for Industry, decided to sponsor on a broad and continuous scale, research and development for offshore oil exploration and production. Associated in this effort were IFP, the oil companies CFP and Elf/ERAP, and interested industrial companies such as Compagnie Generale de Geophysique, Neptune (drilling rigs), DORIS (engineering), etc. The program is coordinated by a specialized committee, CEPM (Comite d'Etudes Petrolieres Marines), and research is performed by the various members or subcontracted to specialized organizations. In the past ten years, more than 300 million Francs ($60 million) have been spent on this program, not including separate proprietary research performed by members.

Among the main sectors studied for this offshore development are (1) geology: geographical zones studied are the Mediterranean basin (correlation between seismic studies offshore and continental structural geology and strata studies), the Indian Ocean, and the Gulf of Guinea; (2) Geophysics: flexitir (small explosive charges of about 50 grams at a depth of 10 meters or more) and flexichoc (acoustical energy created by implosion) have been extensively developed, together with hydrophones, seismic streamers, and digital recording and processing systems; (3) sea-bottom exploration: side-looking sonar, automatic navigating system, and numerous tools have been studied and tested, such as ocean-floor electrocoredrill, vibrocorer, flexocoring and flexodrilling and deep-sea electrocoring; (4) offshore drilling: well known is the Pentagone 81 semisubmersible platform (used by Neptune Co. since July 1969) progressively modified to Pentagone 68 (six are being constructed now, two of which are for the United States), the drilling-ship Pelican from Total/CFP, and the oscillating platform from Elf/ERAP; and (5) production: subsea production well heads are tested (such as CFP experiments on the Zakum field in the Persian Gulf), and robots have been extensively studied (mainly by IFP).

It is expected that these studies will be progressively extended to greater depths, and to Arctic conditions.

Most of the participating organizations in these developments have also recently founded a specialized association for research on the action of the natural elements, aimed at studying such phenomena as the mechanisms of the effects of swell on fixed obstacles, the movement of floating structures, and harmonic analysis.

These studies, leading to a better understanding of the actions of natural elements, have made a valuable contribution to the original design of the concrete oil platform for the Ekofisk field in the North Sea, by the French DORIS company.

**Energy-Related Applications.** Four sectors can be mentioned in which IFP and oil companies are performing research related to energy uses: (1) engines: mechanisms of pollutant formation, catalysts for exhaust combustion gases, "variable geometry cylinder," mathematical model of engine operation; (2) industrial heating: burners for thermal plants, and formation of pollutants (mainly nitrogen oxides); (3) fundamental studies of combustion processes (including formation of pollutants); and (4) fuel cells: studies are based on $H_2$/air fuel cells, and IFP study the conversion process from methanol to $H_2$. First applications foreseen in the coming years are for special vehicles (in closed spaces, for instance, where pollution is the most dangerous), or for remote communications systems, etc.

**International Cooperation.** IFP is actively participating in international activities, and one of its subsidiaries is especially devoted to promoting international cooperation, a good example of which is its help in organizing similarly oriented institutes abroad.

In the oil companies sector, three European oil companies joined together in 1971 to found an association for research. The three participants are Elf/ERAP, AGIP (from the Italian ENI group) and Belgium's Petrofina. It is too soon to draw conclusions about the success of the first example of European cooperation in the sector of oil research and development.

### Gas Research and Development

Almost all research and development is performed by Gaz de France[f] through the specialized Directorate of Studies and New Techniques (DETN—Direction des Etudes et Techniques Nouvelles). About 620 people were employed in 1970, and the same figure was foreseen for 1975. The budget was 32 million F in 1970 ($6.4 million), growing roughly 6.5 percent per year.

All sectors, from gas production to gas utilization, are covered. The main research center is at Landy (near Paris), with experimental facilities for production processes, gas transportation, testing gas-burning equipment (industrial and domestic), and includes a 13-level 100-ft testing tower to simulate various room distribution, gas circulation and flue gas exhausts.

Under the Landy research center are three specialized testing

---

f. For unknown reasons, Gaz de France was unwilling to provide up-to-date information or to discuss R&D programs. Topics presented here can be incomplete or somewhat out of date. However, papers were announced, to be presented at the World Power Conference in Detroit, in September 1974.

stations: (1) Alfortville, near Paris, near the gas station where gas arrives from Groningen and Lacq. The different properties of these feed gases are adjusted for consumption, (such as nitrogen removal for Groningen gas); industrial equipment for transportation or distribution is tested full scale; (2) Nantes, for liquefied natural gas: liquefaction, storage, and maritime transportation. This is where equipment was developed and tested for the first LNG operation, Arzew (Algeria)—Le Havre, and the second one, Skikda (Algeria)—Fos; (3) Toulouse: mainly used in connection with the gas field of Lacq, and includes equipment for studying gas flames (International Flames Study Committee).

**Production.** Research on new processes or improvements in existing processes (for instance using naphtha as a feed material) was performed for a long time, apparently in close association with American Gas Association and British Gas. Research seems presently to be discontinued.

**Storage.** This is an important subject, especially in a country like France, where gas storage is the cheapest way to build up safety reserves. Various forms of storage have been developed, and are now in operation at different locations, on a growing scale: underground storage in aqueous layers, such as the big Chemery reservoir of more than a billion $Nm^3$ (37 billion $ft^3$) at a depth of 4,000 ft; and underground storage in salt-mine vaults (at Tersanne, at depths down to 5,000 ft). Research is performed not only to find new reservoirs, but also on the properties of the reservoirs.

In association with the French Atomic Energy Commission (CEA), long-term possibilities of artificial cavities by nuclear explosions are studied.

The studies on LNG storage have been used for the operational storage facilities at Le Havre and Fos terminals.

**Transportation.** Interesting studies have been performed on sea-gas lines for Algerian gas. It seems that such studies have recently been resumed.

GDF and its subsidiary Gaz-Transport are world reknowned for the development of LNG maritime transportation, mainly based on nickel-based alloys (9 percent Ni, Invar alloy). Most present studies seem to be oriented toward improvements, and to the problems of large LNG ships.

**Distribution and Utilization.** Studies are aimed at improvements of equipment, and to promote gas utilization by industry or for domestic needs. Computers are extensively used for studying pipe networks (low and high pressures, high number of nodal points, and so on).

**Special Studies.** Two are worth mentioning (on which unfortunately it has not been possible to gather up-to-date information): (1) fuel cells: studies have been sponsored over many years by DGRST, and are mainly aimed at medium scale conversion plants; (2) hydrogen production: water-splitting thermochemical processes have been studied for several years (different from the European Communities Ispra–Mark I process), and the coupling to a nuclear process heat reactor is the object of joint research with the CEA.[g]

It is clear that, taking into account some uncertainties on future European gas supplies, such studies can become of the highest importance for further potential of Gaz de France.

### Electricity Research and Development

Electricity research and development is carried out by the French utility EDF and by the electrical industry. EDF owns three main laboratories. The first is Laboratoire National d'Hydraulique de Chatou, initially for hydraulic studies on dams, reservoirs, etc. (and at the beginning also for water transportation, studies performed for another Ministry). This laboratory has broadly increased its interest to include fluid dynamics and thermodynamics, water intakes, water turbines or pumps, to burner studies, diffusion of pollutants in the atmosphere, dust removal, heat transfer (with $CO_2$ for gas-cooled reactors), and even sodium experiments (magnetic pumps). The second is Station d'essais et Laboratories de Clamart (Fontenay). Founded in 1946, this laboratory has studied circuitbreakers (3.8 million kVa), transformers (50 Hz, 1,000 kV) and cables for underground or undersea transmission. The third is Laboratoire des Renardieres, the most recent (1966), connected to a station 400 kV, and equipped for testing circuit-breakers up to 15,000 MVA, high-voltage transmission (1,200 kV). In this laboratory can be found a "climatic station" to study isolation and electrical domestic heating, as well as a station of 50 MWth for testing sodium steam-generators for LMFBR. EDF has mentioned spending about 2 percent of gross income in R&D activities.

Among industrial laboratories, the most important are those of the CGE group, with 420 million francs ($84 million) in 1971 for R&D activities (about 5 percent of total sales), and 5,800 staff (1,500 of academic level). The main laboratories are at Marcoussis (basic studies, 500 employees), Massy and Belfort for Alsthom, etc. There are also the laboratories of the Compagnie Electro-Mecanique, from the Brown-Boveri Group.

**Electricity Production.** There has been important research on combustion processes (EDF is burning about 28 million metric tons of fuel oil

g. In particular, GdF studies potassium cycles, such as:

$$K_2O_2 \; + \; H_2O \; \rightarrow \; 2\,KOH \; + \; 1/2\,O_2 \qquad (\; 150°C, \quad 300°F)$$

$$2\,KOH + \; 2\,K \; \rightarrow \; 2\,K_2O \; + \; H_2 \qquad (\; 700°C, \; 1,290°F)$$

$$2\,K_2O \qquad \qquad \rightarrow \; K_2O_2 \; + \; 2\,K \qquad (1,000°C, \; 1,830°F)$$

Temperatures for this cycle are rather high, but the cycle is relatively simple (few reacting materials, only three steps).

per year), mainly aimed toward a better knowledge of the combustion process and optimization of burners. Some of these studies have been performed in close association with IFP. Due to future plans to "go fully nuclear," emphasis has been mainly shifted to short-term pollution problems, with studies of fuel and exhaust-gases treatment, atmospheric diffusion and high stacks, effects on microclimates, thermal effluents in rivers and estuaries, and noise control.

The CEA is doing most of the studies on nuclear reactors, but EDF is performing studies on environmental problems, and on some aspects of LWR, such as a mock-up experiment of hydro-elasticity problems of internal core structures. Most important has been the construction and three-year operation of a testing circuit (50 MWth) for sodium-steam generators, with which three full-scale modules of the Phenix steam-generators have been tested, as well as many pieces of sodium equipment for Phenix or for the future 1,200 MWe LMFBR.

In close cooperation with EDF, Alsthom is studying: (1) 1,000–1,300 MWe steam-turbines (50 Hz), extrapolating GE technology; (2) cryo-alternators: a four-year program (1972–1975) is aimed at studying cryoalternators of 1,200 to 3,000 MWe, including testing of selected critical components and design for a first prototype. This study is partially sponsored by DGRST industrial aid program. CGE-Marcoussis laboratories participate in the studies.

**Transmission.** Many studies have been performed in the laboratories of Clamart and les Renardieres on power transmission, and on fully interconnected large networks. Although there seems to be no feeling of urgency in France, or in Europe as a whole, regarding very high-voltage transmission, above the 380–400 generalized system now in use, EDF has performed and continues studies on very high voltage, in close cooperation with other European utilities (British CEGB, Italian ENEL, etc.). A testing line has been installed for experiments in Les Renardieres: 1,200 meters long, 3 supports, 1,100 kV. Accompanying theoretical studies already allow fair estimation of losses and radioelectrical perturbations.

Let us remember that a direct-current line has been installed between the United Kingdom and France to exchange power (160 MW, 100 kV, 800 A). Studies are being made for a much more powerful DC connection between the two countries.

**Storage and Peak Power.** Geography and hydraulic reservoir distribution (including possibilities for pumped storage) are rather favorable. Some studies have been made on compressed-air storage, hydrogen possibilities, and gas turbine use. With acceleration of nuclear development programs, storage and peak-power problems become more acute. Various studies have recently been performed on hydrogen production and storage, with or without association with possible complementary industrial markets (oil refining, for example).

**Electricity Utilization.** This sector is of growing importance to EDF, and various original studies are being performed. Many theoretical calculations and experiments are developed on electrical heating, and the "all-electrical home" (the main advantage of which will be not only to increase electrical consumption and correspondingly to reduce oil consumption and imports, but also to improve very considerably the load factor and flatten the daily load curve). A special laboratory, the "Climatron," allows the simulation of many parameters such as wind, temperature, varying sunshine, etc., and the design of the best isolation techniques and heating or control/regulation equipment.

Many other possible applications of electricity are studied: in agriculture, mechanization and thermal uses, but also new prospects for conservation of crops, animal plants, etc.; and in industry, heat pumps, accelerated hardening of concrete, etc. Many of these studies are in fact performed with other research and industrial organizations, such as the Steel Institute, the Petroleum Institute, and the Agricultural Institute.

EDF, and some car manufacturers such as Renault, are also studying extensively electrical cars, mainly for urban use. EDF is testing a fleet of about 100 experimental electrical cars.

In conclusion, EDF has recently developed a strong coherent program that could be one possible solution to the French energy situation: rely more and more on (*nuclear*) electricity; and at the same time develop and promote varied and new electrical applications.

**Nonconventional Power Sources.** Various possibilities have been, or still are, studied in France in relation to electricity: (1) tidal plants. As is well known, the 240 MWe Rance plant is currently operating. Studies of a very large plant (20 billion kWh per year) based on Chausey islands have been discontinued; high capital charges are considered unattractive. For the Rance, bulb-groups have been developed, and are now used on the Rhine and on the Rhone, for low differences of levels; (2) MHD, once a big program (EDF–CGE–CEA), has been stopped, except for liquid MHD (Compagnie Electro-Mecanique); (3) wind power has also been studied by EDF, and two prototypes (1,000 kW) were built and tested a few years ago. But capital charges were considered too high, compared to coming nuclear power; (4) fuel cells: Alsthom (at equal shares with Exxon, in a joint research venture) is studying methanol fuel cells, and has obtained very encouraging results; (5) solar energy: although apparently not directly concerned with solar power, EDF seems interested in possible applications of solar energy for homes, and the possible coupling of solar energy uses in homes with supplementary electrical power. There are various solar energy studies in France, mostly performed by the CNRS, including the world-famous solar furnace at Odeilho (1,000 kW), but the research is apparently not coordinated, and did not receive much support from DGRST, whose interest was quite low. It is not known whether the present situation will change this;

(6) geothermal energy: an experiment has been performed, near Melun, where about 3,000 homes are heated with hot water from the Dogger layer (90°C, 200°F) at 4,500 ft. This hot-water layer is very broad, and new studies are aimed at using it on a very large scale around the Paris area. Other geothermal possibilities are now being assessed in France, and these studies have received impetus with the energy crisis.

As a whole, the heavy commitment to nuclear power (on which EDF has based its future developments) seemed to be considered as excluding strong R&D efforts in other directions until the energy crisis. Although many exploratory studies are now being done, no change of plans has as yet been published.

### Nuclear Energy Research and Development

Most of the nuclear energy research and development is performed by the Commissariat a l'Energie Atomique (CEA—Atomic Energy Commission). Founded in 1946, CEA is a powerful organization ruling the biggest energy R&D program in France (by far!), together with performing a very large amount of research, from biology to military weapons, and from fundamental particle physics to nuclear process heat applications. Only a small part of all the research is contracted to other research organizations, such as the university laboratories, or to industry (mainly development work). The biggest part is done in CEA-owned laboratories, at the Nuclear Research Centers of Saclay, of Fontenay aux Roses (both near Paris), of Grenoble, and of Cadarache (nuclear reactor testing station), not to mention the various specialized military laboratories. Moreover, CEA owns various industrial plants, such as plutonium-producing reactors and tritium-producing reactors in Marcoule, gaseous diffusion enrichment plant in Peirrelatte, etc. The total number of employees has been reduced from a high of 31,000 in 1968 to about 27,000 at the end of 1972. For the last few years, CEA's annual budget has been more or less stabilized (even slightly decreasing in constant francs or in relative percentage to the GNP) at around 4,400 million F ($880 million) (including military activities, about 50 percent of the total).

It must also be mentioned that CEA has progressively created about two dozen industrial and commercial subsidiaries that it owns totally or shares with industry. If some of these creations are straightforward, others may be more questionable (answering to an intention of "public usefulness"), and raise some problems of "competition" with the other industrial companies. Finally, as other nuclear research centers have been doing, CEA is diversifying somewhat into nonnuclear research or applications; its nonnuclear and nonenergy activities in 1972 represented in fact only 10 percent of total activities.

Excluding the military research and its corresponding budget, the three main sectors of CEA activities are (1) nuclear industrial applications, mainly reactors and enrichment, 964 million francs in 1972 ($193 million), 41 percent of civilian budget; (2) raw materials, mainly uranium, 474 million F ($94 million), 20 percent; and (3) fundamental research, 492 million F ($95 million), or 21 percent. Fundamental research includes thermonuclear fusion, which will be dealt with below. The remainder of this section will be chiefly devoted to raw materials and reactor research and development.

**Uranium Production.** The production of uranium by French interests reached in 1972 about 2,500 metric tons of yellow-cake, 90 percent from French mines and about 10 percent from Nigerian (Somair) mines. Not including foreign mines in which CEA or French industry has a major interest, uranium reserves in France are estimated at about 57,000 metric tons of uranium, three-quarter from CEA and one-quarter from private industry.

A decision was made in 1972 to increase production in 1973 by 10 percent, in order to prepare the French mining industry for the increases in production necessary later on for growing uranium needs.

The search for new uranium deposits is continuing in France, Africa, Canada, Indonesia, the United States and Australia, by the CEA alone or in association with French and foreign interests.

**Uranium Enrichment.** Although the Pierrelatte plant is for military application, it began in 1972 to produce low enriched uranium for future needs of EDF's LWR.

Main developments are aimed at the study of a civilian European gaseous diffusion plant of 9–12 million metric tons SWU, to be on line around 1980. Sweden, Belgium, Italy and Spain have been associated with France in the Eurodif study group. Similar study groups have been formed with Japan and with Australia.

In addition to numerous design and optimization studies, and full-scale components testing, pilot circuits of various stages of the future plant have been built and tested at full scale. A decision was made in late 1973 to build this plant, at Tricastin, near the military plant of Pierrelatte. Capacity will be at least 9 million metric tons SWU. Belgium, Italy and Spain have maintained their partnership with France, but Sweden has retired (for political reasons). Production of enriched uranium is planned to begin in 1979. At the beginning of 1974, 100 percent of 9 million metric ton SWU capacity were already committed.

Some studies are also performed on ultracentrifugation processes.

**Light Water Reactors.** Five LWR (Westinghouse license) are now in construction at Tihange (in association with Belgium), Fessenheim, and Bugey; the first one, in Tihange, is due to operate in 1974–1975, and the first one in Fessenheim in 1976.

French experience on LWR dates back to the French Navy reactor program. Two nuclear subs are already in operation, and two others are under construction. There is also the land prototype PAT (Prototype a Terre), which has been operating for many years, and a new advanced prototype CAP (Chaudiere Avancee Prototype), now under construction; CAP is also used for developing civilian maritime applications, and small power plants (300 MWe) for isolated areas.

Based on this experience, CEA has initiated a light water reactor development program named "Champlain." Working closely with industry, this program would improve and gallicize components like fuel, safety, internal structures, prestressed concrete vessels, etc.

**High Temperature Reactors.** Due to past experience with gas cooled reactors and an active participation in the Dragon Project, there has long been an interest in high temperature reactors, although there was no specific project.

In 1972 various agreements were signed between CEA, French industry (GHTR, Groupement Industriel Français pour les Reacteurs a Haute Temperature), and General Atomic for licensing reactor systems, components and fuel. CEA will partially pay the cost of the license by performing a broad research program for General Atomic, mainly in the field of fuel and graphite irradiations. A proposal on a General Atomic type 1,160 MWe power plant is presently being worked out.

Some studies are also devoted to possible applications of such types of high temperature reactors for nuclear process heat (such as the studies already mentioned on hydrogen production, in association with Gaz de France).

**Sodium Cooled Fast Breeder Reactors.** This is by far the largest reactor-development program, with a budget of about 450 million F ($90 million) in 1972.

Many sodium facilities have been built (mostly in Cadarache, plus the steam generator of EDF–Les Renardieres), including the 20 MWth experimental reactor Rapsodie up-rated to 40 MWth (Rapsodie–Fortissimo), and the 250 MWe prototype Phenix (on line since March 1974).

More than 5,000 fuel pins have been irradiated in Rapsodie, higher than 6 percent fima[h] burnup (50,000 MWD per metric ton), and a few of them over 12 percent fima.

Many safety experiments are being performed, such as sodium-water reactions (for instance, one experiment with 1.85 m$^3$ sodium at 350°C with 22 kg water at 250°C and 2,500 psi).

A detailed design has been made for Super-Phenix, a 1,200 MWe plant decided on by the beginning of 1974 (to be built at Creis-Malville, on the Rhone river).

h. Fissile material initially present.

Reprocessing of fast reactor fuels is being studied by the aqueous process as well as by a fluoride volatility process (small pilot plant at Fontenay-aux-Roses).

**Fuel Reprocessing.** There is a reprocessing plant in Marcoule for military application, and a large reprocessing plant in La Hague, initially for HDF gas-cooled reactors and being modified for LWR fuel and fast reactor Phenix fuel reprocessing.

In a pilot plant, fuel from Rapsodie (part of it irradiated over 80,000 MWD/t) has already been reprocessed.

CEA is associated with British BNFL and German KEWA in United Reprocessors for commercial reprocessing. The two main plants of United Reprocessors are the Windscale and La Hague reprocessing plants. A third plant will be built later in Germany.

**Thermonuclear Fusion.** Research on plasma physics and controlled thermonuclear fusion is concentrated in the two research centers of Fontenay-aux-Roses and Grenoble, in the framework of an association with Euratom. The purpose is a better understanding of fundamental plasma phenomena and the study of the various types of magnetic containment. A particular emphasis is devoted to achievement of a large Tokomak machine, and related heating and measuring equipment. The new association contract signed in 1972 with Euratom has assigned a common budget of 346.5 million francs.

Many experimental facilities are being used: (1) high-frequency heating: Petula (Tokomak type) and WEGA (Stellarator type), frequency about 1 MHz; (2) neutral atoms injection heating; (3) most important is TFR (Tokomak Fontenay-aux-Roses), which began operation in 1973: large diameter, 2 m, small diameter of plasma, about 40 cm, toroidal magnetic field, 60 kilogauss, duration of the field, 0.5 seconds.

Moreover, the Department for Military Applications of the CEA, in its center of Limeil, is studying laser fusion. One of the experimental facilities, in the center of Limeil, uses four converging laser beams on a target of deuterium (laser power, 150 joules).

## REFERENCES

### Energy Situation

Atreize. *La planification francaise en pratique.* Editions Economie et Humanisme.

Comite Professionnel du Petrole. "Petrole, 1972," "Petrole, 1973" (very complete statistical yearly publication).

M. Grenon, *Ce monde affame d'energie.* R. Laflont, 1973.

———. *Pour une politique de l'energie.* Marabout, 1972.

MacArthur, J., et B. Scott. *L'industrie francaise face aux plans.* Les editions d'organisation, 1970.

Masse, P. *Le Plan et l'anti-hazard.* Gallimard, 1965.

*Revue Francaise de l'Energie.* (Main monthly publication on energy problems.)

VI eme Plan. Travaux des Commissions et Sous–Commissions: Energie; Petrole; Carbon Gaz Electricite.

Vilain, M., ed. *La politique de l'energie en France.* Cujas, 1969.

### General Organization for Research and Development

Delegation Generale a la Recherche Scientifique et Technique. "La Recherche en France." (Brochure.)

*Le Progres Scientifique.* Monthly Review published by DGRST.

"Les methodes de programmation economique et financiere de la recherche a l'echelon national," *Le Progres Scientifique,* No. 148–149.

VI eme Plan (1971–1975). *Rapport de la Commission Recherche.* (2 vol.).

### Coal Research and Development

CERCHAR (descriptive brochure of facilities).

CERCHAR. *Rapport sur l'activite du Centre en 1971.*

_____ . *Rapport sur l'activite du Centre en 1972.*

"La recherche dans les Houilleres." Publ. Techn. CdF, 1972 (No. 5).

"Le CERCHAR et la recherche de la securite." Ann. Mines, Juillet 1972.

Table rond, "Valorisation chimique du charbon." Paris, 9 Mai 1972.

### Oil Research and Development

Elf/ERAP. *Annual Reports,* 1971 and 1972.

_____ . Private communications.

_____ . "La recherche scientifique et technique." (Brochure.)

_____ . Brochures on research laboratories.

Institut Francais du Petrole. *Annual Reports,* 1971 and 1972.

IFP. "L'avenir des piles a combustible."

_____ . "Techniques for offshore petroleum prospection, drilling and production."

Sixth Plan. Commission for Oil. *Report.* Chapter IX: Recherche Scientifique et Technique.

Total Compagnie Francaise des Petroles. *Annual Reports,* 1971 and 1972 (and private communications).

### Gas Research and Development

Gaz de France. *Direction des Etudes et Techniques Nouvelles.* (Descriptive brochure.)

Gaz de France/DTEN. "Quelques exemples de travaux executes 1970–1971."

### Electricity Research and Development

Alsthom. Private communications (fuel cells, cryoalternators).

Compagnie Generale d'Electricite. *Annual reports.*

EDF. "Quelques faits marquants—1971" Direction des Etudes et Recherches.
_____ . *Symposium Electricite 2000* (Paris, 1973).
_____ . "25 ans de vie-technique et economique d'EDF." (Brochure.)
"Electricite de France et Gaz de France ont 25 ans." *Revue Francaise de l'Energie,* No. 230, 1971.
L'economie electrique (UNIPEDE, special publications): *Le chauffage electrique et la climatisation des locaux* (No. 66); *Le vehicule electrique* (No. 65).

**Nuclear Energy Research
and Development**

Commissariat a l'Energie Atomique. *Rapports annuels,* 1971–1972.
Geneva Conferences.

# Chapter Nine

# Japan

Many people were surprised when Japan became the third economic power in the world. Extrapolating the curves, it has been forecast that Japan will become, without *any* domestic natural resource, the second most powerful economic nation. Hermann Kahn has predicted that it will rank first by the end of the century.

However, this superdynamic nation suffered a dramatic shock around 1970, when it was faced with an unprecedented environmental crisis more severe than anywhere else because industry had for much too long been reluctant to undertake any nonprofitable pollution abatement.[a] And now Japan is suffering a second shock, the world energy/oil crisis. The first was internal, the second is external. Both affect it deeply, and both will require effort and money; but Japanese people are naturally ingenious, and they have patiently accumulated a powerful financial wealth. But it is premature to assess how the Japanese economy will possibly be reoriented.

Japanese economists like to make plans . . . and to revise them, being sometimes oversensitive to short-term conditions such as the 1971 recession, from which the economy recovered in a remarkably short time. Because of the environmental and energy crises mentioned above, some of the prospects presented here will be modified, with the goal of increased self-sufficiency.

Imported technologies, including, of course, those for the energy sector, have played a prominent part in the postwar economic development of Japan. As much valuable information as we were able to collect indicated that the total amount of R&D (as well as energy R&D) is somewhat low compared to U.S. and European standards. But it is our opinion that all the conditions now point to a noteworthy change; Japan will probably not be able to import tailor-

---

a. "Le drame est que ce pays est trop etroit pour l'industrie qu'il veut porter"–Robert Guillain. ("The drama is that this country is too small for the industry it wants to bear.")

made solutions to its particular problems, and will have to build them up urgently . . . to survive.

### The Energy Situation

Japan's self-sufficiency in energy in 1970 was about 15 percent, and was supposed to decrease to a low 5 percent in 1985, as can be seen from Table 9–1. There is apparently no simple solution for changing this uncomfortable situation. However, one of the objectives of the Tanaka administration was that Japanese interests should control about 30 percent of raw and energy materials supply in 1985. Even under normal conditions, this would be a formidable task; but with the recent move toward self-control by oil-producing countries, it is even questionable if such a goal will ever be feasible politically. In any case, this explains Japan's active prospecting abroad for oil, uranium, and many other minerals.

Energy policy in Japan is administered by MITI, the powerful Ministry for International Trade and Industry, and its various Bureaus (Heavy Industry, Mine, Coal, Public Utilities, etc.), with guidance for long-term energy policy prospects from the Advisory Committee for Energy. Close coordination is maintained with the Science and Technology Agency (one of its major subjects is nuclear energy developments), and with the Economic Planning Agency, both under the authority of the Prime Minister.

All enterprises in the Japanese energy industry are privately operated, as a rule, and most are privately controlled, apart from a few governmental organizations. But MITI exercises very strict control over industry operations,

### Table 9–1. Primary Energy Supply: Actual and Forecast, 1965–1985
*(in million m³ oil)*

|  | 1965 | 1970 | 1975 | 1980 | 1985 |
|---|---|---|---|---|---|
| Electric power | 20 | 22 | 41 | 82 | 138 |
| (hydro) | (20) | (21) | (25) | (27) | (35) |
| (nuclear) | – | (1) | (16) | (55) | (103) |
| Coal | 53 | 71 | 67 | 78 | 88 |
| (indigenous) | (38) | (30) | (15) | (15) | (15) |
| (imported) | (15) | (41) | (52) | (63) | (73) |
| Petroleum | 102 | 234 | 379 | 524 | 671 |
| (for power generation) | (14) | (44) | (66) | (69) | (57) |
| Natural Gas | 2 | 2 | 2 | 2 | 2 |
| LNG | – | 1 | 8 | 25 | 42 |
| *Total* | 177 | 330 | 497 | 711 | 941 |

Note: Mining and manufacturing account presently for 50% of the total energy demand.

mainly in the oil sector, where many regulations are somewhat similar to those of France.

**Coal.** Domestic coal is produced chiefly in Hokkaido and Kyushu. Production, which reached a high of 55 million metric tons in fiscal year 1961,[b] decreased slowly until fiscal 1968 (a period of "scrap and build"), when production was still 46 million metric tons, and dropped sharply over the next four years (period of "curtailment") to a level of about 26 million metric tons in fiscal 1972. The number of coal mines has decreased accordingly, from 700 to less than 100, and the number of employees from 250,000 to less than 40,000.

Since 1958, there have been various government plans and countermeasures to improve the coal industry situation, mainly through the creation of the Coal Mining Industry Rationalization Corporation; but without success. The mid-1972 plan of the Coal Mining Council aimed toward a domestic production reduced to a low 20 million metric tons per year; from 1975 on the government will take over the long-term debts of coal mining enterprises (the third such measure since 1966). The Government will also step up a variety of subsidizing and supporting measures for coal industries. Of the two main large-scale users, the electric power industry is urged to buy about 8.5 million metric tons per year, and the iron and steel industry is urged to buy about 8 million metric tons per year. For the period from fiscal 1973 through 1976, the government's fiscal contribution is estimated at from about 470 billion yen ($1.9 billion) to 500 billion yen ($2 billion) during the period.

It was questioned by industry (and by "forced" large-scale users) if even such measures will be sufficient to keep the production up to a level of 20 million metric tons. It is not known how far the energy crisis will now change this opinion.

**Oil.** As can be seen from Table 9–1, oil covers more than 70 percent of the total energy mix in Japan, and will in principle continue to do so for the next fifteen years. Practically speaking, at least 99 percent of this oil is imported. Although there is an active search for oil in the various offshore areas surrounding the islands, no significant discovery has been recorded so far.

Through various successive laws (such as the most important, the Petroleum Industry Law, enacted in 1962), the Japanese government regulates all business activities of the petroleum industry, from exploration to refinery extensions, and selling or merging of companies. The government first joined (50 percent) in the Japan Petroleum Exploration Company, which has been succeeded by the Petroleum Development Corporation (100 percent government-owned). This corporation participates, mainly by financial sharing, in a high number of oil enterprises.

The situation of the oil industry in Japan is somewhat similar to

b.  Fiscal year begins April 1 and ends March 31 the following calendar year.

Germany's, although foreign companies do not dominate the industry or the market to the same level. There is no large domestic integrated oil company, but many large corporations deal with one sector or another of the oil business.

In 1973, there were about forty companies in oil exploration (most of them created after 1970), searching for oil all over the world. Share-owners of these companies were, respectively, big industrial concerns, electric power companies, steel companies, shipyards, banks, insurance companies, financial and commercial companies, transportation societies, or various associations of oil users. The Petroleum Development Corporation was participating in more than half of these exploration companies, with share percentages varying from a few up to 50 percent. Moreover, to supplement a scarce oil research expertise, many of these companies included as minority partners foreign oil companies, or else were associated with foreign oil companies in joint ventures. Overall results (including some positive ones in Indonesia, Sabah, Zaire and Nigeria) were still somewhat limited, and could illustrate that it will be a difficult task to reach a 30 percent control of oil supplies by purely Japanese interests.

Other actions to secure oil supplies have included a deal to share BP's oil reserves and production in Abu Dhabi. Another transaction, between a Japanese maritime company and Abu Dhabi, was one of the first international participation purchases. The high costs of this contract have caused criticism. Long-term supply contracts are actively sought.

There are ten major oil refining companies, including Idemitsu, Nippon, Kyodo, Maruzen, and Mitsubishi (some of them recently formed as a group). Some foreign companies (Exxon, Mobil, Shell, Caltex, Getty) are share-owners, for a maximum of 50 percent of refining subsidiaries.

A major problem for Japanese oil refiners is to find new sites, due to a very active environmental opposition. The possibilities of building refineries abroad, mostly in producing countries, are actively studied. This solution would simultaneously satisfy the environmentalists and improve relationships with producer governments. If this tendency would be confirmed, for refineries as well as for petrochemical complexes or big steel or manufacturing plants, we can wonder if this would correspond to a new Japanese economic development era, a kind of "diaspora" of heavy Japanese industry . . .

**Natural Gas.** There is little production of natural gas in Japan, and a growing flow of imports of LNG (from Alaska, Brunei, and Abu Dhabi). Various contracts already signed cover a supply of 8.1 million metric tons per year in the coming years; other contracts being negotiated (including the long-awaited negotiations with the Soviet Union for 10 million metric tons LNG from Siberia, possibly in a joint project of USA–USSR–Japan) could raise the level of imports to 30 million metric tons in 1985.

The consumption of city gas (from coal and oil) and LNG is expected to increase at a high rate; however, its weight among the gross energy demand will be no more than a mere 2 percent.

**Electricity.** Total electricity production in fiscal 1971 reached 385 billion kWh. Total capacity in 1972 was 76,480 MWe, from which 66,000 MWe was owned by utilities, and 10,000 by industry for its own needs. Since 1963, thermal capacity has passed hydro capacity, and the policy was "thermal-primary and hydro-secondary," although huge pumped storage stations were being built or planned. In 1972, there was a total of 56,000 MWe thermal against 20,000 MWe hydro.

Oil is the dominant fuel for thermal production, with about 87 percent of total fuel consumption in 1971. Heavy oil accounted for 35 million $m^3$, (630,000 bpd), and crude oil for 11 million $m^3$ (200,000 bpd). Incidentally, because of pollution countermeasures, consumption of crude oil is on the increase year after year. One unit (Minami-Yokohama) uses LNG, and a few other units are planned, for environmental reasons. Besides LNG, natural gas liquid and methanol are also in study for the fuel. It is expected that oil's share in power generation will decrease from 60 percent in 1970 to about 27 percent by 1985, because of LNG and nuclear energy.

There is a growing tendency for very large units (1,000 MWe and more), and for very large plants (4,000 to 5,000 MWe). But the siting problem becomes more and more acute, and utilities meet growing difficulties of acceptance, which could become so severe in the near future as to cause a threat to the power supply. In the summer of 1973 (since 1968, peak demand has shifted from the winter to the summer period), Japan experienced a severe shortage; capacity in reserve was at a low 3 percent, and some limitations on uses were imposed.

There are nine major utilities with local monopoly under government control for production, transmission and distribution, plus the government-owned Electric Power Development Company. This company deals with special projects, such as the Sakuma frequency conversion station (Japan is divided in two parts, one 60 Hz and one 50 Hz), and acts as consultant to any enterprise developing electric power resources in overseas countries. Coordination and exchange of power between the various utilities is accomplished through the "Wide Area Coordinative System Operation." There is a project for connecting Hokkaido to Honshu by a 380-km long 500 kV DC 300 MW capacity line in 1977.

Although geothermal potential is rather high (many volcanoes accompanying a great many hot spring resorts), and has been estimated at 20,000 MWe (about one-third of present installed capacity), only a few small plants have been built: Matsukawa, 20 MWe (1965); and Otake, 11 MWe (1967). About 135 MW (including Hacchobara 50 MWe and Kakkonda 50 MWe) are under plan for development. Many more projects are now being studied (see addendum).

**Nuclear Energy.** At the end of 1972 there was a total of 1,823 MWe generating nuclear capacity in Japan, with 7.3 billion kWh generated during fiscal 1971. Apart from the first plant—Tokai I of JAPCO (joint enterprise of the utilities) commissioned in 1967, of the Magnox type—all other nuclear plants are of the LWR type. There were 18 more units totalling 14,763 MWe under construction by the end of 1972, plus two reactor prototypes (discussed in the Energy Research and Development section).

Long-term nuclear plants, as proposed by the Japanese Atomic Energy Commission, have been revised towards a higher capacity: 32,000 MWe in 1980, 60,000 MWe in 1985 and 100,000 MWe in 1990, representing respectively 18 percent, 25 percent, and 33 percent of total capacities; most of these plants will be of the LWR type.

Many industrial companies (some critics, mindful of the British experience, say too many) are engaged in nuclear development, and the overall organization of the nuclear industry is not very easy to understand. The three main reactor manufacturers are licensed by American companies—Mitsubishi for PWR by Westinghouse, Hitachi and Toshiba for BWR by General Electric—but there is apparently a lack of engineering or architect-engineer companies. Fuel fabrication is performed by reactor manufacturers, but other companies (such as Sumitomo) aim at the reload market.

Uranium procurement is a major problem, because there are only very tiny domestic resources. Long-term contracts have been signed, and joint ventures are the second possibility; Japan presently has such contracts or enterprises with five countries: the United States, Canada, United Kingdom, Australia and France/Nigeria. Enrichment is another major problem: contracts with USAEC, negotiations to participate in foreign enrichment plants (such as the United States, France/Europe), and projects for a domestic enrichment plant for 1985 (based on centrifuge) are actively explored.

### General Organization for Research and Development

By importing and adapting foreign technology (as defined by the special 1949 and 1950 laws), it is generally considered that Japan was able to achieve her industrialization without going through the stage of independent research and development. The situation is changing now rather quickly, and it is thought that national R&D must play a growing role. Total expenditures are estimated at a low 2 percent of the GNP; but unlike many countries where public funds are equal to, or slightly above, 50 percent of total R&D expenditures, the ratio is only about 30 percent in Japan, and industry covers the remaining 70 percent. During the last few years there has been a clear trend for research as a whole to be less technology/industry oriented, and somewhat more devoted to social development and improvement, such as environmental research (including interesting studies on recycling).

**Government and Research.**   There is no centralization of research in Japan. Many ministries (MITI, Agriculture-Forest-Fisheries, Transportation,

Communication, Education, etc.) have their own research organizations and laboratories. Some coordination is accomplished by the Advisory Scientific Council, or by the Prime Minister agencies. In fact, a change of attitude toward scientific research has been initiated by the decision to develop nuclear energy on a national scale.

In 1956, the Science and Technology Agency, under the Prime Minister, was created, and its budget has steadily increased (very often by more than 20 percent per year) to reach 109 billion yen ($400 million) for fiscal 1973. About 60 percent of this budget is devoted to nuclear energy, and major parts of the remainder cover space research and oceanography. The STA budget was somewhat more than half the total public budget for R&D of 210 billion yen ($840 million), not including the research budgets of state universities, generally of a comparable amount. University research is very active; the first Japanese satellite (Feb. 1970) was developed by the University of Tokyo; moreover, university laboratories perform a good deal of R&D for industry.

In addition to its coordination or orientation functions, STA directs the activities of six laboratories: National Space Laboratory, National Institute for Research on Metals, Radiology Institute, National Research Center to Prevent Natural Disasters, National Institute for Inorganic Materials, and National Institute for Resources.

An office for national R&D programs was created in 1965; its three main objectives were to study desulfurization, computers, and energy. Moreover, the government and ministries have institutionalized: (1) special research projects, generally performed jointly by research organizations of the different ministries, such as countermeasures against natural disasters, environmental studies, oceanographic projects, safety in industry, and so on; (2) special research institutes, financed by grants, public subsidies, and private industry, considered more flexible than purely public organizations. These include, among others, the Atomic Institute, Institute for Physical-Chemistry Research, Space Development Corporation, Nuclear Ship Development Corporation, and Power Reactor and Nuclear Fuel Development Corporation (PNC); (3) large-scale projects, which are long-term and important projects requiring a special public effort, such as: (a) MHD, with 5.3 billion yen ($21 million) for 1966–1972 (extended to 1976); (b) desalting, with 5 billion yen ($20 million) for 1964–1975); (c) remote-control oil drilling, with 5.1 billion yen ($20 million) for 1970–1974. Other projects are sponsored mainly by MITI and Agricultural Ministry. In fiscal 1973, two new large scale projects have been added by MITI: (a) nuclear steel-making, with 7.3 billion yen ($29 million) for 1973–1978; communication-control of automobile-traffic, with 5 billion yen ($20 million) for 1973–1977.

The biggest large scale project so far appeared to be the development of a very large computer, with 10 billion yen ($40 million) already spent between 1966 and 1971.

**Industrial Research.** As mentioned above, industry is funding about 70 percent of R&D activities. In fact, the biggest part of this effort is products and production-oriented, most of it having been related to adaptation and improvement of imported technologies. According to statistics for 1970, for instance, of a total R&D budget of 252 billion yen ($1 billion) spent by 287 enterprises (above 500 million yen [$2 million] assets), an average 4.5 percent was devoted to environmental research, 16 percent for paper industry, 10 percent for power-producing and gas, and 2.5 percent for steel.

Three main sectors (between 20 and 25 percent each of the total) performing R&D were chemistry, electrical and electronic equipment, and transportation.

Some companies have central research laboratories, others subcontract research to specialized organizations or to university laboratories.

## ENERGY RESEARCH AND DEVELOPMENT

Japan, with its lack of centralized R&D, especially in the energy field, presents the same difficulties as Germany to those trying to survey its activities. For this reason, it was impossible to get a complete picture of the various energy R&D projects performed in Japan.

In any case, it was our impression that, aside from a few sectors (mainly power production and nuclear energy), there was only a small amount of R&D performed in the energy field. This may be due to economical reasons (such as in the coal industry, the difficulties of which have already been mentioned), or to structural reasons—such as the organization of the oil industry, widely spread among rather small entities—or due to the fact that Japan, during its fantastic development period, decided to rely on commercial exercise, dynamic production and financial investment instead of painful and uncertain scientific research.

There are already many signals that this is no longer true. As an example, we will conclude this section with a short survey of a recent assessment of nonconventional energy resources.[c] There is no doubt that, due to its particular situation Japan can contribute to original new energy research and development.

### Coal Research and Development

Statistics on the coal industry, in general, were obtained from the Coal Ministry Industry Rationalization Corporation, but no information useful for this study was available.

### Oil Research and Development

Complete information could not be collected from the Japan Petroleum Development Corporation, from the Petroleum Producers Association, or from MITI offices.

c. This will be further expanded in the addendum.

Apart from R&D for petroleum chemistry, some programs are related to offshore exploration and offshore equipment. The geological studies start from a modest base: In the past, seismology in Japan has meant earthquake seismology, not petroleum exploration. As far as offshore exploration is concerned, most companies, as we have mentioned, are rather small and concentrate only on one area, and do not perform much research; many of the participants do not have any oil experience.

For fiscal 1973, the budget for oceanographic development was 930 million yen ($3.7 million). Part of it was to be used to study a submarine research vehicle able to reach depths of 20,000 ft, or for developing various underwater working tools.

As mentioned above, among the Large Scale Projects is the development of an underwater remote-controlled oil-drilling tool.

Finally, some information was obtained on desulfurization process equipment being installed by Ube Kosan in a pilot plant of about 250 metric tons per day for a power plant of 40–50,000 kW. Processes being used are Catacave, and French IFP. Other studies on fuel and stack gas desulfurization are performed by the electricity industry.

### Gas Research and Development
No useful information could be collected.

### Electricity Research and Development
This is apparently one of the main sectors where industrial R&D are performed on a larger scale, by utilities and by electrical equipment manufacturers.

The Central Research Institute of Electric Power Industry (CRIEPI) was founded in 1951 as a nonprofit organization; it is financed by the nine electric utilities and the Power Development Company. CRIEPI performs research on request of sponsoring organizations (part of it of an applied nature, aimed at improvement of existing equipments and systems), but also performs some research of its own. CRIEPI includes various research committees (such as the Research Committee for Air Pollution Control, the Research Organization on Advanced Power Transmission and the Council for Industry Planning), an Economic Research Institute, and various laboratories.

With reorganization in 1970, the former Technical Laboratory has been separated into two independent organizations. Technical Laboratory No. 1, consists of research departments for electric power, machinery, chemistry, nuclear engineering and physics. Technical Laboratory No. 2 studies civil engineering and geology problems related to power plants, hydro, thermal or nuclear. There is also an Agricultural Laboratory, at Abiko, with two departments: an Environmental Biology Department, which has studied desulfurization of heavy oil by microorganisms, utilization of thermal discharges of power plants, and reduction of bacterial corrosion on condenser tubes, etc., and the Agrielectrification Department, which studies new possible applications of electricity in agriculture (heating appliances for nursing plants, environmental conditions in green houses and plastic houses, etc.). At the time of reorganization in 1970, CRIEPI staff amounted to about 600 people.

Technical Laboratories 1 and 2 are situated at Komae, southwest of Tokyo. They cover practically all sectors of electricity production and distribution, with extended facilities, such as for research on insulation, and on thermal and mechanical problems of power-transmission systems. Since one particular problem in Japan is salt contamination of equipment, mainly in the coastal area, many studies are permanently devoted to this problem. The extensive power-transmission system is 275 kV, although there is already a substantial part of the system (mainly around the biggest cities) at 500 kV. Dependent on the Technical Laboratory No. 1 are the 600 kV Shiobara Testing Laboratory for high-voltage AC and DC transmission, and the Akagi Distribution Testing Laboratory, devoted to modernization of distribution system. In Technical Laboratory No. 2 are concentrated the Hydraulics Department, including a Coastal Hydraulics Section and the important Structure Department, studying foundation engineering, soil mechanics and earthquake engineering.

Research is also actively pursued on electric cars, sponsored by STA; the program has been raised since fiscal year 1971 by MITI to the level of a Large-Scale Project (1971–1976). Various types are studied, including vehicles with fuel cells.

### Nuclear Energy Research and Development

As in many—if not all—other countries, this is by far the largest energy R&D program. The budget of STA for nuclear development for fiscal year 1973 was 62.6 billion yen ($250 million) a "small" increase of 12.1 percent only relative to the 1972 budget, because some large development projects are now in the completion stage. About 20 percent was for Japanese Atomic Energy Research Institute (JAERI), and more than 60 percent for the Power Reactor and Nuclear Fuel Development Corporation (PNC), the remainder being split between nuclear ship development and various institutes on atomic physics, chemistry or medicine.

JAERI was established in June 1956, as a center for basic research and applied R&D of atomic energy. JAERI has three research establishments, at Tokai, Takasaki and Oarai, and a radioisotope center. Its total budget for fiscal 1973 was approximately 15 billion yen ($60 million); it has approximately 2,200 employees, of which 800 are qualified scientists and engineers. It also supports R&D projects undertaken by PNC and the Japan Nuclear Ship Development Agency (JNSDA). JAERI does R&D on LMFBR and ATR,[d] and PNC does basic

d. Advanced thermal reactor (heavy water reactor).

research on fuels and materials of LWR, research on HTGR (nuclear process heat with VHTR, very high temperature GCR), research on thermonuclear fusion, and on radiation utilization technology.

Near the JAERI Research Center, PNC owns and operates the important Oarai Engineering Center, including the experimental FBR "Joyo," among various large experimental facilities (1 MWth and 50 MWth sodium-steam generator facilities, large components test facility, etc.).

**Uranium.** Prospecting for uranium resources has been underway since 1956. As a result a total of approximately 8,000 metric tons ($U_3O_8$ equivalent) has been discovered as estimated ore reserves (Ningyo-Toge and Tohno mines). In refining techniques, the "PNC process" has been developed, from which uranium can be produced directly from ore without passing through the intermediate stage of yellow cake (direct production of $UF_4$).

**Enrichment.** The Enrichment Survey Committee has been created by the government, electric utilities and major manufacturing industries within CRIEPI. Enrichment needs have been estimated at about 8,000 metric tons SWU for 1985, probably doubled by the year 2000.

Japan negotiates actively with various countries, as mentioned above, and performs her own studies, mainly based on centrifugation; this latter process has been selected for national development in 1972, aiming at a domestic production by 1985.

**Light Water Reactors.** Industry is building LWR under American licenses, and performs developmental research. National equipment already represent some 90 percent of the last power plants. Moreover, JAERI is engaged on studies on safety as well as on tests of fuels and materials, by using JPDR (Japan Power Demonstration Reactor, 12.5 MWe BWR–GE plant). Blow-down tests are performed with "Rig of Safety Assessment" (Rosa–I, remodelled Rosa–II), and from 1973 on reactivity accident experiments will be performed with a Triga–ACPR named Nuclear Safety Research Reactor NSRR.

**Advanced Thermal Reactor ATR.** An Advanced Thermal Reactor, ATR, has been developed and is being built by PNC at Tsuruga. Named Fugen, this is a 165 MWe (later on, 200 MWe) heavy water steam-cooled slightly enriched uranium (or plutonium enriched) reactor, expected on line in 1975–1976.

**High Temperature Gas Cooled Reactor (HTGR).** Interesting studies are performed on nuclear process heat, mainly for nuclear steel-making. As mentioned above, this is now a national Large Scale Project, with a budget of 7.3 billion yen ($29 billion) for five years. The aim is to build a 50 MWth reactor by the end of the 1970s, with a test loop, a reformer loop, and possibly a helium gas turbine.

JAERI has already operated 1,000°C (1,830°F) and 1,100°C (2,000°F) helium gas loops, to study heat transfer, helium gas purity-control techniques, and prevention of hydrogen gas diffusion in heat loop in the JMTR (Japan Material Testing Reactor, 50 MWth, at Oarai). Development of the secondary system for nuclear heat utilization started in 1973, in the framework of the above-mentioned MITI Large Scale Project.

**Fast Breeder Reactors.** PNC is carrying out the development of the experimental fast reactor "Joyo" and the prototype fast breeder reactor "Monju."

Construction of Joyo, a sodium-cooled reactor using plutonium-uranium mixed oxide (50 MWth first stage, 100 MWth final stage), was started at PNC—Oarai Engineering Center in 1970, and is expected to reach a critical stage in 1974.

Construction of Monju, a 300 MWe prototype FBR, loop type, could start in 1975–1976. Research studies, including safety experiments, are performed by JAERI.

**Nuclear Ship Propulsion.** A nuclear ship, "Mutsu," with a 36 MWth PWP reactor (by Mitsubishi), has been built, and has started operation, with early troubles.

Other studies (most of them in association with Germany) are devoted to high-speed (30 knots) large container ships.

**Reprocessing.** The first commercial fuel processing plant of 0.7 metric tons/day throughput is under construction at the site of Tokai, being scheduled to go into full operation from January 1975.

As for nuclear waste disposal, various studies have been done on ocean disposal of low-activity wastes in concrete containers. A very complete report recently published by the Japanese Atomic Industrial Forum on waste management problems defines some 20 work programs, including studies on ultimate disposal by deactivation (fusion reactors, or accelerators).

### Thermonuclear Fusion Research and Development

JAERI performs various research on thermonuclear fusion. The most important machine is the JFT–2 (JAERI Fusion Torus–2), a Tokomak type, with a plasma diameter of 50 cm (20 in.), a major diameter of 1.80 meters, (70 in.) a toroidal magnetic field strength of 15 kilogauss, and an estimated maximum plasma current of 250,000 A. It is expected to reach ion temperatures of 2.8 million degrees and plasma confinement times of 40 msec by the end of 1974.

JAERI is also making studies on technical problems related to nuclear fusion reactors.

JAEC has created a Council on Thermonuclear Fusion R&D, and is preparing a second five-year plan (1975–1980), aiming to build an experiment able to reach a 30 million degrees temperature during 0.1 second.

### Nonconventional Energy Research and Development

Various research has been performed in Japan for many years, though on a low scale, on nonconventional energies. They have been reassessed not long ago, and could be the starting point of original energy R&D in this country (see Addendum).

**Solar Energy.** Solar batteries are manufactured by some Japanese companies, such as Sharp, Matsushita Electric Apparatus, and Nippon Electric, for remote location applications (near Nagasaki, 300 W). Most of the studies are oriented toward satellite applications, but it is expected that the present high fabrication costs will be drastically decreased (related to microcircuit uses).

Some studies also have been performed since 1970 on solar power forms, according to ideas similar to the Meinel projects in the United States, for power production on a large scale as well as for housing air-conditioning.

MITI established the Study Committee for Solar Energy in March 1973. Solar energy is expected to be used on a reasonable scale in the 1980s.

**Ocean Energy.** Among the various energy resources of the oceans, one has been developed by Japan—energy of the waves. In 1964 the first small plant went into operation (for aerial navigation). A small power plant has been in use since 1967 on the Ashika island; to be sure, it is a very low power, around 40 W. Another alternator of 500 W was shown at the Osaka Fair in 1970.

Although installed kilowatt cost will probably remain very high, it has been decided to continue such studies, some applications being feasible for remote areas; and the Okinawa Maritime Exhibition in 1975 is expected to display a 10 kW unit. Developments could point to the possibility of generating 2 kW of power per meter offshore.

Some thinking has also been given to ocean gradient thermal energy (Frenchman George Claude's process), mainly in the proximity of nuclear thermal power plants, as well as to the possibilities of tidal plants, although there are few favorable sites in Japan (Ariake Sea, maximum difference of level about 5 m).

Finally, some studies of the Kurushio Stream (mainly between Hachijo and Mikura islands, with a speed of 3–4 knots) have been proposed.

**Geothermal Energy.** As mentioned above, Japan is very far from having used her potential geothermal energy, estimated at about 20,000 MWe. This is often given as an example of insufficient interest in new technologies R&D. But various studies are now being planned, and in 1973 STA began detailed studies on thirty possible promising sites, and technical research on geothermal power generation.

Some exotic studies involve trying to master part of the energy of the volcanoes.

**Wind Energy.** A few experiments have already been performed in this field, such as a wind-generator of 4.5 kW with a wheel of 9 m diameter, and they are expected to be extended.

**Fuel Cells.** It is worth remembering that since 1972, Tokyo Gas and Osaka Gas have participated in the U.S. TARGET program. Also, Matsushita Electric and Hitachi have fabricated hydrazine-air fuel cells for Japanese TV stations, and for other special users. These fuel cells are studied for possible applications to electric cars.

**MHD.** As mentioned above, MHD is a large-scale national project that has been extended to 1976.

Various experiments have already been performed, such as Mark–V, and Mark–VI. Mark–V is a 1,000 kWe experiment (but of short duration, planned to be extended to more than 10 hours from 1973 on), and Mark–VI is a long duration experiment. It is expected that at the end of the present program, in 1976, the next phase of industrial development will possibly begin.

## ADDENDUM

### Japan's Sunshine Project

In April of 1974, the Japanese Ministry for International Trade and Industry (MITI) and the Science and Technology Agency decided to found the General Delegation for Implementing the "Sunshine Program." This program aims to develop on a broad scale the utilization of solar energy, of geothermal energy and the use of hydrogen as a secondary energy, for the year 2000. All three energies are clean, and theoretically nonexhaustible, and they are expected to replace conventional polluting resources as they are exhausted, principally oil, in the next century. This program is being given highest priority in Japan.[e] For the first fiscal year (1974), a budget of 2.5 billion yen ($10 million) has been funded, including some research on coal and oil, distributed as follows:

| | | | |
|---|---|---|---|
| solar energy | $873 \times 10^6$ yen | = | $3.5 million |
| geothermal | $551 \times 10^6$ yen | = | $2.2 million |
| coal liquefaction | $443 \times 10^6$ yen | = | $1.7 million |
| general research | $217 \times 1C^6$ yen | = | $0.8 million |

e.  Apparently Japan is the first industrialized country (after the United States with Project Independence) to launch a strong energy R&D program as a result of the oil situation.

During fiscal 1974, the following research will be done:

**Solar Energy.** (1) Building of a heating and air-conditioning system, and development of components; (2) design of a solar plant (1,000 kW) and development of components; (3) basic studies on various thermal solar plants and on a space solar plant.

**Geothermal Energy** (1) Basic research on geothermal resources in thirteen regions; (2) basic research on hot water fields; (3) basic research on volcanic power plant.

**Hydrogen.** (1) Design of a pilot plant using high-temperature electrolysis under high pressure; (2) basic studies on thermochemical water-splitting; (3) studies on hydrogen storage.

**Coal Gasification and Liquefaction.** (1) Development of electrical process of gasification; (2) basic studies on gaseous plasmas.

Some of the technology to be developed with possible dates of achievement are given in Table 9–2.

Owing to a new policy on electricity generation (Law of Control of

**Table 9–2.  Timing of Technological Developments**

| Energy | Technology | (Tentative) Operation in: |
|--------|-----------|------------|
| Solar energy | Air conditioning | 1980 |
| | Power Plant: | |
| | 10,000 kW | 1980 |
| | 100,000 kW | 1985 |
| | large power | 2000 |
| Geothermal energy | Hot water power plant | |
| | 10,000 kW | 1978 |
| | 50,000 kW | 1985 |
| | Power plant with very deep well | |
| | 100,000 kW | 1985 |
| | Volcanic power plant | |
| | 10,000 kW | 1980 |
| | 300,000 kW | 1990 |
| Hydrogen | Thermochemical water-splitting | 1985 |
| | Beginning of hydrogen economy | 1995 |
| Coal gasification and/or liquefaction | Syngas plant | |
| | 40,000 m³/d (1.5 million ft³/day) | 1980 |
| | 1,000,000 m³/d (37 million ft³/day) | 1985 |
| | Power plant using gas from coal | |
| | 200,000 kW | 1980 |
| | Liquefaction plant | |
| | 10,000 bpd | 1990 |

January 16, 1974), all electric utilities are pushing hard to find new sources of clean fuel. Geothermal energy is benefiting from such a new orientation, and during the first three months of 1974 about six new plants (ranging from 10 to 500 MWe and totaling 660 MWe) have been announced. Most of these plants will be built by Mitsubishi Heavy Industry (in connection with Mitsubishi Mining) and by Toshiba.

In the same way, there is an active reconsideration, and an acceleration, of hydraulic power plant construction.

Toyo Kogyo is studying wind power, and plans to install a wind plant on top of its administrative building. If successful, another plant could be installed for the Bofu factory (Yamaguchi).

Finally, in addition to the Sunshine program mentioned above, various organizations are devoting a lot of effort to solar energy development: (1) solar heating and air-conditioning (Toshiba, Hitachi, Matsushita); (2) solar heating combined with an oil heating plant (Nippon Oil), aiming at 30 percent fuel oil economy; (3) various water heaters (Nippon Thermo-Industry, Showa Aluminium); (4) photovoltaic batteries: Sharp, the main manufacturer, expects to get a 70 percent decrease in the near term in producing cost of solar batteries (from 30,000 yen ($120) to 10,000 yen ($40) per watt), and plans to invest 700 million yen ($2.8 million) in 1974; (5) special lenses of 150-ft diameter, made of plastic material—with a mechanics allowing best orientation toward the sun, this instrument could allow one to get 3,000°C (5,400°F) to 4,000°C (7,200°F), and operate a 1,000 kW power plant (Ushio Electric and Yupe).

## REFERENCES

### Energy Situation

Coal Mining Industry Rationalization Corporation. "Outline of Business Activities."
Guillain, Robert. "Japon, Troisième Grand." Seuil.
Institute of Energy Economics, Tokyo. "Energy in Japan." (Quarterly reports.)
———— . Private communications.
Overseas Electrical Industry Survey Institute, Tokyo. "Electric Power Industry in Japan, 1972."
*Statistical Handbooks of Japan, 1971–1972.*

### General Organization for Research and Development

"Nouvelles scientifiques et techniques du Japan." Published quarterly by Japanese Embassy in Paris.
OCDE. "Science Policy–Japan."
"White Paper on Scientific Research, 1970." Tokyo.

### Oil and Gas Research and Development
"Japan—An Emerging Power in Offshore Oil and Gas Exploration," *Ocean Industry* (Sept. 1972).

### Electricity Research and Development
Central Research Institute of Electric Power Industry. Descriptive brochures and organization charts.
CRIEPI. Technical Laboratory No. 1 and No. 2 *Annual Reports.*

### Nuclear Energy Research and Development
Japan Atomic Energy Commission. "General Review of the Long-Term Program of the Development and the Utilization of Atomic Energy." June 1, 1972.
Japan Atomic Industrial Forum. "The Role to Be Played by Japan's Nuclear Industry. A Nuclear Vision for Year 2000." Sept. 1971.
*Nouvelles Scientifiques et Techniques du Japon* (Japanese Embassy, Paris). Special issue for nuclear energy, No. 16 (March 1972).
Power Reactor and Nuclear Fuel Development Corporation (PNC). *Annual Reports.*
"Survey of Japan," *Nuclear Engineering International* (July 1973).

### Thermonuclear Fusion and Nonconventional Energy R&D
*Nouvelles scientifiques et techniques du Japon* (Japanese Embassy, Paris). Special issue No. 19 (September 1973).

# Chapter Ten

# Sweden

From the geographical point of view, Sweden is a relatively large European country, with an area of 450,000 square kilometers (176,000 sq. mi), having a length of 1,600 km (1000 mi) and a maximum width of 300 km (180 mi). The northernmost part lies north of the Arctic circle. Sweden's geography has an important influence on its energy situation: water resources are in the north, and its population is in the south, resources and population being separated by long distances; and the climate is very cold. The population in 1972 was slightly over 8 million people, most of them living in the south; with 75 to 80 percent living in urbanized areas. Forests, iron ore and water constitute the main natural resources; the country is highly industrialized (high technical level) with one-third of the economically active population working in industry and less than one-tenth in agriculture. Some 20 to 25 percent of the GNP is exported.

## The Energy Situation

The absence of domestic supplies of fossil fuels, offset by access to hydraulic power, and the high consumption of energy per capita, are some of the characteristic features of the Swedish energy situation, which has been completely dominated by electrical power and petroleum products.

**Conventional Fuels.** Sweden does not produce any oil. About 20 percent of the oil products are refined in the country, the remainder imported. Forecasts are that oil products will continue to be the predominant kind of energy used in industry, as well as in transportation (in 1965, there was one car for every four persons; for 1985 the forecast is one car for every 2.25 persons). All other consumers, such as private dwellings, offices, commerce, schools, and hospitals, are responsible for about 40 percent of the total energy consumption. The consumption of fuel is completely dominated by space heating, including

223

**Table 10–1.  Consumption of Energy in Sweden**

| | Coal | | Oil | | Primary Electricity | | Total Energy | |
|---|---|---|---|---|---|---|---|---|
| | $10^6$ $mt^a$ | % Energy | $10^6$ $mt^a$ | % Energy | $10^9$ kWh | % Energy | $10^6$ tee | tce/cpt$^b$ |
| 1960 | 2.4 | 10% | 11.6 | 73% | 31.1 | 17% | 23.7 | 3.5 |
| 1970 | 1.7 | 4% | 27.1 | 85% | 41.6 | 11% | 47.6 | 5.9 |
| 1971 | 1.5 | 3% | 25.0 | 83% | 52.1 | 14% | 45.5 | 5.7 |

a. Metric tons.
b. Metric ton coal equivalent per capita.

production of hot water. In population centers, heating is provided to an increasing extent in the form of oil-fired district heating; plants for combined power and heat production are used in the largest towns.

Seven enterprises account for more than 90 percent of the supply of oil; two are Swedish-owned, and the others are subsidiary companies of international concerns. A company has recently been formed in order to prospect for oil and gas in Sweden and offshore along the coastline, without any discovery so far. (The absence of an integrated oil industry was not favorable to petroleum energy R&D.)

The small amount of domestic coal is used for processing; coke is imported for the steel industry. Town gas is manufactured and distributed by about twenty municipal works; no natural gas is imported or used at present.

**Electricity.** Up to now, electricity production has been dominated by hydropower. Although hydroelectric power worth exploitation will continue to be available to a certain extent even after 1975, most of the economically profitable sites have already been installed. New construction of hydroplants will be mainly devoted to peak-power regulation capacity (together with gas turbines and simplified condensing plants). Additional new production will therefore consist mainly of thermal power, and nuclear power is expected to play an important role; in the longer term, pumped storage plants and air storage plants will have to be considered in connection with nuclear power plants.

Electricity has a large and growing share of the Swedish energy market, and the electrical supergrid (400 kV) is strong and well integrated and thus able to accommodate very large units. It is expected that nuclear installations will total about 8,000 MWe during the 1970s, as shown in Table 10-2. Moreover, the construction of nuclear plants for combined power and heat production is planned; these plants will be sited within (underground) or outside the city areas; a 10 MW prototype has already been built south of Stockholm, at Agesta. Electric space heating has also been developing very rapidly since the mid-1960s.

In the electricity market, eight enterprises account for a good 90 percent of the produced power. The State Power Board supplies about 45 percent, municipal enterprises about 12–14 percent, and private enterprises (in which the state and/or municipalities are sometimes joint owners) the remainder, either for their own use, or for sale and distribution. Transportation of electricity is more and more performed by the trunk line (200 and 400 kV) of the State Power Board. Distribution is performed by a high number of enterprises (more than 1,000), but here also there is a growing concentration in fewer but larger units. As far as nuclear power is concerned, reactor development was initially started on heavy water/natural uranium. Then the whole program was reoriented on light water reactor systems. Sweden has the only type of LWR

**Table 10–2.  Swedish Nuclear Power Situation, 1970–1980**

| Unit | Power MWe (net) | In Commission | Owner | Type | Main Supplier | Pressure Vessel |
|---|---|---|---|---|---|---|
| Oskarshamn I | 400 | 1971 | OKG | BWR | ASEA–ATOM | Gutehoffnungshutte |
| Ringhals I | 760 | 1974 | SV | BWR | ASEA–ATOM | Babcock & Wilcox, U.K. IHI Co. Ltd., Japan |
| Ringhals 2 | 820 | 1974 | SV | PWR | Westinghouse | Rotterdam Dry Dock |
| Oskarshamn 2 | 580 | 1974 | OKG | BWR | ASEA–ATOM | Uddcomb |
| Barseback I | 580 | 1975 | SSK | BWR | ASEA–ATOM | Uddcomb |
| Ringhals 3 | 900 | 1977/78 | SV | PWR | Westinghouse | Uddcomb |
| Forsmark I | 900 | 1978 | SV | BWR | ASEA–ATOM | Uddcomb |
| Barseback 2 | 580 | 1977 | SSK | BWR | ASEA–ATOM | Uddcomb |
| Oskarshamn 3 | 900 | – | OKG | | | |
| Ringhals 4 | 900 | 1979/80 | SV | PWR | Westinghouse | Uddcomb |
| Forsmark 2 | 900 | 1980 | SV | BWR | ASEA–ATOM | Uddcomb |

Notes:
BWR = Boiling water reactor.
PWR = Pressurized water reactor.
OKG = Oskarshamnsverkets Kraftgrupp AB (private utility).
SV   = Statens Vattenfallsverk (State Power Board).
SSK = Sydsvenska Kraft AB (private utility).

system in industrialized countries that has been developed completely independently of U.S. reactor technology.

The Swedish government has been actively engaged in the creation of a viable nuclear industry. The program is under the Ministry of Industry, created in 1968. It is responsible for general energy policy, executed largely by boards and agencies that are, by tradition, relatively independent. The State Power Board has been engaged in nuclear development work from the very beginning. The government has a half share in both ASEA–ATOM (the main nuclear company) and Uddcomb (pressure vessels, Uddenholm-Combustion Engineering). The main responsibility for research and development rests with AB-Atomenergi, which is government-owned.

### General Organization for Research Development[a]

The total amount of money spent on R&D in Sweden represents about 1.5 percent of the GNP. About two-thirds of the current R&D expenditures are spent on development, which is mainly performed in industry. In 1969–1970, Swedish industry spent about 1,200 million S.Kr ($275 million) in research.

**The Government and Scientific Research.** The institutions responsible for the foundation of the Swedish science policy are the Parliament and the government. For long-term problems, the government consults the Science Advisory Council (established in 1962, eighteen members).

The most important ministries, so far as research is concerned, are the Ministry of Education and the Ministry of Industry (followed by the ministries of Agriculture, of Communications, of the Interior and of Social Welfare). Swedish ministries are comparitively small, working as secretariats for the ministers. Most specialized matters are delegated to attached authorities, which enjoy a high degree of freedom, as mentioned above.

The two most important organizations for research are the Board for Technical Development, and the Research Councils. Moreover, there are government foundations, private foundations (Nobel, Wallenberg, etc.), for a total share of about 10 million S.Kr (2.3 million dollars) per year, and academies: the Royal Academy of Science (the oldest, founded in 1739, which annually decides the award of Nobel Prizes for Chemistry and Physics), the Royal Academy of Agriculture and Forestry, and the very active, important Royal Academy of Engineering Sciences, formed in 1919 to promote industrial development in Sweden (the Academy works with special committees for different technical fields).

a. Many statistics on R&D are somewhat old, going back to a study performed for OECD in 1969. The few recent ones are almost always published in Swedish. Energy R&D statistics have been brought up to date as often as possible.

**The Board for Technical Development (STU).** STU was formed in 1968 by a fusion of the Technical Research Council, the Iron Ore Foundation for Scientific Research and Industrial Development, the Institute for Utilization of Research Results, the Foundation for Exploitation of Research Results and the Inventor's Office. STU is the central authority for support of technical and industrial research, and is responsible for planning and coordination of technical R&D, and for the planning and development of the semi-government-owned cooperative research institutes. The creation of STU was an important step toward a greater centralization and coordination of applied research, which earlier had been very decentralized; the budget for STU in 1970–1971 has been estimated at 95 million S.Kr ($22 million). Research projects on energy are partially coordinated at this level.

**Research Councils.** Of the ten bodies that may be classified as Research Councils, five of them chiefly support basic research (from humanities to nuclear sciences) and come under the Ministry of Education, and the others are under the control of different ministries. All Research Councils have great freedom in the allocation of their resources at their own judgment. They make grants in response to applications from individual researchers, research groups or institutions, or, in some cases, they promote the development of new projects on their own initiative.

The bulk of the fundamental research in Sweden is done in the universities, institutes of technology and other colleges. The research is financed partly through the regular budget, partly by grants from Research Councils and public and private foundations, and for the institutes of technology, partly also by way of contracts. Central supervision is entrusted to the Office of the Chancellor of Universities. The largest government-sponsored laboratories are the Atomic Energy Company (AB-Atomenergi) and the Research Institute of National Defense.

**Research in Industry.** The main branches are chemical, metals, and metal products, machinery (excluding electrical), transportation, and electrical products. The last is the most important, and represents about one-fourth of the total effort (compared to petroleum and coal products, which receive less than 1 percent); it is generally the only branch spending more than 10 percent of its value added on R&D (according to OECD statistics).

A large part of the research connected with industry is carried out in the cooperative research institutes, of varying nature and organization, about half of the most important being semi-governmental, based normally on three-year agreements between the government and an industrial foundation (for wood, textiles, metallurgy, food preservation, corrosion, etc.). They are important factors in Swedish technical research. The large amount of research undertaken by industry is a characteristic feature of Sweden.

## ENERGY RESEARCH AND DEVELOPMENT

### Electric Power

There are a number of institutes dealing with electric power, mainly at Chalmers University of Technology in Gothenburg, and a number of departments and divisions in the Royal Institute of Technology in Stockholm and in the Lund Institute of Technology. Most of these research groups (two to five professors and assistants) work generally on fundamental problems.

Most of the applied research is done by the State Power Board and the biggest power utilities, together with the very powerful company, or group, ASEA (total assets 5.7 billion S.Kr [$1.3 billion] and total sales 4 billion S.Kr [$900 million] in 1971; no precise figure on R&D is available, but it ranks internationally at a high level). A brief review of achievements follows.

**Power Production.** ASEA generators have a worldwide reputation. Research is continued on efficient internal cooling systems.

STAL–LAVAL Turbin A.B. (an ASEA Group company) has the same world position for steam and gas turbines. R&D is performed on large steam turbines for nuclear power stations (up to 600 MW output), and on high rating gas turbines. In 1972 the company signed an agreement with United Aircraft-Connecticut, for the joint development of industrial gas turbines.

ASEA–ATOM builds nuclear plants of Swedish design (BWR), and fabricates fuel. ASEA–ATOM is 50 percent owned by the Swedish Government, and most of the research is done at Studsvik. Technology development is done in Vasteras laboratories (for instance, 9 MW FRIGG loop for testing electrically heated full-scale fuel assemblies for studying core hydraulic characteristics, or use of internal pumps for the main circulation), or in cooperation with Studsvik, such as prestressed-concrete pressure vessels (advantages in safety and construction). Some studies have also been done on underground siting of nuclear power plants, for electricity generation and district heating.

**Power Transmission.** Swedish developments in this field are very prominent. Most of the R&D is performed in the famous Ludvika laboratories.

1. High voltage alternating current (HVAC). Harspranget transmission line (first 400 kV system in the world) came into service in 1952. Then Swedish industry in the late 1960s helped Canada (Province of Quebec) with the installation of a completely new 735 kV system. Although system voltages around 700 to 765 kV are still in the introductory stage, R&D has begun on ultra-high-voltage (UHV) systems, above 1,000 kV. ASEA has been engaged since 1969 in a research and development agreement with the American Electric Power Service Corporation (AEP). After encouraging results of a first phase on possibilities of designing UHV equipment, a second stage includes, for the Swedish partner, development work on UHV equipment and manufacture of a

transformer for 1,500 kV, and its testing. R&D is being performed on insulation and insulator strings (polluters), corona effects (such as radio and television interference and audible noise), and on the magnitude of induced voltages and currents in people and objects under the line. A full-scale prototype of a 1,500 kV transformer had already been built by 1971, 333 MVA (compared to a future three-phase bank of 3,000 MVA).

      2.  High voltage direct current (HVDC).  Swedish industry has been working in this field since the end of the 1920s on development and manufacture of static converters and mercury-arc valves for voltages up to 1,000 kV, or even more. In 1954, Sweden began the world's first power-transmission system using HVDC, linking continental Sweden to the island of Gotland: 20 MW, 200 A, 100 kV. Since then, high-voltage thyristor valves have been developed as an alternative to mercury-arc valves. Possibilities of applications are: long-distance bulk-power transmission from remote energy sources (high interest for northern territories), interconnections between power systems or pools, and a high-power underground distribution system.

      **Energy Storage.**  In addition to continuous interest in pumped storage in a rock cavity (450 m [1,500 ft] below ground level) or compressed-air reservoirs for gas turbines, some studies have been done on thermal energy storage in rock chambers, connected to the possibility of using power produced during the night (period of low demand) by a nuclear power plant. Variations in feed-water temperature are foreseen between day, 73°C (163°F), and night, 217°C (420°F), with excess feed water being recirculated. Most of the research work has been theoretical: circuit design, accumulator design to meet requirements concerning thermal insulation (to avoid exposing the rock walls to daily temperature cycles), avoidance of risk of leakage of slightly radioactive feed water to the surrounding ground water even in case of pipe or tank ruptures, and water chemistry to avoid water containing impurities or dissolved gases from reaching the feed-water circuit. Preliminary investigation has shown major economic and technical benefits: nuclear power plants complemented by thermal stores could take over the medium-load duties from fossil fuel plants at a much earlier date, and eventually the major part of the peak-load duty.

### Nuclear Energy
      This is by far the biggest energy R&D program in Sweden. A part is done by industry (ASEA–ATOM, Uddcomb, Monitor/Westinghouse, Axel-Johnson Group, Sandvik Steelworks, STAL–LAVAL Turbin AB), but most of it is financed by the government. In 1971 the grants-in-aid to AB-Atomenergi totaled about 83 million S.Kr. ($19 million) of a total of 120 million S.Kr. ($28 million). Most of the other funds came from research contracts, domestic and international (75 percent from industrial institutions). In 1972, the total was slightly reduced, the decrease in government's grant to 65 million S.Kr. ($15

million) being almost counterbalanced by an increase of other items and sales.

The AB-Atomenergi has administrative offices in Stockholm, a main laboratory at Studsvik, and a uranium mine at Ranstad. The research program is decided by the Company's Programme Council, which includes representatives from the State Power Board, the Atomic Power Group (Utilities, AKK), ASEA–ATOM, Sandvik and Uddcomb.

**Light Water Reactors.** Development work for Swedish Boiling Water Reactor (BWR) is shared by supplier and AB-Atomenergi. Fuel assemblies are tested in the KRITZ reactivity facility, operating up to 245°C (470°F) (steam is produced by a rapid reduction of pressure). Boiling is studied in the heat-transfer laboratory.

A model pressure vessel in prestressed concrete has been built and operated at pressures up to 215 bars, more than 3 times the working pressure of current BWRs, without any damage to the vessel. Other Scandinavian countries—Denmark, Finland and Norway—participate in these studies, as well as ASEA–ATOM. Reactor designs are being made, together with an assessment of residual verification tasks to be completed before a large nuclear 900 MWe BWR with this type of vessel can be committed.[b]

**Fast Breeders.** This is a long-term program for which international cooperation is actively sought (i.e., an exchange agreement on R&D with the British atomic energy authority, UKAEA, and short-term agreements with Atomics International). The fast zero-power reactor FR–O was decommissioned in 1971 after eight years of experimental work. Research is also done on materials: corrosion and mass transport loops in sodium, and swelling and creeping irradiation of stainless steel in the R–2 (ORR-type) reactor. At this time, there is no fast reactor project, as such.

**Uranium Extraction.** There are huge deposits of uranium shale in the southern central part of Sweden, although the content, 0.03 percent U, is very low.[c] The Ranstad mine and mill (800,000 tons of ore a year) are the main parts of a development program. Preliminary conclusions at the end of 1971 described how the capacity of Ranstad could be extended to about 1,250 tons of uranium per year, i.e., ten times the capacity of the present plant; this should correspond to about half the Swedish requirement for 1985. For further improving the economics of uranium extration, suggestions have been made to extract other metals (primarily vanadium and molybdenum) at the same time, and to

b. The third and last phase of this program was decided in late 1973, covering the period till autumn 1975, costing around S.Kr. 10–12 million ($2.3–2.8 million). At the end of this period, all necessary information to build a reactor with a prestressed-concrete pressure vessel will be available.

c. These shales contain also about 15 percent extractable hydrocarbons.

use the rock excavation left by the large-scale mining of the shale as the lower water reservoir of a pumped storage power plant. Even so, according to 1971 estimates, uranium prices will still be about $8/lb U O. Under a three-year (1972–1974) program of development for 20 million S.Kr. ($4.6 million), AB-Atomenergi and the State Power Board (10 million S.Kr. each) decided to create a reliable basis for cost estimates and cost developments from both technical and environmental points of view.[d]

**Uranium Enrichment.** Enriched uranium is bought from any supplier (U.S., USSR). Studies have been made on centrifugation, and on gaseous diffusion. Sweden joined the Eurodif, a European group on gaseous diffusion under France leadership, and is said to have proposed sites in the northern territories, where huge hydroelectric power could be available. But in early 1974, when the decision was made by France to go ahead and build the Eurodif plant, Sweden had retired from the European association.

### Environmental Aspects

Legislation on pollution was passed in 1969. Fuel oil used for heating must have less than 2.5 percent sulfur content; incidentally, this has given a strong impetus to district heating (fuel oil now, nuclear projects in the future) for big cities. Since January 1973, lead in gasoline must be less than 0.4 gr/l, and leadless gas is being foreseen.

Fundamental research on pollution is performed in universities and institutes of technology, and sponsored by STU.

As far as nuclear safety is concerned, a special budget provides funds for research on safety devices, pressure suppression, reactor containment, and environmental effects, mainly with the studies for locating the reactors near cities. In early 1973, a proposed one-year moratorium on further expansion of nuclear power was defeated by a 218 to 70 vote after debate in the Parliament, leaving intact the present program of expansion until the 1980s. Beyond the present program, however, further nuclear commitments will depend on the findings of special committees studying ECCS, radioactive waste disposal, reprocessing, potential diversion of fissile material, and other points raised by the moratorium backers.

d. An experiment on underground mining has been started in a 100 × 5.0 × 3.5 m gallery at Ranstad (300 × 15 × 12 ft). The same dimensions will also be required by future large-scale operation. The experiment's primary function to give information about the eventual development of methane and radon with underground mining (for radon, a special alpha spectrometer is being used). During the test period at Ranstad, experiment will also be done with varying methods for top heading anchoring, an important economic aspect of all underground mining.

**Energy Conservation**

In 1973 the Royal Academy of Engineering Sciences started two special studies in the energy sector. One is a study of the possible future of energy supply and demand in Sweden and the technology that may create the future energy system. The second is a study concentrated on the potential for energy conservation in heating, transportation and industry. Both of these studies work in close connection with a governmental committee of five members, whose task it is to make a forecast for energy consumption in Sweden in the next fifteen to twenty years, and to assess alternative possibilities regarding the rate of expansion and the mechanisms and structure of the energy sector.

## REFERENCES

UNO and OECD publications.
*Scandinavian Research Guide.*
A.B. Atomenergi, *Annual Reports* and *Research Reports.*
ASEA, *Annual Reports* and ASEA technical information.
Office of Statistics, Stockholm. *Research and Development in Technology and Natural Sciences in Industry.*
Office of Statistics, Stockholm. *Research and Development in Technology and Natural Sciences in Agencies, Research Institutes and Foundations.*
District Heating, Stockholms Elverk (Stockholm).
Swedish State Power Board. *Integration of Nuclear Units in the Swedish Power System.* Geneva IV A/Conf. 49/P/306.
Margen, P. H. *Thermal Energy Storage in Rock Chambers.* Studvik. Geneva IV A/Conf. 49/P/798.
Personnel communications: Gunnar Hambraeus-Director, Royal Academy of Engineering Science; Skjoldebrand, IAEA.

# Chapter Eleven

# United Kingdom

For a long time the foremost industrial country in the world, the United Kingdom has had a difficult period since World War II, and its economy and its industry have undergone cloudy development. Although the United Kingdom has tried to become the world leader in the nuclear energy revolution, and has made some noteworthy achievements, it has not had the success it expected. The biggest change in its energy situation came from the unexpected bonanza of North Sea oil and gas.

There is a very high potential for research and development in Great Britain.

## THE ENERGY SITUATION

Until 1967 the energy economy was based mainly on two resources: domestic coal and imported petroleum.[a] In 1967 the government announced, in a White Paper on Energy Policy, a shift to a four-energy system, adding natural gas and nuclear energy to the other two resources. In fact, nuclear energy has expanded much more slowly than expected (see Table 11-1).

The British fuel and power industries, with the exception of petroleum, are under public ownership. General responsibility for the effective and coordinated development of fuel and power resources lies with the Secretary of State for Trade and Industry, who has an Advisory Council on Research and Development. Research is undertaken by the fuel and fuel-using industries.

**Coal.** Coal has been worked in Britain for over 700 years, and an organized coal-mining industry has been in existence for over 300 years, some

---

a. From 1959 to 1968, the increase of energy consumption in the United Kingdom was quite slow—less than 2 percent per year—compared to an average near 5 percent per year in OECD countries.

**Table 11-1.   Energy Consumption, 1950–1971** *(in million tons coal equivalent)*

|                | 1950  | 1955  | 1960  | 1971  |
|----------------|-------|-------|-------|-------|
| Coal (net)     | 201.1 | 213.5 | 195.5 | 136.7 |
| Oil            | 22.2  | 34.5  | 65.5  | 147.3 |
| Nuclear energy | –     | –     | 0.9   | 9.7   |
| Natural gas    | –     | –     | 0.1   | 25.9  |
| Hydro-Power    | 0.9   | 1.0   | 1.7   | 1.8   |
| *Totals*       | 224.2 | 249.0 | 263.7 | 321.4 |

200 years longer than in many other countries. British coal exports dominated the world market until about 1910. In 1913–the peak production year–the industry produced 287 million tons of coal, exported 94 million tons, and employed over a million workers.

The demand for coal grew steadily until the end of the 1950s. Then growing competition from oil, increasing efficiency in the use of coal, and the reduced requirements of the gas, steel, railway transport and other industries, contributed to a fall in demand, which is continuing. In 1971 the coal mined in the country was responsible for about 43 percent of primary energy consumption.

Nearly half of total consumption is by the electricity authorities, and over one-quarter by domestic and industrial users together, coke ovens are other large users, while consumption by the gas industry is falling rapidly with the switch to natural gas. Consumption by the electricity industry has increased by 38 percent since 1960–to 71.7 million metric tons in 1971–whereas the requirements of most other classes of consumers have declined.

In 1947 the coal mines passed into public ownership by means of the Coal Industry Nationalization Act 1946, which set up the National Coal Board as a statutory corporation to manage the industry. The NCB is answerable to the Secretary of State for Trade and Industry (and through him, to Parliament) for its efficiency.

**Petroleum.**   Full-scale exploration activities in the North Sea began in 1964, following the enactment of the Continental Shelf Act, and the subsequent award of rounds of licenses in 1964, 1965, 1969–1970 and 1971–1972. Oil in significant quantities was first found in the British sector in 1970; development plans were announced for the Forties field to provide for output of 12.5 million metric tons a year (250,000 bpd) by late 1975. Due to other discoveries (such as Auk, Brent, and Piper), a production rate by the mid–1970s of 25 million metric tons a year (500,000 bpd) has been estimated, with a possible rise to 75 or 100 million metric tons (1.5–2 million bpd). Possibly, during the

1980s 50 percent of the energy used by Great Britain will come from the North Sea.

Inland consumption of oil in 1971 totalled about 96 million metric tons (1.9 million bpd), having more than doubled since 1960. Fuel oil consumption constituted 43 percent of the total. The most important uses of gas and diesel oils were for nonindustrial heating, agricultural tractors and the railway; electricity generation accounted for 35.1 percent of total fuel oil consumption (excluding that used in oil refineries). At the end of 1971, rated refinery capacity in Britain amounted to 120 million metric tons a year (2.4 million bpd); it was about 135 million metric tons (2.7 million bpd) at the end of 1973.

The petroleum industry is represented by two very powerful private companies, Royal Dutch-Shell (owned 40 percent by Britain) and British Petroleum, in which the British government owns almost 50 percent of the shares. In 1972 production by these companies (especially in the Middle East, Far East, Africa and Caribbean areas) amounted to about 18 percent of total world production; and they operated a tanker fleet (partly owned by them and partly on charter) amounting to over one-fifth of the world's tanker tonnage.

**Gas.** The single main source of gas in Britain is now natural gas, accounting for well over 90 percent of the total demand in 1971. The first productive well in the North Sea was discovered in 1965. Five major gas fields have now been located, all now in production: Leman Bank, West Sole, Hewett, Indefatigable and Viking. During 1971 the average daily quantity of natural gas received by the Gas Council amounted to some 50 million cubic meters (1,800 million cubic feet).

Three-fifths of all gas sold is for household use and the remainder for industrial and commercial purposes. About 45 percent of the domestic load is used for central heating, with gas fires and cookers accounting for a further 45 percent. In industries, gas has traditionally been used extensively when an accurate control of temperature is required (pottery, some iron and steel products), or as a chemical feedstock and in bulk fuel markets.

The Gas Act of 1948 brought the gas industry under public ownership and control, with a Gas Council coordinating twelve area Gas Boards. The British Gas Corporation now has taken the place of the Gas Council. Appointed by the Secretary of State for Trade and Industry, it is both a coordinating council and, since 1965, a trading body.

**Electricity.** As Britain has abundant supplies of coal, together with good rail and water transport for moving it, most of its electricity is produced by coal-fired steam-generating stations. Since 1965, nuclear energy has become relatively important.

The output capacity of the generating stations of the electricity boards at the end of 1971 totalled 60,789 MW, an increase of nearly 50 percent since 1965. Generation for the public supply in Great Britain reached nearly 230 TWh ($10^{12}$ Wh) in 1971; conventional steam power stations provided 88 percent of the total, nuclear stations 10 percent, and hydro, 2 percent. A high rate of expansion of output has been a feature of the industry since its earliest years, but the rate has decreased considerably in recent years (net overcapacity). Generation of electricity outside the public supply system is relatively small.

The electricity authorities take nearly half the British consumption of coal and about 10 percent of the consumption of oil. Many stations have been converted to dual firing. The average thermal efficiency of conventional steam stations rose from 20.75 percent in 1947 to 29.1 percent in 1971; the twenty most efficient stations had an average thermal efficiency of 32.86 percent in 1970–1971.

Some 10 percent of Britain's public-supply generation was in nuclear power stations in 1971, and the proportion is expected to rise to about one-sixth by the mid-1970s. Britain accounts for some 25 percent of world nuclear generation. Under the first commercial program, originally announced in 1955 but since twice modified, nine stations—with a total design capacity of 4,500 MW—were in operation in 1971; these stations, like Calder Hall and Chapelcross, are all Magnox stations. Under a second program announced in 1964 and extended in 1965, a further 8,000 MW of nuclear capacity is planned, of which 6,500 MW will be commissioned by 1976; the reactor design chosen for the program is based on the AGR at Winscale (slightly enriched uranium dioxyde fuel canned in stainless steel). A large prototype fast reactor (PFR) of 250 MW capacity is to be commissioned in 1974 at Dounreay.

The development of the grid system has made the British system the largest fully interconnected power network under unified control in the world.

In England and Wales, electricity is generated and transmitted by the Central Electricity Generating Board (CEGB), and distributed by twelve separate area electricity boards, coordinated by the Electricity Council. In Scotland, two boards (NSHEB or North of Scotland Hydro Electric Board, and SSEB or South of Scotland Electricity Board) both generate and distribute electricity.

To summarize the energy situation in Great Britain: (1) very old, and nationalized, coal industry (the biggest in Europe); (2) large electricity system, still mainly based on coal, but with a growing nuclear share; there was some slowing down, due to overcapacity; largest electricity organization in the Western world; (3) growing national gas industry; (4) two major oil companies, and important discoveries of oil fields in the British sector of the North Sea.

### General Organization for Research and Development

The government is the main source of funds for scientific R&D as a whole, though private industry contributes a larger proportion of funds for civil R&D. Considerable sums are also provided by public corporations, independent trusts and foundations, and learned societies.

Total expenditure in Britain on scientific R&D has risen from £657.7 million ($1.5 billion) in 1961–1962, to £1.016 billion ($2.4 billion) in 1968–1969, while remaining at about 2.7 percent of the gross national product at factor cost. The proportions of total research and development carried out in the various sectors have not changed appreciably since 1964–1965, with the government (including the research councils) carrying out 25 percent and universities between 7 and 8 percent. The proportion of research and development financed by the government is slowly decreasing, but remains at about 50 percent. In 1970–1971, total government support was estimated at £580 million ($1.39 billion), £230 million for defense ($550 million), £350 million ($840 million) for civil sector.

**The Government and Scientific Research.** The Central Advisory Council for Science and Technology was established in January 1967, under the chairmanship of the Chief Scientific Advisor to the Government, to advise the government on the most effective national strategy for the use and development of the country's scientific and technological resources.

Under the Science and Technology Act of 1965, central responsibility for basic and applied civil science rests with the Secretary of State for Education and Science who, advised by the Council for Scientific Policy (now changed into the Advisory Board for the Research Councils), is responsible for directing and financing the Research Councils. Responsibility for technology rests with the Secretary of State for Trade and Industry; other government departments (Transport, Environment, Defense, and so on) are responsible for research and development related to their executive responsibilities. It can be stated that R&D in Britain is less centralized than in France, but more centralized than in Germany.

The Department of Education and Science (DES) is responsible for government policy regarding the universities through the University Grants Committee, and for basic and applied civil science mainly through the five Research Councils: the Science Research Council, the Medical Research Council, the Agricultural Research Council, the Natural Environment Research Council and the Social Science Research Council. The Science Research Council coordinates the space research program. The total grant-in-aid to the Research Councils for 1970–1971 was about £110 million ($264 million); current funding is estimated at about £130 million ($312 million) in 1974–1975. Of the total estimated university expenditure on scientific research in the academic year 1969–1970 (over £90 million [$216 million]), the largest government contribution, £60 million ($144 million) was through the University Grants Committee. Scientific research in the universities is also supported through other channels, such as other government departments, the Royal Society, industry and the independent foundations (all of them, about 30 percent of the total).

The Department of Trade and Industry (DTI), which came formally into being in 1970, took over responsibility for the United Kingdom Atomic

Energy Authority (AEA) and the National Research Development Corporation, as well as most of the nonaviation functions of the former Ministry of Technology. The responsibilities of the DTI now include that for civil aviation and the sponsorship of most industries (excluding aircraft) in both the public and private sectors. The DTI is responsible for research into safety and health of mineworkers. The coal, electricity and gas industries settle their general program of research with the Secretary of State for Trade and Industry, who is assisted by an Advisory Council on Research and Development. The public corporations that run the nationalized industries have their own research organizations.

The DTI has direct control of six industrial research establishments: the National Engineering Laboratory, the National Physical Laboratory, Warren Spring Laboratory (which works on air pollution, clearance of oil and recyling of waste), the Laboratory of the Government Chemist, the Safety and Mines Research Establishment, and Torrey Research Station. The total net expenditure of the DTI for 1970–1971 on these establishments was about £12 million ($29 million). The DTI also sponsors research by grants-in-aid to research associations and by extramural contracts with industry and universities.

Following suggestions contained in the Rothschild Report on R&D laying down the principle of the "customer-contractor basis,"[b] the system of control depends essentially on Requirement Boards deciding on research objectives, and by whom the work can best be done.

The Requirements Boards (in effect, "the customers") have a twofold function in the technological and industrial fields within which they operate: (1) to help the department identify those areas within its jurisdiction that will most benefit from government-supported R&D; (2) to determine the objectives and balance of R&D programs to support departmental policies, within the board allocation of funds available to them.

The initiative for new research may come from the boards themselves, from the DTI customer division, or through bids for support from potential contractors.

Within their terms of reference (and subject to the approval of the Minister for Aerospace and Shipping), the Requirements Boards have wide responsibilities for commissioning R&D in the Industrial Research Establishments, the UKAEA (nonnuclear), the Research Associations, industrial organizations, the universities and Research Councils. (In the addendum, analyses are given of R&D gross expenditure for DTI by main objective and by main contractors for 1972–1973 and 1973–1974.)

The National Research Development Corporation (NRDC) is an independent public corporation to promote the adoption by industry of new products and processess developed in government laboratories, universities and elsewhere, advancing money where necessary to bring them to a commercially

b.   "The customer says what he wants, the contractor does it; and the customer pays."

viable stage; and to speed up technological advance by investing money with industrial firms for the development of their own inventions and projects. Financed by government loans through the DTI, the borrowing power of NRDC, originally £5 million ($12 million), has been progressively increased to £50 million ($120 million).

There are research associations with firms having similar interests to the government. The research associations carry out industrial research cooperatively and are co-financed by grants administrated by the DTI. They are autonomous bodies governed by their own councils, the members of which are mostly representatives from industry. Progressively, through a reduction of the DTI grants, industry bears an increasing proportion of the cost of its associations.

**Industrial Research.** The greater part of industrial research in Britain is undertaken in the research organizations of the largest firms and in government research establishments. Research organizations in industry vary widely between the largest firms employing thousands of qualified staff and some employing few.

Total expenditure of scientific R&D carried out within industry's own establishments or financed by industry in 1969–1970 was £711 million ($1.7 billion), covering private industry, public corporations, and the industrial research associations already mentioned. Of this total more than £500 million ($1.2 billion) represent expenditure from industry's own funds and some £200 ($480 million) expenditure by industry from government funds. Most of the work (roughly 90 percent) is carried out within private industry, 6 percent is carried out in the laboratories of the public corporations, and 2 percent in research associations; while a further 2 percent is financed by industry but carried out elsewhere. Of the £697 million ($1.67 billion) spent on work carried out within industry, about 10 percent, £68 million ($163 million) was capital expenditure on land, buildings, plant and equipment; 90 percent was current expenditure. The relative importance of capital and current expenditure is similar for private industry, public corporations and research associations.

Private industry devotes the greater part of its resources and effort to development (over three-quarters of the total expenditure). The public corporations are interested in rather long-term projects; less than half their expenditure is on development and about one half is on applied research. The industrial research associations spend a fifth of their resources on basic research— compared with private industry, which spends about 4 percent; this latter percentage is similar to that in industry in the United States.

The aerospace industry has spent about £170 million ($408 million) for R&D, including air-cushioned vehicles; on motor vehicles about £50 million ($120 million). Of the £186 million ($446 million) spent by the electrical engineering industry, 65 percent was devoted to electronic components and apparatus, including telecommunications, and 13 percent to electrical machinery. Finally, from the £ 109 million ($260 million) spent by the chemical industries, about 11 percent went to petroleum industry.

## ENERGY RESEARCH AND DEVELOPMENT

The fact that most of the energy industry (apart from petroleum) belongs to the public sector has resulted in a good deal of research and development related to energy in the United Kingdom, with a fair balance between short-term and long-term objectives.

### Coal Research and Development

For a number of years the National Coal Board spent just over £ 4 million per year on specific research and development programs. The NCB has two research organizations: a Mining Research and Development Establishment near Bretby, Derbyshire, for the investigation of underground problems, developing new machines and testing equipment; and a Coal Research Establishment at Stoke Orchard, near Cheltenham, Gloucestershire, providing facilities for fundamental research and coal applications.[c] A few examples of R&D during recent years are shown here.

### Mining Research and Development

Emphasis is being given to improving reliability and efficiency of existing machines and systems for the short term. For the longer term, the principal developments are related to the effects of the depths at which mining is and will be carried out in Great Britain; long-term evaluations are being made of the feasibility of extending systems for manless operations and remote control together with their effect on safety and efficiency. The overriding aim at all times is to reduce the hazards of mining.

To refine and improve the performance of the main power-loading equipment in advancing systems, early experiments with ROLF (remotely operated longwall face) demonstrated the possibility of remote control of coal face equipment, but also exposed the limitations of electrohydraulic controls of roof supports and the crudeness of prototype power-loader steering. An all-hydraulic support control system has been developed; and a nucleonic sensing device to steer the machine within the seam has been introduced, feeding to a minicomputer. Semiautomatic control of face and face-end operations is now possible. Various sets of automatic steering equipment based on the production prototype were ordered for installations during the last few years.

In the ancillary operations, improvements have also been made. In particular, various systems for the elimination of stables at both main- and

---

c. There is also the well-known Safety and Mines Research Establishment, from the DTI. In 1972–1973, expenditures for SMRE were £ 562,000 ($1.35 million), and for 1973–1974, £ 522,000 ($1.25 million).

tailgate have been developed, including the more difficult and congested main-gate environment, or for seam sections below four feet. Several separate systems are currently in advanced stages of development and extension of these into general use is expected to be rapid.

Materials transport systems, both to and from the face, have been developed due to the increased rate of extraction and face advance, such as remotely controlled high-capacity coal transport systems involving conveyor/bunker complexes. High-speed manriding systems have been developed that are capable of safely transporting the face labor-force at speeds of over 20 mph.

Research has been directed toward experimental confirmation, by a number of methods, of the channelling of seismic waves in coal seams, following earlier theoretical work, so as to be able to detect unknown faulting up to 300 yd forward of the face line. Furthermore, refinements in seismic methods of detection have enabled larger faults to be located with improved accuracy and certainty from the surface, by large-scale testing of methods and equipments.

R&D is also performed to decrease the production of dust and fine coal by developing rock- and coal-cutting equipment of high mechanical efficiency, such as drums with small numbers of large cutting picks, flushed internally by water and operating at much lower rotational speeds than normal. Similar developments have been made to reduce and control the heat at the coal face, and to reduce the contamination of the air by methane migration. Dust physics is studied in a specialized laboratory at Swadlincote Test Site, containing both a high-speed and low-velocity wind tunnel.

On the surface, research is continued on coal preparation plant design to permit automatic operation in combination with sampling and blending facilities to ensure a consistently acceptable product. Radiometric ash monitors and homogenizing bunkers have been developed to ensure consistent ash contents in power-station fuel.

Finally, the Mining Research and Development Establishment works continuously to improve basic electrical techniques (such as methane monitoring, intrinsically safe power supplies, and small digital computers for collieries), instrumentation, control and power engineering. It also performs much research on design projects, engineering principles, metallurgy and materials (cutting tools, wear of materials used with fire-resistent fluids, corrosion protection), and develops proving and acceptance techniques and mining trials and investigation.

### Coal Processing Research and Development

All the R&D programs on coal utilization for the future are very strongly market-oriented. The NCB's largest market is electricity. Work was initiated in 1966 on fluidized bed combustion with the objective of developing power-plant boilers having lower capital and operating cost than pulverized fuel boilers. The research has been successfully performed at the NCB's Coal Research Establishment (CRE) and at British Coal Utilization Research Association (BCURA, now a unit of NCB) laboratories, Leatherhead. In the past four years attention has been given to the ability of fluidized combustion to retain sulfur from the fuel by adding limestone or dolomite to the bed. An extensive research program on this aspect (jointly financed by the NCB and the Office of Coal Research, Department of the Interior) was carried out at both CRE and BCURA laboratories. It has established the technical feasibility of reducing $SO_2$ emission from coal-fired fluidized bed combustors to the levels required. The effect of plant operating parameters on the efficiency of the reduction in $SO_2$ emission has been determined; under optimum conditions, it is possible to retain 95 percent of the sulphur by the addition of about 1.8 times the theoretical requirement of limestone. This would allow an emission of 100 ppm of $SO_2$ in flue gas to be achieved even when burning a coal containing 3 percent sulfur. Responsibility for promoting this technique abroad has been passed by NCB to the National Research Development Corporation.

Coking is the second largest market. Research is continuously carried on to extend the range of coals from which metallurgical coke of the best quality can be made, to include those hitherto regarded as unsuitable for the purpose. Blends of coal for coke-making have been developed, which use prime coking coals as additives rather than as major constituents. This research has highlighted the need for considerable refinement in the technique of coal blending, with close control of the preparation of coke smalls at washeries. An effort is also devoted to the methods to assess the strength of coke, for improving the measurement method, and for enlarging its range of application. There is also an investigation on steam assisted vacuum filtration.

In the commercial/residential market, some developments are having an important impact on coal requirements and marketing procedures, with a new generation of appliance design intended to give a wide range of sizes and styles to meet all domestic needs, burning bituminous coal smokelessly ("smoke eaters"). An automatic ash removal system for industrial boilers has been developed with a manufacturer. Projects related to control of the environment and the use of waste include methods of pollution control at coal processing plants (collaboration with CEGB on NOx measurements) and basic work on the formation of emissions. Research has also been in progress on making a skid-resistant paving material by heat treatment of colliery spoil.

A large activity of CRE is related to the aim of creating materials of high value derived from coal, such as special coke and carbons for the electrometallurgical industries by direct extraction of coal, using solvents (extractions of coal with "supercritical" gases is also studied). The mixture obtained by treating coal with a solvent without subsequently separating undissolved coal and mineral matter is referred to as "coal digest." This mixture is very similar to pitch, for which it has been successfully used as an alternative in making briquettes. Research is also being continued on the process for making carbon fiber, and has resulted in a great improvement in mechanical properties; fiber being produced is now as strong as and stiff as the best available fiber (made from polyacrylonitrile by NRDC patents). Many other products from coal are being developed, including pitch plastics, Hyload sheets for roofing, sealants, foams, and coal-tar based resins.

**Reclamation.** During World War II, there was extensive surface mining of coal, reaching an output of 8 million metric tons by 1945, and progressively increasing to 14 million metric tons in 1958. Since 1958, output has been controlled and reduced to between 5 and 7 million metric tons, which has included a substantial proportion of anthracite and other scarce coals needed for the smokeless fuel market; output increased again to around 10 million metric tons a year in 1971–1972. Since 1952, the total area of land used for opencast work, including reclamation, has been about 150,000 acres. Each site must be individually authorized by the Secretary of State for Trade and Industry, and there are local hearings in which community authorities and citizens participated.

Various methods of surface mining and land restoration have been developed. Land may be restored to woodland (in South Wales, for instance), to agriculture, or, recently, to Country Parks. Agricultural rehabilitation takes a five-year period, in order to reestablish a good soil structure. The British technique for success during this phase is based on segregating and saving the topsoil during the mining process itself, so that it may be replaced.

NCB has always paid close attention to restoration. Current restoration techniques are generally considered as unsurpassed elsewhere in the world, the closest rival being the brown coal industry of West Germany. On a national basis, NCB's restoration cost averaged £230 ($550) (1971 estimate), per acre.

**Coal Gasification.** Experimental work on the production of methane by hydrogenating coal was pioneered by the United Kingdom gas industry in 1937 (research group at Leeds, led by F. J. Dent). Two Lurgi plants were built at Coleshill and Westfield, enriching the Lurgi gas with light petroleum fractions. Two other plants were built during the 1950s at Solihull and Leatherhead, employing the slagging process for ash disposal as an improvement (Gas Council, BCURA, and Ministry of Power). But the availability of cheap oil in the 1960s led to the abandonment of all the proposed processes.

There is now an agreement between British Gas and Conoco to continue work on the Westfield Lurgi coal gasification plant in Scotland. British Gas will also conduct trials at Westfield for the U.S. Office of Coal Research and the American Gas Association, with four American types of coals (OCR/AGA-sponsored program estimated at £1 million).

A second joint development associates National Research and Development Corporation, British Coal Utilization Research Association, and the

American Cogas Development Company (including FMC Corporation), to design, construct and operate a large pilot plant using the Cogas process (extension of FMC's Coed process).

Finally, some researchers have explored the possibility of using a nuclear reactor to provide the heat required for gasification in the context of the manufacture of iron and steel, using the Dragon type reactor.

But at present, the NCB is doing no experimental work on coal gasification, although proposals have been made to the EEC in connection with power generation for a project on coal gasification to low Btu gas.

### Petroleum Research and Development

Research into problems of petroleum technology is carried out mainly by the leading oil companies, which have also endowed research at the universities on a substantial scale. Research centers are situated at Sunbury-on-Thames (the British Petroleum Company), Thornton in Cheshire, Woodstock in Kent (Shell), and Abingdon in Berkshire (Esso). Only the first one covers the full range of petroleum research and development, from geology and production to product utilization and petroleum chemicals.

In general the remainder are concerned with the evolution of new and improved fuels and lubricants and the development of new uses for petroleum products and of new products based on petroleum, especially chemicals. It is well known that very much more money is spent on chemical research than is spent on oil research. This reflects the fact that the chemical industry is generally more research-intensive than the oil industry because of the complexity and changing nature of the chemicals produced and of the technology used for their manufacture. Moreover, for companies like Royal-Dutch-Shell and Exxon, most of the research, and especially the research for exploration and production, is performed in the mother countries, i.e. the Netherlands for RDS (Risjwick and Amsterdam laboratories), and the United States for Exxon (Linden and Houston laboratories).

**British Petroleum.** The principal research center—more than 1,700 people, one of the largest in Europe—is at Sunbury-on-Thames, near London. Specialized work is handled at other centers in Britain, France and West Germany.

Exploration techniques (for which BP has a high reputation), including work on reservoir evaluation and crude oil production, are examined and developed at Sunbury. Fundamental petroleum research and process development (such as BP Ferrofining process and BP isomerization process) is also handled at Sunbury. Applied research is carried out at the Kent (Isle of Grain) and Llandarcy (South Wales) refineries in Britain, and at the Dunkirk and Lavera refineries in France, and at the Neuhof refinery at Hamburg, West Germany. Product development is handled at Sunbury, the Llandarcy refinery, the Dunkirk refinery and at centers in Hamburg.

Apparently there is no important program on tertiary recovery, because BP had generally good reservoirs.

BP is sponsoring a broad study on a world energy model with Queen Mary College (Professor Deam, formerly from the BP staff).

**Royal-Dutch-Shell.** The RDS group is said to spend about 1.1 percent of net sales proceeds in R&D (exploration and production, natural gas, marine, refining, chemicals, etc.). No detailed information could be collected on the budgets per country, or per item, nor on the research programs.

**Esso Research Center, Abingdon.** The Esso Research Center is a £4 million ($9.6 million) complex of research facilities. About 380 chemists, physicists, chemical and mechanical engineers and supporting staff are engaged in research in support of worldwide Exxon activities. Work ranges from continuous engine testing to check and improve existing products, to the pioneering of completely new techniques. The research center, while having interests in many aspects of petroleum and chemical technology, specializes in work on lubricants, gas, heavy fuel oils and additives, in close relationship with the other European laboratories in Brussels, Hamburg, Rome and Rouen.

A major research program at the Abingdon center is the development of a desulfurization process for high-sulfur, heavy fuel oil. The process, called the Chemically Active Fluidized Bed (CAFB), uses a shallow fluidized bed of lime, which removes almost all of the sulfur in oil. The hot gasified oil is then combusted in a slightly modified conventional burner unit (a bonus is that the process also removes vanadium). The six-phase program aims at the conversion of a 100 MW power station in the United States. The program was in phase II at time of writing, with a pilot plant CAFB gasifier of 10 million Btu/hr capacity (equivalent to about 1 MW of power-generation capacity). This program is actively supported by the U. S. Environmental Protection Agency (£250,000 [$600,000] since June 1970 for Phases I and II).

### Gas Research and Development

The British Gas Corporation has a worldwide reputation for its technology and experience. Its annual R&D budget is £5 to 6 million ($12–14.4 million). In 1971–1972 the main items of the R&D budget were:

| | | |
|---|---:|---:|
| Production and treatment | £516,000 | $1,240,000 |
| Storage | 100,000 | 240,000 |
| Transmission | 1,100,000 | 2,640,000 |
| Distribution | 480,000 | 1,152,000 |
| Utilization | 2,700,000 | 6,480,000 |
| General studies | 210,000 | 504,000 |

R&D is performed in four Research stations: (1) London Research Station, for Physical, Chemical and Life sciences, applied mathematics and computing; (2) Midlands Research Station, for gas production and industrial gas utilization; (3) Engineering Research Station at Killingworth, Northumberland, for transmission, distribution, storage and compression; (4) Watson House in London, for domestic and commercial gas utilization and appliance testing and approval.

**Production and Treatment.** With the advent of natural gas, production research is now aimed primarily at a synthetic substitute for North Sea supplies.

In recent years, the effort devoted to the development of both catalytic and noncatalytic processes for the manufacture of natural-gas substitutes has been substantially increased. The raw materials of choice are petroleum-based, and processes suitable for crude oil and distillates of various kinds are at different stages of development. The most advanced are those based on the Catalytic Rich Gas Process (CGR), in which light hydrocarbon oils are converted with steam into a methane-rich gas, under conditions which have been improved and give improved catalyst performance and higher process efficiencies. One variant, the CRG Hydrogasification Process, has been successfully demonstrated on a full commercial scale at a converted town-gas plant. These CRG-based SNG processes have been adopted by various U.S. gas transmission and utility companies.

There is also increased development of the fluidized bed hydrogenation process for gasification of crude oil and heavy fractions. A pilot-scale plant has been constructed for conducting feedstock classification trials, supplementing the collaborative development work at semicommercial scale being pursued with the Osaka Gas Company. Methods of controlling the combustion properties of the product gas are also being investigated.

Work is also performed on the determination of the accurate composition of gases from new and existing sources, on odorants added to natural gas, on the thermodynamic properties of natural gas mixtures (for design of compressors, high-pressure transmissions mains, and heat exchangers for liquefaction plants).

**Storage.** Work is carried out on the storage of natural gas both in the gaseous and the liquid form. The former includes structural studies of storage vessels and optimization studies, and analysis of potential fatigue-failure situations in welded vessels. Work on liquefaction is concerned with the effective pretreatment of the gas to remove carbon dioxide and water.

**Transmission.** Great emphasis is placed on the integrity and safety of high-pressure pipelines and work on the design, and evaluation of pipelines and their components is tackled from both theoretical and practical viewpoints.

Theoretical studies into the mechanisms that control the initiation and propagation of pipeline cracks, and the development of structural analysis techniques to predict the behavior of highly stressed components are undertaken. Work is also being done to determine the fatigue life of components under cyclic pressure conditions, together with extensive research on metallurgy (including behavior of heat-affected zones of welded pipelines), welding (new techniques such as explosive, friction and electron beam), and corrosion and coatings.

Pipes and components (such as compressors, pressure and flow-regulator valves, and release and slam-shut valves) are evaluated and tested in a unique flow test facility at Low Thornley, with a wide range of operating pressures from 5 in.wg to 1,000 psi) and flows.

Mathematical models and programs for the control and operation of the transmission grid, and network-analysis computer programs used in the design and operation of pipe works, have also been developed.

**Distribution.** The low-pressure distribution network comprises over 100,000 miles of mainly cast-iron pipes. It is a system built up over the years that span the industry's transition from one based primarily on coal gas to one based on oil and now on North Sea gas (oil gas and natural gas are dry, and cause a drying-out problem in mains accustomed to wet gas like that based on coal).

Research and development work was devoted to studying the effect of natural gas on vegetation and the measures to prevent damage; to improve equipment for use in field operations, including flow-stopping equipment and equipment for excavation and for cleaning of live mains; to leak-sealing methods, including the use of gas-borne and "fill-and-drain" sealants, and of a minimum-cost approach to the choice of leakage-control action; and to the evaluation, specification and development of plastic pipe and fittings for use in new mains and for insertion replacement in old mains.

**Industrial and Large Commercial Utilizations.** About one-third of the money spent for R&D on utilization of gas is devoted to the industrial and large commercial sector. New large-scale applications and new plant and equipment are being developed (mainly at the Midlands Research Station), with increasing concern for the control of the environment, both inside and outside the factory. Many unexploited opportunities remain.

The R&D program is concerned with combustion and the design of burners, with aerodynamics and heat transfer, with controls, and with the development of specific kinds of applications of gas firing, for instance: in steam-raising power generation, metal heating and melting, and in the pottery and brick industries.

Major activities are directed at ensuring safety in gas-fired plants and at satisfactory performance of large steam boilers, particularly with dual-fuel burners (related to "interruptible" supplies), such as comprehensive trials of the performance of a number of shell boiler-burner combinations when changed over to natural-gas firing. Research has gone into the development of process-heating plants, the emphasis being on the exploitation of the smaller rapid-heating machines and on the development of improved recuperative burners. Part of the studies on steam-raising (field trials, firing shell, water tube and other types of boiler) are made in relation with the Central Electricity Generating Board. An effort is oriented toward a total energy concept, using heat from the exhaust gases of turbines or reciprocating engines.

**Domestic and Other Massed-Produced Systems.**  With almost two-thirds of the overall R&D budget, the aim is the improvement of appliances and services provided by the gas industry for the benefit of domestic and commercial consumers, all the aspects of utilization being covered.

The Combustion Group studies the physical and chemical mechanisms of combustion (better ignition and combustion systems for all types of appliance). The Thermal Engineering Group studies how the best use can be made of the heat released by combustion and the best way of releasing the waste gases. These are supplemented by environmental engineering (to measure, for instance, the sound output from appliances or the environmental effects of heating systems), and materials research (corrosion, plastics).

Development of appliances covers all sectors (including conversion from manufactured to natural gas), from cooking and catering to air-conditioning, water heating, burners, etc.

**General Utilization and General Studies.**  Research is done on fundamental properties and reactions of fuel gases and flames, in order to be able to predict flame behavior over a wide range of conditions, to understand better the mechanism of formation of carbon and other products of hydrocarbon pyrolisis.

New analytical techniques and new techniques applied to operational problems of the industry are continuously developed, together with long-term research in pure physics and chemistry (transport-property, surface chemistry, etc.)

### Electricity Research and Development

The Electricity Council, in consultation with the Secretary of State for Trade and Industry, is responsible for drawing up a general program of research, comprising direct research carried out by the electricity boards themselves, supported by cooperative research with selected industrial research associations and by research contracts placed with universities and other organizations. The council itself is empowered to conduct research. It is advised by the Electricity Supply Research Council. Collaboration on research between the supply industry and the plant manufacturers is coordinated by the Power Engineering Research Steering Committee (PERSC), set up in 1966.

The main research establishments of the industry are run by the CEGB and comprise the Central Electricity Research Laboratories at Leatherhead, Surrey; the Berkeley Laboratories in Gloucestershire, concerned with nuclear problems; and the Engineering Laboratories at Marchwood, on Southampton Water. CEGB devoted £9.6 million ($23 million) to R&D (not including depreciation of equipment, rents, interest, and so on) in 1971–1972. Research on distribution technology and electricity utilization is undertaken at the Electricity Council Research Center at Capenhurst, Cheshire, and by the area boards.

Both Scottish electricity boards carry out research and experimental work either on their own or in cooperation with other electricity authorities. The SSEB undertakes a wide range of research and development work, both independently and in conjunction with the universities and manufacturers, and, with the NSHEB, is associated with the activities of the Electricity Council and CEGB.

The R&D discussed below is chiefly that performed or sponsored by CEGB, whose major part is related to improvements in the performance and availability of generating and transmission plants. Effort is also being expanded on the establishment of basic data for new designs of equipment, on environmental matters, and into possible types of nuclear reactors (in connection with AEA).

**Conventional Production (Coal and Oil).**  By far the greater part of CEGB's production is by coal-fired power station boilers. For this reason, many studies are related to combustion problems. For instance, based on aerodynamic studies of the classifiers associated with the mills, improvements in the present degree of separation of fine and coarse particles (returned to the mills for regrinding) aim at a reduction of unburnt carbon in the ash, and to less ash deposited on the walls of the combustion chambers of the boilers. Automatic control systems are continuously developed, improved and tested, supplemented by new instrumentation (such as the electronic gauge "Hydrastep" for measuring water levels in boiler drums).

Metallurgy research and welding research support studies on pressure-vessel integrity, and on the growth of cracks in heavy section metal structures stressed by high pressures and operating under high temperatures; correlations between general creep properties of the material and the propagation of defects have been established, using new equipment to measure crack growth up to $700°C$ ($1290°F$). An experimental facility has been built to carry out internal pressure testing of large vessels (8 cells), at operating temperature and pressure. Full-size steampipe joints have been developed and tested (for AGR nuclear stations).

For improving turbine designs, stress analysis is performed with new types of strain gauges (good stability at high temperature), as well as methods of measuring running clearances between rotating and fixed components, in radial and axial directions. Turbine behavior is being studied by measuring the vibration pattern with accelerometers. Efforts are being made to develop a systematic diagnostic technique that would enable remedial measures to be planned well in advance of an overhaul.

Studies are in progress related to stresses and vibration fatigue at end windings of the stator of present-day 500 and 600 MW alternators (where higher current density in the conductors and magnetic flux in the stator iron impose higher temperatures and forces due to large eddy currents in the end laminations). Hot spots are found with a method using infrared photography. The distribution of temperature in the winding while a generator is in normal or faulty operation is also measured with a telemetry system fixed to the rotor. Drying-out methods of stator insulation (after a long shut-down) have been developed, and are extended with the hope of establishing conditions that may dispense completely with the need for drying out large machines.

Novel wind-tunnel techniques have been developed to estimate both mean and fluctuating wind-induced stresses in cooling-tower shells. Scale models can be tested for new power stations under simulated atmospheric conditions. A mechanical draft cooling tower has been developed (35 cells of cross-flow fans between the packing and the tower shell), and tested on a scale model. If successful, it would reduce dramatically the impact on visual amenity (one unit instead of three conventional natural draft towers for a 1,000 MW power station).

A new method has been developed for measuring the natural frequencies, mode shapes and damping of large multiflue chimneys from their response to wind excitation. It is expected that the results (already tested at some plants) will be applied to the assessment of the wind loading on future large chimneys. Wind-tunnel experiments are also assisting chimney design for gas-turbine power stations in urban or industrial sites where the stack height is critical, to study the ground-level concentrations of plume gas to be expected over the regions downwind of the stations.

**Nuclear Power.**   Inside CEGB, the main efforts on Magnox reactors are related to fuel performance and development of canning material to increase the "in-reactor" life of the elements, and to the research for inhibitors to reduce the rate of corrosion of mild steel components, the corrosion being carefully monitored (with a new instrument using a laser beam to measure the thickness of oxide).

Supporting research work during the construction of the AGR reactor power stations is continuing (AGR fuel cycle simulator, studies on the nature of contact between solids in hostile environment).

Many evaluations are made of possible reactor types. As is well known, CEGB is hesitating, for the third program, between continuing gas-cooled reactors (on which £1.25 billion [$2.5 billion]) have already been invested or committed), possibly with HTR development, or on the steam generating heavy water reactor (SGHWR), which has been developed as an alternative by AEA, or possibly on LWR. The decision has not been urgent, due to the slowing down of electricity consumption during recent years, which has led, as noted above, to some overcapacity.[d] The development of the fast breeder reactor adds to the dilemma, for as this advances and a decision on the next thermal reactor type is delayed, the interval between the stage when large-scale prototypes of each can be ordered diminishes. As there is already experience on the operation of prototype- or commercial-scale water reactors, only a small program of research has been initiated into the technology of SGHWR or LWR.

A research program has been established to study the basic problems of safety and reliability of fast breeder reactors. Specific advances have been made in instrumentation for monitoring impurities in sodium and in methods for extracting particles and gas bubbles from the flowing metal. A million volt electron microscope is also extensively used in studies on radiation damage in fast reactor materials.

**Transmission.** Research activity is continuing related to the 400/275 kV supergrid, mainly to reduce maintenance requirements and to establish data enabling the maximum possible use of all the installed plants (including ice accretion on conductors at high altitude). Tunnel cable parameters are also studied.

High-voltage transmission laboratories have been extended to facilitate exploration of the transmission of electrical energy at voltages in the range 765 to 1,500 kV (possible needs of transmission voltage higher than 400 kV in the 1990s, but possibly later than in various other countries, because of short distances and high density of population). These studies are closely coordinated with French EDF and Italian ENEL (for voltages higher than 1,000 kV).

Research on the technical and economic feasibility of superconducting cables for underground transmission is continuing: measurements of the losses in niobium/copper composite superconductors at A.C. currents of up to 4,000 amps and of the dielectric losses of polyethylene, at superconducting temperatures (conductors up to 100 mm (4 in.) diameter, suitable for one phase of a cable with a rating of 1,000 MVA).

A 400 kV cable system and accessories is being developed with gas-pressurized $(SF_6)$ polyethylene tape, following positive results and economic assessment of a 275 kV similar system.

**Fuel Cells and MHD.** Efforts in both fields have been discontinued. R&D on fuel cells was related to the use of natural gas fuel, with an eutectic of

---

d. Over the last two years organizations have adopted, and then sometimes changed their position, and CEGB is generally willing to adopt LWR. Finally, SGHWR was adopted in late, with a small program of development.

lithium, sodium and potassium carbonate at 600°C as an electrolyte.

Work on duct electrodes for MHD proceeded as part of a collaborative program with French EDF and CGE (Compagnie Generale d'Electricite).

### Nuclear Energy Research
### and Development

It had been expected that uranium would become the main fuel for electricity production before the end of the century. Slowing down of electricity demand, North Sea discoveries, a possible comeback of world interest in coal, and some internal difficulties with industrial organization—or reorganization—of the nuclear industry have caused second thoughts on nuclear prospects in the United Kingdom. But the research and development program remains vigorous.

The United Kingdom Atomic Energy Authority (AEA), set up under the Atomic Energy Authority Act 1954, is responsible for research and development; it is answerable to the Secretary of State for Trade and Industry. As an essential part of the British government's nuclear power program, the AEA has carried out research and developed new types of nuclear power stations for the generation of electric power on a commercial scale; and for this purpose it builds and operates experimental and prototype nuclear reactors.

Under the Science and Technology Act of 1965, the functions of AEA were extended beyond nuclear energy. Nonnuclear work is absorbing a rising proportion of the AEA's research resources, mainly at the Harwell establishment, in Berkshire. This includes research into desalination, hydrostatic extrusion, satellite design, tribology, nondestructive testing, atmospheric pollution, carbon fibers, and so on. Forecasts are that in 1976, about 40 percent of profits for Harwell will originate from private industry, such as ICI, British Leyland, General Electric, Westinghouse, and Gulf Oil. Most of the research items are not necessarily energy-oriented, although there were and still are some proposals to change the Atomic Energy Research Establishment at Harwell into an Energy Research Establishment.

From the numerous facilities owned by AEA, the ones related to the nuclear fuel business (say, Springfields for fuel fabrication, Windscale and its reactors for plutonium production and fuel reprocessing, and Capenhurst for enrichment) were transferred in 1971 to a new company, British Nuclear Fuels, Ltd.

The main AEA laboratories are Harwell, Winfrith Heath, Dounreay and Risley. The main reactor development programs are the gas cooled reactors, the water cooled reactors and the fast breeder reactors.

### The Gas Cooled Reactors

All the stations of the first nuclear program have been completed: eleven stations, totaling 5,000 MWe, called "Magnox" stations or Mark I Gas Cooled Reactor Stations. Ten reactors (five stations totalling more than

6,200 MW) of AGR type or Mark II are under construction; the last ones will be connected to the grid in 1976. A good part of R&D related to gas-cooled reactors is now oriented toward the high temperature helium cooled reactor, Ma:k III.

Departing from the OECD Dragon concept, which is based on a uranium 233-thorium cycle, AEA has studied a slightly enriched uranium alternative, more compatible with the fuel policy aimed at plutonium production for future fast reactor plants. Progress in the development of coated-particle fuels and in their fabrication technology has made it possible to develop a coated-particle fuel having a higher heavy metal density to permit the use of low-enrichment uranium. Designs of Mark III reactors with prestressed concrete pressure vessels and high efficiency steam cycles with conventional turbines have been established by AEA with industry, and proposed to CEGB for evaluation.

Fuel development is based on a large-scale irradiation program (in AEA test reactors, in Dragon, and in facilities abroad). Several tons of coated particles and many thousands of fuel inserts have been manufactured. An out-of-pile testing program studies wear, fretting and strain between compact and fuel tube and between fuel pin and channel wall induced by thermal cycling, vibration and accoustic effects. Other fuel-element designs are being considered, such as compacting process of fabrication, thinner coatings, and smaller core components.

The other large part of the program is related to materials corrosion arising from impurities in the helium coolant (or from water inleakage or hydrogen ingress). The development program is concentrating on providing comprehensive data at appropriate temperatures up to 800°C (1,470°F) on a few alloys selected for their corrosion resistance, physical properties, cost, and general engineering suitability. Experiments are also carried out on friction behavior and on ceramic fiber material proposed as the basic component in the insulation of the reactor vessel (thermal and irradiation performance).

For the longer term, direct gas-turbine cycle possibilities are explored, assuming temperature increases from 750°C to about 850°C (1,380°F to 1,560°F).

**Water Cooled Reactor.** A significant effort has been devoted to the development of a water cooled reactor. A 100 MWe prototype of the steam generated heavy water reactor (SGHWR) has been successfully operating since the beginning of 1968. The expected fuel performance has materialized, and the prototype has given valuable experience with which to assess the prospects for water reactors in general. Regarding safety, very interesting dry-out experiments have been performed in a 9 MW experimental rig (in the reactor itself).

**Fast Breeder Reactor.** This is by far the biggest R&D program in the United Kingdom. From 1965 to 1970, roughly £100 million ($240 million) were devoted to fast reactors. A total of about £230 million ($552 million) were devoted to all reactor systems R&D (gas cooled Mark II, gas cooled Mark III, water moderated, and fast breeder). About 700 people of a total of 1,500 were working in the fast reactor program. The main tool is, of course, the PFR in Dounreay, which reached criticality beginning of 1974. Initially, the date for ordering the first commercial plant CFR of 1,000–1,300 MWe was set for 1973; it has slipped back now to 1976. The R&D effort is now sustained with a yearly £15 million ($36 million) development program on FBR components.

Overall development for fast reactors gives detailed consideration to the very many factors involved in the acceptance by the electricity boards of the first commercial unit. Various existing sodium facilities are used for further development of pumps, control and shut-off rod mechanisms, and for investigations into the effects of sodium/water reactions following boiler-tube failures. Engineering experimental work is directed toward reactor safety, including development of subassembly protection instrumentation and alternative shutdown devices. There is also a large amount of theoretical work (such as detailed neutron physics and heat-transfer calculations, determination of cross-sections and their relation to reactor performance).

**Enrichment.** AEA is a member of the three-country organization joining the Netherlands, the Federal Republic of Germany and the United Kingdom (through the Treaty of Almelo, 1970) for ultracentrifuge research and development. A pilot plant (40,000 SWU) has been built at Capenhurst under this program.

**Thermonuclear Fusion.** There is a continuing effort on thermonuclear fusion in the United Kingdom, mainly at AEA Culham laboratories Among the main devices are straight systems (8-meter [24 ft] Theta Pinch, and Stamp), toroidal pinches (Zeta, HBTX), Stellarators (Proto-Cleo), toroidal quadruple, and mirror machines (Phoenix II, MTSE II).

In early 1973, the government authorized a substantial increase in funds available for fusion research at Culham, to restore spending on fusion research almost to the 1967 level (after which time it was reduced 10 percent a year for five years), approaching £5 million ($12 million) a year. The fusion review committee has suggested that the British program form part of the European Communities program. The committee also suggests that a new large experimental assembly be built at Culham, probably a large Tokomak system named JET (Joint European Tokomak); £500,000 ($1.2 million) has been allowed for initial work so that a start can be made during the three-year program.

## ADDENDUM

Table 11–2 gives an analysis, updated to 1974, of gross R&D expenditures on energy in the United Kingdom. The first part of the table breaks out expenditures by main objectives; the second part by specific R&D contractors.

**Table 11–2.   Analysis of R&D Gross Expenditure for 1972–73 and 1973–74**

## Analysis of R & D Gross Expenditure by Main Objectives

| Objective | *$million* 1972–73 | 1973–74 | *$million* 1972–73 | 1973–74 |
|---|---|---|---|---|
| 1 Nuclear R & D (safety) | 0.1 | 0.2 | 0.24 | 0.48 |
| 4 Exploration and exploitation of the earth | 0.7 | 2.7 | 1.68 | 6.48 |
| 5 Protection and promotion of health (e.g. control of pollutants) | 1.5 | 1.2 | 3.60 | 2.88 |
| 6 Planning of environment | 0.4 | 0.5 | 0.96 | 1.20 |
| 8 Promotion of industrial productivity and technology: | | | | |
| 8.0   General | 5.0 | 5.9 | 12.00 | 14.16 |
| 8.1   Fuel (including electrical power) | 0.1 | 0.1 | 0.24 | 0.24 |
| 8.2.1 Chemical | 2.6 | 2.8 | 6.24 | 6.72 |
| 8.2.2 Metals | 0.3 | 0.3 | 0.72 | 0.72 |
| 8.2.3 Electronics | 1.1 | 1.7 | 2.64 | 4.08 |
| 8.2.4 Aerospace: | | | | |
| Civil aeronautics | 13.9 | 17.5 | 33.36 | 42.00 |
| Space technology | 9.1 | 14.1 | 21.84 | 33.84 |
| 8.2.5 Other transport | 1.9 | 2.3 | 4.56 | 5.52 |
| 8.2.7 Mechanical engineering products | 3.6 | 3.9 | 8.64 | 9.36 |
| 8.9   Other research | 0.2 | 0.5 | 0.48 | 1.20 |
| 9 Computer science and automation | 12.8 | 15.6 | 30.72 | 37.44 |
| Unclassified (grants to Research Associations, etc.) | 4.5 | 3.6 | 10.8 | 8.64 |
| | 57.7 | 72.8 | 138.48 | 174.72 |

## Analysis of Gross Expenditure on R & D by Contractors

| Performer | *$000* 1972–73 | 1973–74 | *$000* 1972–73 | 1973–74 |
|---|---|---|---|---|
| DTI Research Establishments: | | | | |
| National Physical Laboratory | 6,624 | 6,875 | 15,890 | 16,500 |
| National Engineering Laboratory | 3,704 | 3,801 | 8,890 | 9,122 |
| Warren Spring Laboratory | 1,640 | 1,540 | 3,936 | 3,696 |
| Safety in Mines Research Establishment | 562 | 522 | 1,349 | 1,253 |
| Laboratory of the Government Chemist | 45 | 31 | 108 | 74 |
| Computer-aided Design Centre | 398 | 525 | 955 | 1,260 |
| Research Associations | 2,977 | 2,932 | 7,145 | 7,037 |
| UKAEA | 5,489 | 5,986 | 13,174 | 14,366 |
| Other Government departments | 6,871 | 5,910 | 16,490 | 14,184 |
| Industry | 27,556 | 34,573 | 66,158 | 82,975 |
| Universities | 491 | 496 | 1,178 | 1,190 |
| Natural Environment Research Council | 190 | 520 | 456 | 1,248 |
| Other | 1,170 | 1,320 | 2,808 | 3,168 |
| | 57,717 | 65,031 | 138,537 | 156,073 |

Source: From "Report on Research and Development 1972–73," Department of Trade and Industry.

## REFERENCES

### Energy Situation
*The British Fuel and Power Industries* (November 1970).
*Out of Britain,* 1973.
UN and OECD energy statistics.

### General Organization for Research and Development
DTI. *Report on Research and Development 1972–1973.*
"Industrial Expenditure on Scientific Research and Development in 1969–1970," *Trade and Industry* (21 December 1972).
Private discussions with Mr. P. Goodman, Scientific Counsellor, British Embassy, Paris.
*The Promotion of the Sciences in Britain* (February 1972).
Rothschild and Dainton Reports. *A Framework for Government Research and Development* (November 1971).
*Statistics of Science and Technology.*
*Le Systeme de la Recherche.* Vol 1. Allemagne. Royaume Unit. OCDE, 1972.

### Coal Research and Development
Arguile, R. T. "Reclamation: Five Industrial Sites in the East Midlands," *Journal of the Institution of Municipal Engineers* (October 1970).
Brent-Jones, "Methods and Costs of Land Restoration," *The Quarry Manager's Journal* (October 1971).
CRE. *Annual Reports, 1971/72 1972/73.*
Gasification of Coal in the United Kingdom. Meeting on Nuclear Process Heat, EEC, Brussels, 7 June 1973.
Highley, J. "Reduction in Sulphur Dioxyde Emission by Fluidized Bed Combustion. Salford University Symposium, April 1973.
McLaren, J., "Combustion Efficiency, Sulphur Retention and Heat Transfer in Pilot-Plant Fluidized-Bed Combustors, *Journal of the Institute of Fuel* (August 1969).
Mathematical Modelling of the Limestone-Sulphur Diocyde Reaction."
Mining Research and Development Establishment. *MRDE Reports.*
*Mining Research and Development Review.*
National Coal Board. *Report and Accounts, 1971–1972.*
Private communications from NCB staff.

### Petroleum Research and Development
BP. *Our Industry.* (Chapter on research.)
Esso. Research Center Publications. (Brochure.)
RDS. *Research for Chemicals* (Brochure.)
_____ *Science and Technology Newsletter.*

### Gas Research and Development

British Gas Corporation. *Annual Reports.*
_____ . *Research and Development Facilities.* (Brochure.)
Private communications from British Gas staff (Research Department)
Research Communications List of the Gas Council (GC–156 to GC–206).

### Electricity Research and Development

"Berkeley Nuclear Laboratories." (Descriptive brochure.)
Booth, E. S. *Whither Nuclear Power?* Institution of Electrical Engineers, 1971.
Brown, S. "The Next 25 Years in the Electric Supply Industry, *Electrical and Electronics Technician Engineer* (Nov. 1970).
CEGB. *Annual Reports.*
_____ . *CEGB Statistical Yearbook, 1972.*
"Central Electricity Research Laboratories." (Descriptive brochure.)
Clarke, A. J., D. H. Lucas, and F. F. Ross. "Tall Stacks: How Effective Are They?" Second International Clean Air Conference, Washington D.C., Dec. 1970.
"Marchwood Engineering Laboratories." (Descriptive brochure.)

### Nuclear Energy Research and Development

AEA. *Annual Reports.*
"The Fluctuating Fortunes of Fusion Research in the U.K.," *Nuclear Engineering International* (June 1973).
Fourth United Nations International Conference on the Peaceful Uses of Atomic Energy. Geneva. September 1971, especially:
Papers 467. General Program.
469, 474, Safety of Gas Cooled Reactors.
471, SGHWR.
472, 481, 482, Fast Reactors.
480, 494, 495, HTGR and fuel for HTGR.
488, Fusion.
493, Centrifuge Plants.
496, Plutonium.

# Index

## About the Authors

**J. Herbert Hollomon,** Director of the Center for Policy Alternatives, Massachusetts Institute of Technology and Professor of Engineering at M.I.T. is a past president of the University of Oklahoma (1967–70) and was Assistant Secretary of Commerce for Science & Technology (1962–67) and Acting Undersecretary of Commerce (1967). Long interested in the analysis of public issues involving technology and society, Dr. Hollomon's professional activities, awards and numerous publications reflect these interests. He received his undergraduate degree in physics and an Sc.D. in Metallurgy from the Massachusetts Institute of Technology.

**Michel Grenon,** a graduate of the University of Science (Paris, France), worked in basic science research with the French National Research Center, the French Petroleum Institute and the French Atomic Energy Commission. From 1962 to 1968 he was Deputy Director of the European Communities Establishment in Petten (EURATOM–Netherlands) and worked on the development of liquid fuel reactors. Since 1968 he has served as an International Consultant on energy problems and is presently a visiting professor at the University of Tennessee.